Enrichment Workbook

STRETCH YOUR THINKING

TEACHER'S EDITION
Grade 7

Harcourt Brace & Company
Orlando • Atlanta • Austin • Boston • San Francisco • Chicago • Dallas • New York • Toronto • London
http://www.hbschool.com

Printed in the United States of America

ISBN 0-15-311093-7

1 2 3 4 5 6 7 8 9 10 082 2000 99 98

CONTENTS

CHAPTER 23 Experiments with Probability

CHAPTER 24 Measuring Length and Area

CHAPTER 25 Surface Area and Volume

CHAPTER 26 Changing Dimensions

CHAPTER 27 Percent: Spending and Saving

CHAPTER 28 Showing Relationships

Name ____

All Set!

Venn diagrams show relationships among sets. You don't need to know which elements are in the sets.

- The **union** of sets A and B is written A ∪ B. It refers to all the elements in set A, set B, or both.
- The **intersection** of sets A and B is written A ∩ B. It refers to all the elements in both set A and set B.

You can show union and intersection by shading Venn diagrams.

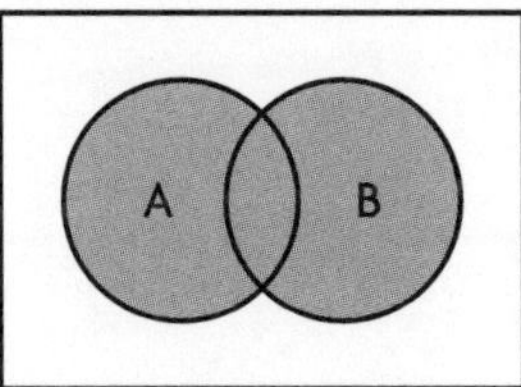

A ∪ B

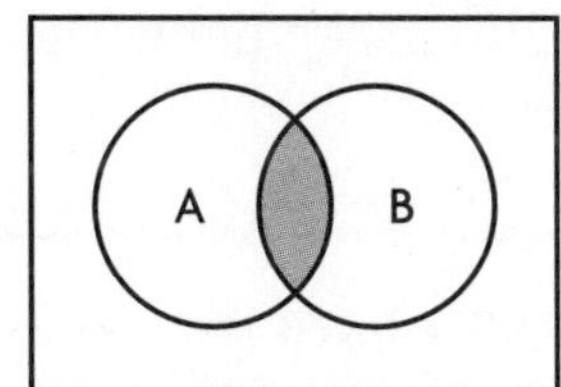

A ∩ B

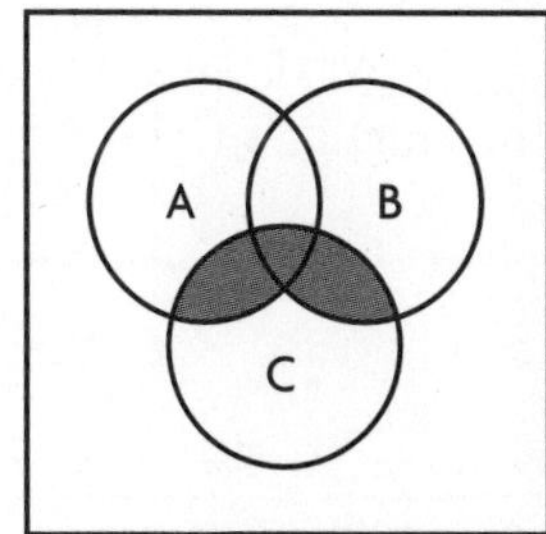

(A ∪ B) ∩ C

Shade each Venn diagram as indicated.

1.

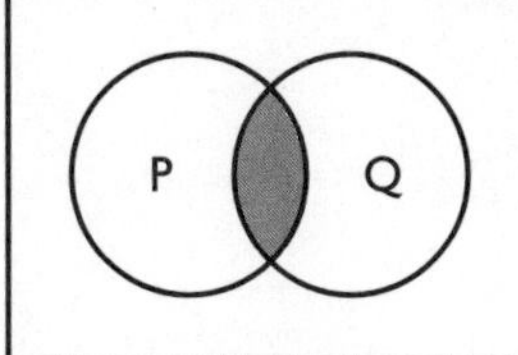

P ∩ Q

2.

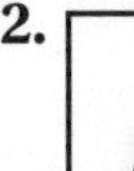
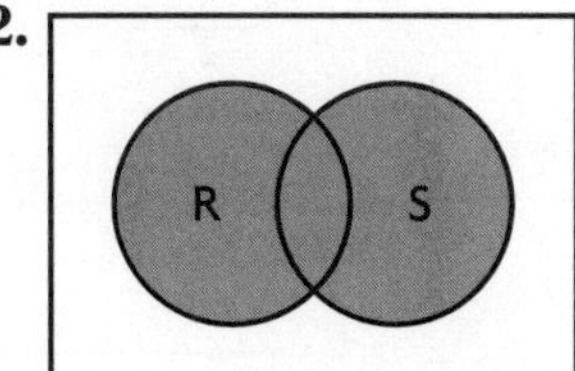

R ∪ S

3.

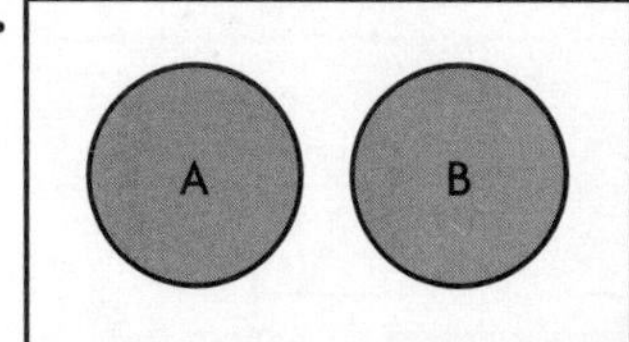

A ∪ B

4.

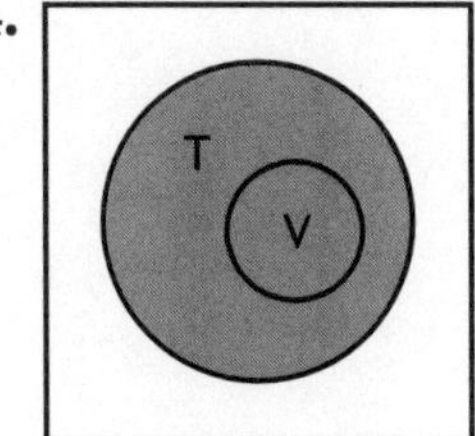

T ∪ V

5.

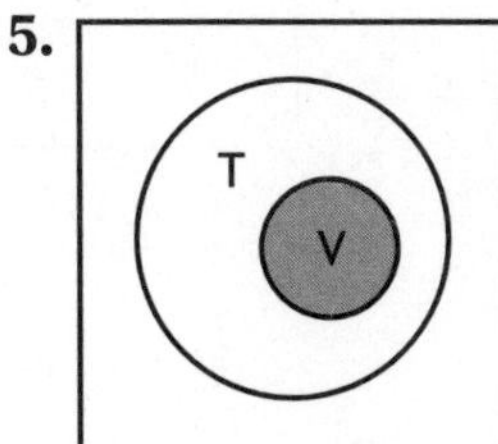

T ∩ V

6.

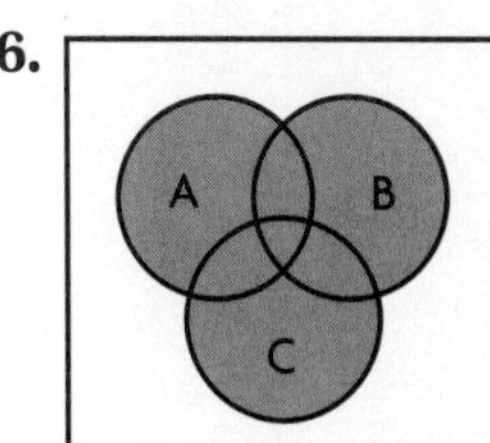

A ∪ (B ∪ C)

7.

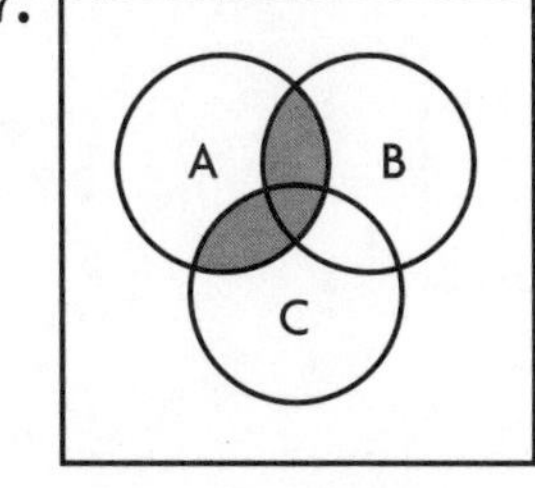

A ∩ (B ∪ C)

8.

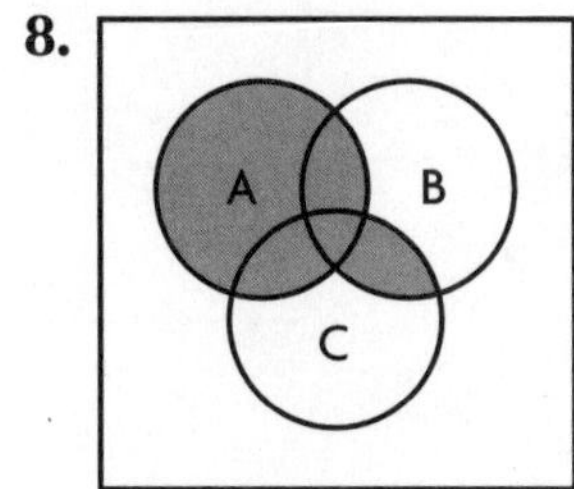

A ∪ (B ∩ C)

9.

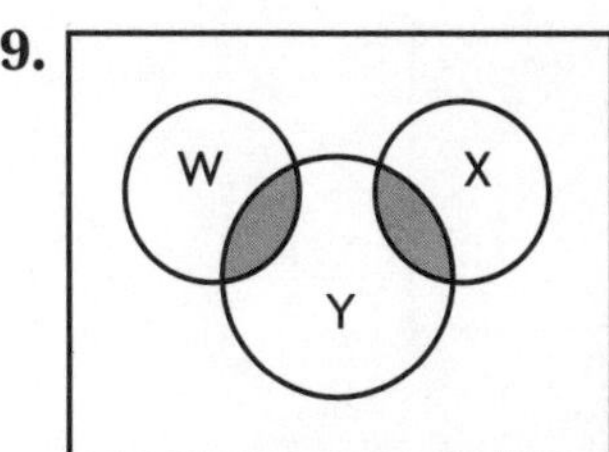

(W ∩ Y) ∪ (X ∩ Y)

Name ______________________________

Square Deal

You draw two overlapping segments, one 6 cm long and another 10 cm long, as shown. If the segments are placed end to end, the length is 16 cm. But as it is drawn, it is only 12 cm. What is the length of the overlapping part?

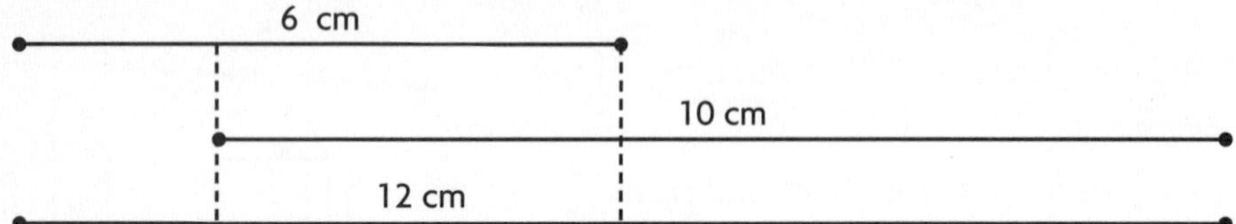

Notice how the vertical rules divide the 12-cm segment. The length of the overlapping part has to be 4 cm.

Each square is 6 in. × 6 in. Find the area where the squares overlap.

1. 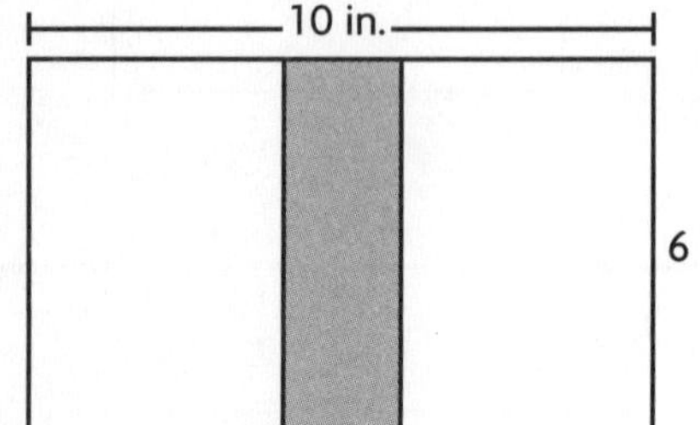

12 in.^2

2. 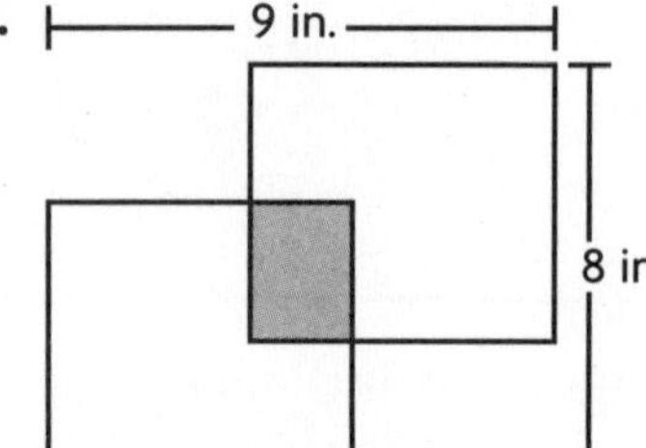

12 in.^2

3. 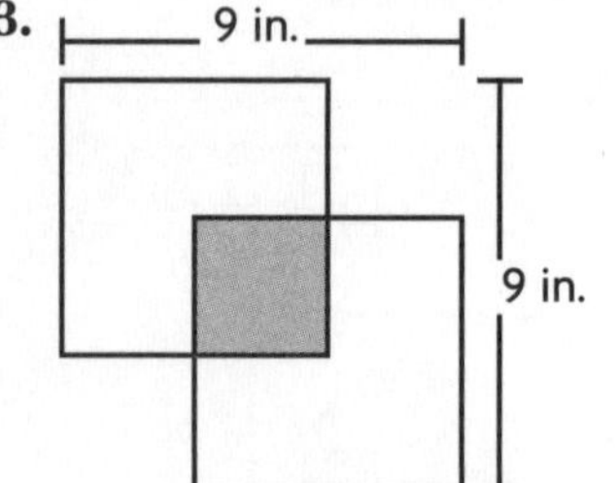

9 in.^2

4. 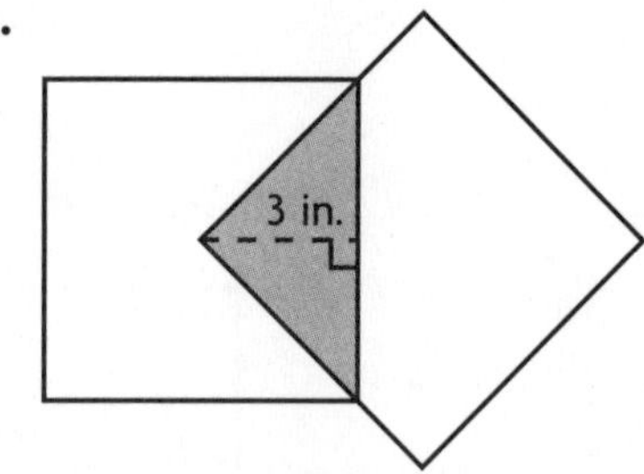

9 in.^2

5. 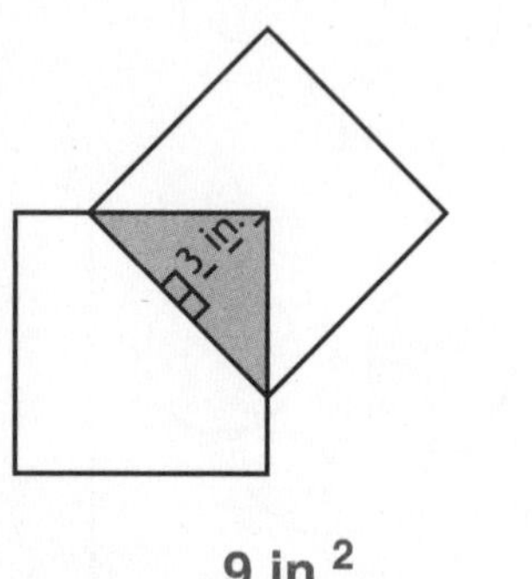

9 in.^2

6. 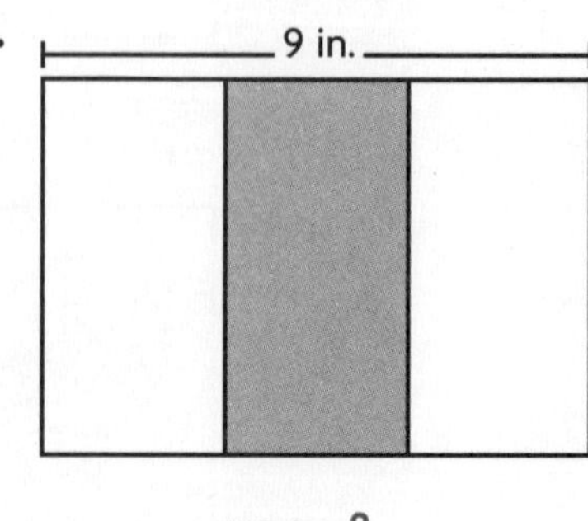

18 in.^2

Name ______________________

Cubes, Cubes, Cubes

A cube has six sides, or faces.
Each of the six faces is a square.

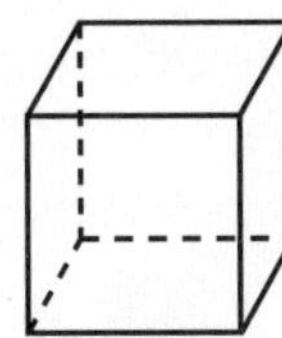

The cube at the right measures 2 units on each edge.
It is painted.

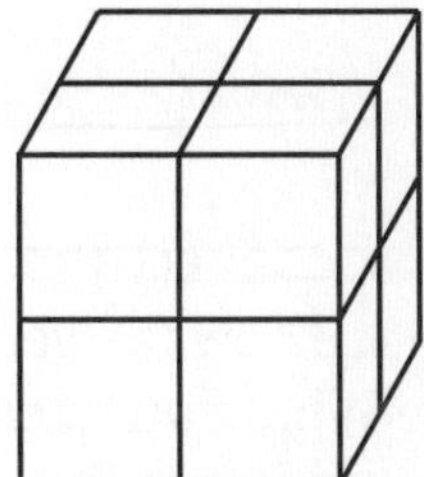

1. How many small cubes make up the large cube? **8 cubes**
2. How many small cubes will be painted on 3 faces? on 2 faces? on 1 face? not at all?

   8 cubes; 0 cubes; 0 cubes; 0 cubes

This cube measures 3 units on each edge.

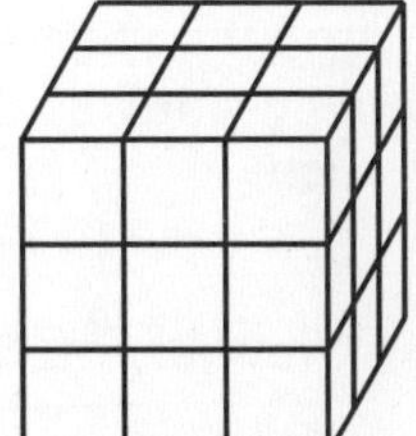

3. How many small cubes make up the large cube? **27 cubes**
4. If the large cube is painted, how many small cubes will be painted on 3 faces? on 2 faces? on 1 face? not at all?

   8 cubes; 12 cubes; 6 cubes; 1 cube

This cube measures 4 units on each edge.

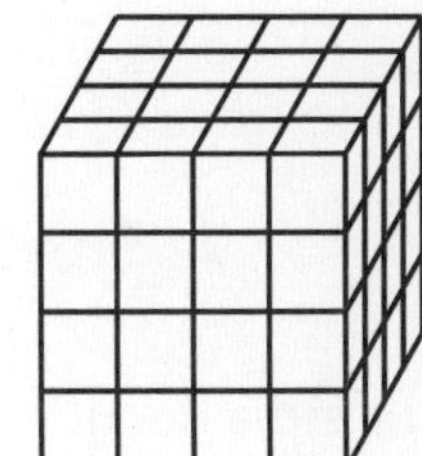

5. How many small cubes make up the large cube? **64 cubes**
6. If the large cube is painted, how many small cubes will be painted on 3 faces? on 2 faces? on 1 face? not at all?

   8 cubes; 24 cubes; 24 cubes; 8 cubes

7. Complete the table below by entering the number of small cubes that will be painted on the given number of faces.

Size of Large Cube	Painted on 3 faces	Painted on 2 faces	Painted on 1 face	Painted on 0 faces
2 × 2 × 2	8	0	0	0
3 × 3 × 3	8	12	6	1
4 × 4 × 4	8	24	24	8
5 × 5 × 5	8	36	54	27

8. Look at your table in Exercise 7. What is the rule for the number of cubes painted on 3 faces?

   always 8

Name ______________________________

Repeating, Repeating

You will need a scientific calculator to do this activity. Set the mode on your scientific calculator to "float," for floating decimal.

Convert the fraction $\frac{1}{3}$ to a decimal by entering 1 [÷] 3.

1. What does your calculator display? **0.333333333**

Now convert the fraction $\frac{2}{3}$ by entering 2 [÷] 3.

2. What does your calculator display? **0.666666667**
3. What is the difference in the calculator displays?

   The decimal for $\frac{2}{3}$ rounds up the final digit.

4. Now convert the fractions $\frac{1}{9}$, $\frac{2}{9}$, $\frac{4}{9}$, and $\frac{5}{9}$ to decimals.

   0.111111111; 0.222222222; 0.444444444; 0.555555556

5. What do you think the calculator will display for $\frac{7}{9}$? for $\frac{8}{9}$?

   0.777777778; 0.888888889

6. Are the decimal numbers you found with your calculator exactly equal to the fractions or do you think they are approximations? Why?

   Approximations; the decimals actually go on and on.

7. Find a decimal approximation for $\frac{1}{7}$. **0.142857143**
8. Find a decimal approximation for $\frac{2}{7}$. **0.285714286**
9. Find a decimal approximation for $\frac{5}{7}$. **0.714285714**
10. Look at your answers to Exercises 7–9. Starting with any digit, write the repeating part of the decimal representation for sevenths.

    Possible answer: 285714

The repeating part of the decimal for nineteenths is 17 places long. You can find it using a strategy similar to that used for sevenths above.

11. Pick 4 fractions with 19 in the denominator. Convert them to decimals. **Answers will vary. Check students' work.**
12. Use your answers in Exercise 11 to find the first 17 decimal places of $\frac{1}{19}$.

    0.05263157894736842

Name ______________________________

How Many Colors?

People who design graphs and maps use different colors to show different regions.

How many colors do you need for a design if no two regions touching each other can be the same color?

When two regions meet at only a point, they can be the same color. For example, the interior of the square shown could be colored using only two colors.

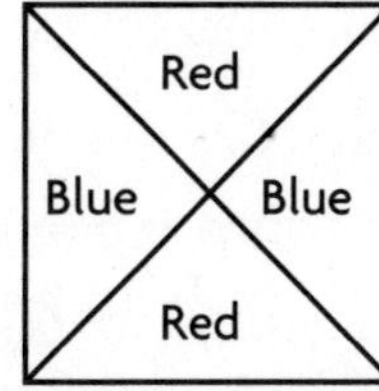

How many colors would be needed to color the regions of a circle graph divided into the number of parts given?

1. 2 parts **2 colors**
2. 3 parts **3 colors**
3. 4 parts **2 colors**
4. 5 parts **3 colors**

5. The design below was drawn without lifting the pencil from the paper. How many colors are needed to color it? Only the areas of the design inside the lines are colored. **2 colors**

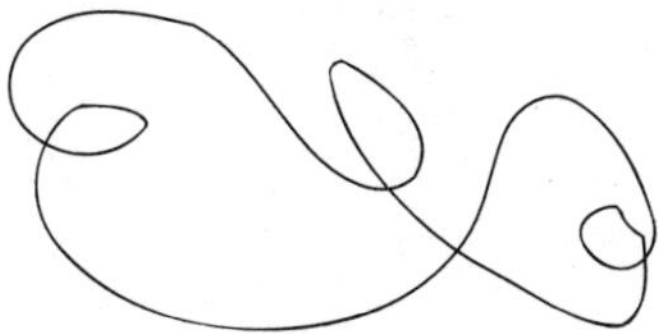

6. Draw a design without lifting your pencil from the paper. How many colors are needed to color it? **Check students' work.**

How many colors are needed to color each of the designs below?

7. **3 colors**

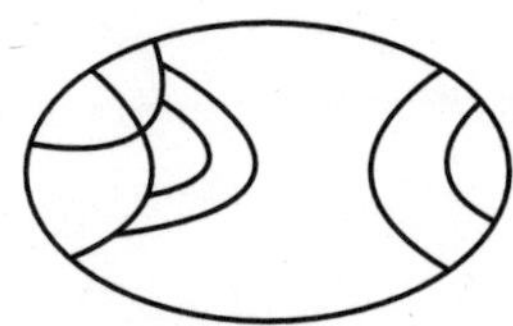

8. **4 colors**

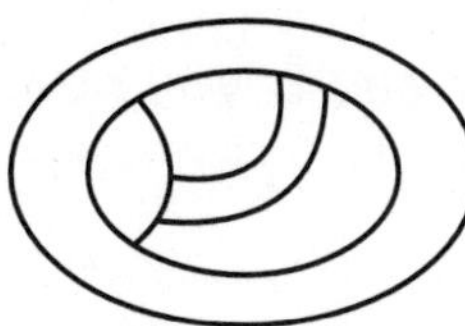

9. Do you think it is possible to draw a design that requires more than 4 colors? Try it. **no**

Name ______________________________

Break It Apart

Using formulas, you can find the areas of more complicated figures by dividing them into rectangles and triangles.

- area of a square = s^2, where s is a side
- area of a rectangle = lw, where l is the length and w is the width
- area of a triangle = $\frac{1}{2}bh$, where b is the base and h is the height

If you want to find the area of this figure, it can be divided into a rectangle and a triangle. Find the area of each, then add them to find the area of the whole figure. HINT: Be careful; the base of the triangle is 12 m − 7 m = 5 m.

area of rectangle $= 7 \times 10 = 70 \text{ m}^2$

area of triangle $= \frac{1}{2}(5 \times 10) = 25 \text{ m}^2$

total area of figure = area of rectangle + area of triangle

$= 70 \text{ m}^2 + 25 \text{ m}^2 = 95 \text{ m}^2$

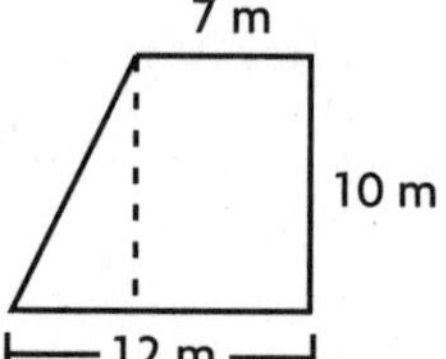

Divide each figure into parts. Then find the area of each part. Add the areas of the parts to find the area of the whole figure.

1. 30 in.^{2}

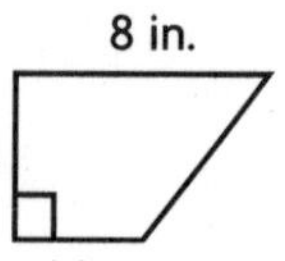

2. 168 ft^2

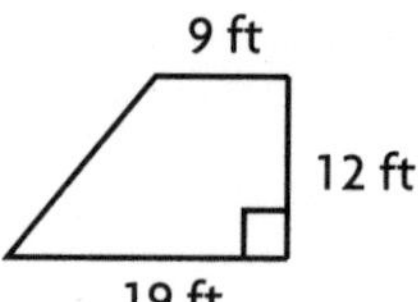

3. 120 m^2

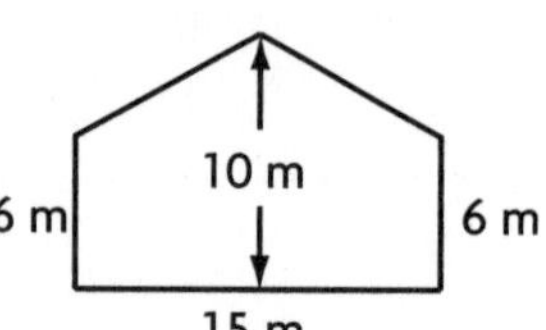

4. 94.5 in.^{2}

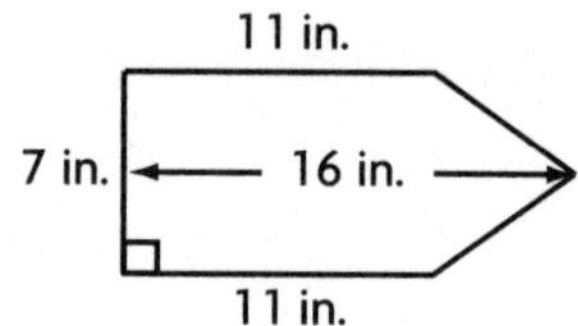

5. 180 cm^2

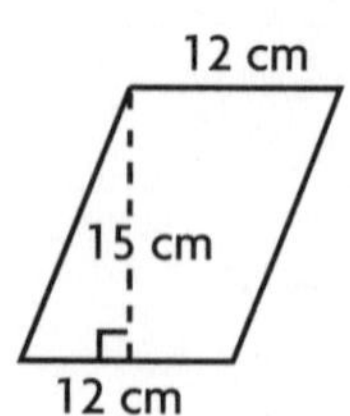

6. 182 cm^2

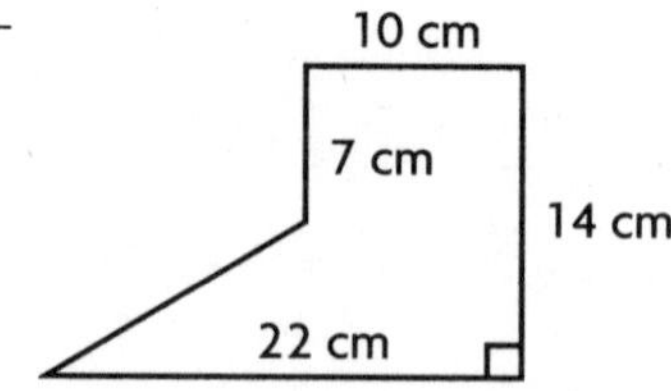

For Exercises 7 and 8, you need to *subtract* an area to find the area of each figure.

7. 234 m^2

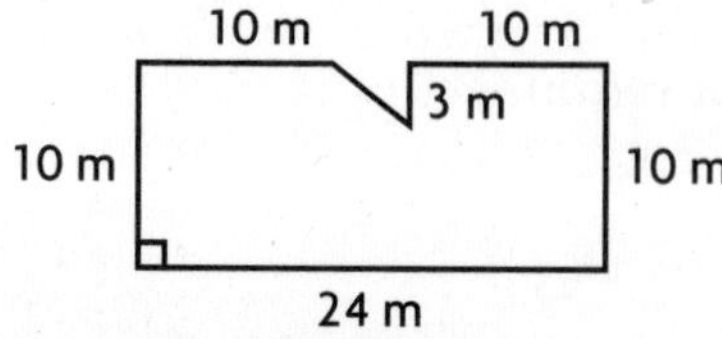

8. 72 ft^2

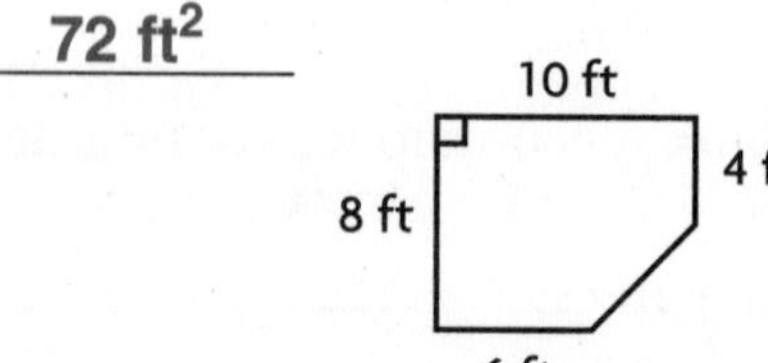

Name ______________________________

LESSON 2.2

A Card Trick

You can use the binary system to make a set of cards for a card trick. You will need five cards. On each card, write 16 numbers in order. Here is how to do it;

- On a separate sheet of paper write the numbers from 1 to 31, using the binary system. The table on page 40 of the text will help you get started.
- Write on the first card, using decimal numbers, every number that has a 1 in the 2^0 or ones column of its binary form. There are 16 such numbers.
- Write on the second card, using decimal numbers, every number that has a 1 in the 2^1 or twos column of its binary form. There are 16 such numbers.
- Write on the remaining three cards the decimal numbers that use the 2^2 or 4, 2^3 or 8, and 2^4 or 16 columns for binary numbers.

To check whether you are getting the correct numbers, the first seven numbers for each card are given. Continue until you have 16 numbers on each card.

1. Card 1: 1, 3, 5, 7, 9, 11, 13, **15, 17, 19, 21, 23, 25, 27, 29, 31**
2. Card 2: 2, 3, 6, 7, 10, 11, 14, **15, 18, 19, 22, 23, 26, 27, 30, 31**
3. Card 3: 4, 5, 6, 7, 12, 13, 14, **15, 20, 21, 22, 23, 28, 29, 30, 31**
4. Card 4: 8, 9, 10, 11, 12, 13, 14, **15, 24, 25, 26, 27, 28, 29, 30, 31**
5. Card 5: 16, 17, 18, 19, 20, 21, 22, **23, 24, 25, 26, 27, 28, 29, 30, 31**

Now that your cards are ready, the trick works like this:

- Ask a friend or family member to pick a number from 1 to 31. Make sure they don't tell you the number!
- Give the five cards to the person, and ask him or her to give you back all the cards that have the picked number on them.
- Find the number quickly by adding the first numbers on the cards.

  Examples:

  The number 17 appears on Cards 1 and 5, that start with 1 and 16.

  The number 12 appears on Cards 3 and 4, that start with 4 and 8.

  The number 31 appears on Cards 1, 2, 3, 4, and 5, that start with 1, 2, 4, 8 and 16.

Name ______________________________

LESSON 2.3

Histograms: Comparisons Made Easy

A *histogram* is a bar graph in which the bars are right next to each other. The interval for each bar is the same.

The histograms below show the percents of the population between certain ages for Nigeria and the United States.

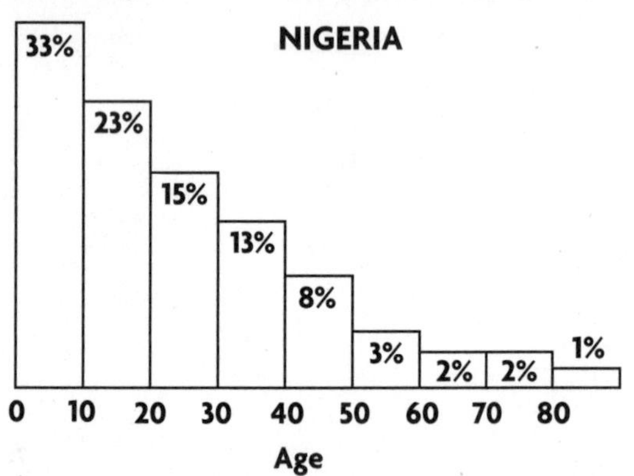

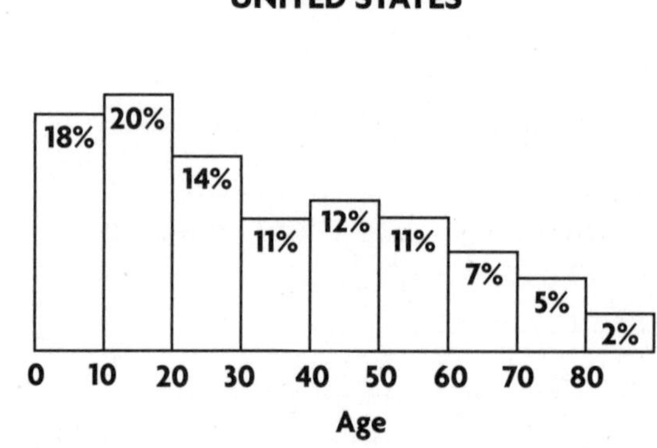

What percent of the population of Nigeria is between 20 and 30 years of age? The histogram shows that 15% of the population is between 20 and 30 years of age.

---

1. What percent of the population of the United States is between 50 and 60 years of age? 11%
2. What percent of the population of Nigeria is between 30 and 40 years of age? 13%
3. What percent of the population of Nigeria is less than 20 years of age? (HINT: This must include those less than 10 years and those between 10 and 20 years of age.) 56%
4. What percent of the population of the United States is more than 70 years of age? 7%
5. What percent of the population of the United States is between 20 and 60 years of age? 48%
6. What percent of the population of Nigeria is between 20 and 60 years of age? 39%
7. If there are 100 million people in Nigeria, how many are under 10 years of age? 33,000,000 people
8. If there are 260 million people in the United States, how many are under 10 years of age? 46,800,000 people

Name ____________________

Simplify Life with Tables

Tables are useful tools for comparing different quantities.

The manager of a rock band earns a fee for each concert. The fee is based on a royalty rate, or a percent of the profits from the concert. The royalty rates for bands and fees for managers differ.

The table shows concert profits, royalty rates, and the manager's fees for five concerts.

Concert	Profit ($)	Royalty Rate	Manager's Fee ($)
Baltimore	45,000	2% or 0.02	900
Philadelphia	75,000	3% or 0.03	2,250
Washington, D.C.	90,000	3.5% or 0.035	3,150
Boston	105,000	2.5% or 0.025	2,625
New York	180,000	1.5% or 0.015	2,700

The manager's fee is found by multiplying the profit by the royalty rate.

---

1. What is the manager's fee for a concert with a profit of $90,000 and a royalty rate of 3.5%? **$3,150**
2. What is the manager's fee for a concert with a profit of $150,000 and a royalty rate of 3%? **$4,500**
3. Emilio Sanchez manages two concerts with profits of $40,000 and $20,000. The royalty rate is 2%. What is the total fee Mr. Sanchez earns for the two concerts? **$1,200**
4. Melissa Harrington manages a concert with profits of $62,000. The royalty rate is 1.6%. What is the fee that she earns? **$992**
5. Jamie Li manages a concert with profits of $180,000 and a royalty rate of 2%. His brother earns a rate of 1.5% on profits of $240,000. Who earns more? How much more? **They both earn the same, $3,600.**
6. Rhoda Weiss manages a concert with profits of $200,000. There is an unexpected expense of $40,000. Her fee is 2.2%. What fee does she earn? **$3,520**

Name ______________________________

Going in Circles

Iterations are often used in programs for computers and calculators. Using iterations, you can write instructions for doing calculations that involve repeated operations.

Some of the key words for programs with iterations are IF, THEN, and ELSE. If the statement after IF is true, then you do the next step. If it is not true, then you go to the statement after ELSE.

What condition will make this program stop?

Line 1 Select any two counting numbers x and y.
Line 2 Add $x + y$.
Line 3 IF $x + y > 100$
Line 4 STOP
Line 5 ELSE
Line 6 Go to 1.

The program will stop when the sum of the two numbers is greater than 100.

In Exercises 1 and 2, find the condition that will make the program stop.

1. Line 1 Select any two counting numbers x and y.
Line 2 Subtract $x - y$.
Line 3 IF $x - y < 2$
Line 4 STOP
Line 5 ELSE
Line 6 Go to 1.

when the difference between the two numbers is less than two

2. Line 1 Select any two counting numbers x and y.
Line 2 Multiply $2x$ and add y.
Line 3 IF $2x + y$ is odd
Line 4 STOP
Line 5 ELSE
Line 6 Go to 1.

when $2x + y$ is an odd number

3. Work with a partner. Each write a short program, but do not tell your partner the instruction in the IF statement that will make the program stop. Give as clues three numbers that will stop the program and three that will not stop the program. Exchange programs and find your partner's missing instruction.

Answers will vary. Check students' work.

The Best Excuse

Joe brought this homework assignment to math class. He said his gerbil had chewed holes in it. Repair the damage by finding the missing digits.

1.
9 7 3
+ 3 6 1
1,3 3 4

2.
5 8 0
−2 5 6
3 2 4

3.
3,0 2 8
1, 2 9 5
+ 4, 0 4 6
8, 3 6 9

4.
8 7 3
× 8
2 4
5 6 0
+ 6 4 0 0
6,9 8 4

5.
2 7
× 3 6
1 6 2
+ 8 1 0
9 7 2

6.
4 3
× 5 6
2 5 8
+ 2 1 5 0
2, 4 0 8

7.
8 2, 6 5 9
− 3 9,4 9 2
4 3, 1 6 7

8.
1 3, 4 9 5
− 8, 5 0 8
4, 9 8 7

9.
9 7 8
+ 9 6 2
1,9 4 0

10.
6 0 3
4 7)2 8, 3 4 1
−2 8 2
1 4 1
−1 4 1
0

11.
4,3 6 9
− 7 8 2
3, 5 8 7

12.
8 4 5
× 3 4
3 3 8 0
+ 2 5 3 5 0
2 8,7 3 0

Name ____________________

Magic Decimal Squares

Fill in the missing decimals to make the sums in each row, column, and diagonal equal. This is called a *magic sum*.

1.

2.4	5.4	1.2
1.8	3	4.2
4.8	0.6	3.6

What is the magic sum? 9.0

2.

0.438	0.073	0.584
0.511	0.365	0.219
0.146	0.657	0.292

What is the magic sum? 1.095

Fill in the missing decimals to make the products of the numbers in each row, column, and diagonal equal. This is called a *magic product*.

3.

0.2	0.9	1.2
3.6	0.6	0.1
0.3	0.4	1.8

What is the magic product? 0.216

4.

25.6	0.2	6.4
0.8	3.2	12.8
1.6	51.2	0.4

What is the magic product? 32.768

This magic square appears in a famous engraving from 1514 by Albrecht Dürer, called *Melancholia*.

16	3	2	13
5	10	11	8
9	6	7	12
4	15	14	1

5. What is the magic sum? 34

6. What is the sum of the four numbers at the corners of the square? 34

7. What is the sum of the four numbers at the center of the square? 34

Name ____________________

Decimal Riddle

Use the numbers below for circles 1–22 to make each number sentence true. Then use the matching letter to fill in the corresponding blank and answer the riddle. HINT: There are unused numbers and letters.

Use in addition sentences.		Use in subtraction sentences.		Use in multiplication sentences.		Use in division sentences.	
N	74.59	W	23.7	O	5	E	3.92
A	72.9	N	8.39	S	6.08	I	1.9
H	7.8	O	5.93	N	10.58	I	0.7
E	15.4	A	12.7	M	12.42	T	5
K	17.87	T	6.4	E	40.3	B	14.6
Y	87.9	H	13.13	H	2.7	E	9.69
A	98.6	M	9.28	S	3.2	C	31.05

(1.) + 7.8 = 106.4 98.6: A

(2.) − (3.) = 7.2 13.13: H; 5.93: O

(4.) × 8.06 = (5.) 5: O; 40.3: E

(6.) ÷ (7.) = 5.16 3.92: E; 0.7: I

(8.) + 57.5 = (9.) 15.4: E; 72.9: A

(10.) ÷ 5.6 = 0.7 3.92: E

(11.) − 0.89 = (12.) 9.28: M; 8.39: N

(13.) × 1.9 = (14.) 3.2: S; 6.08: S

(15.) − 17.3 = (16.) 23.7: W; 6.4: T

4.6 × (17.) = (18.) 2.7: H; 12.42: M

56.72 + (19.) = (20.) 17.87: K; 74.59: N

(21.) ÷ 6.21 = (22.) 31.05: C; 5: T

What does the decimal point say to the dollar sign?

I		A	M		T	H	E		O	N	E		W	H	O
7		1	11		16	2	8		3	12	6		15	17	4

M	A	K	E	S		C	E	N	T	S	!
18	9	19	5	13		21	10	20	22	14	

Name ______________________________

In Need of Repair

Use the tools 3, 5, 6, 7, and 9 and the skills +, −, ×, and ÷ to complete each number sentence. Each tool can be used only once per sentence. There may be more than one correct answer.

1. $\boxed{9} + \boxed{5} - \boxed{6} = 8$

2. $(\boxed{3} + \boxed{7}) \times \boxed{6} = 60$

3. $\boxed{6}^2 - \boxed{3} \times \boxed{5} = 21$

4. $\boxed{3} \times \boxed{9}^2 - \boxed{6} = 237$

5. $\boxed{3} \times \boxed{5} - \boxed{6} = 9$

6. $\boxed{7}^2 - (\boxed{3} \times \boxed{9}) = 22$

7. $\boxed{5} + \boxed{3} \times \boxed{9} = 32$

8. $(\boxed{5}^2 + \boxed{6}) - \boxed{7} = 24$

9. $(\boxed{3} \; (+) \; \boxed{5}) \times (\boxed{9} \; (-) \; \boxed{7}) = 16$

10. $\boxed{3} \; (\times) \; \boxed{5} \; (+) \; \boxed{6} \; (-) \; \boxed{9} = 12$

11. $\boxed{5} \; (\times) \; \boxed{6} \; (\div) \; \boxed{3} \; (+) \; \boxed{9} = 19$

12. $\boxed{5} \; (+) \; \boxed{6} \; (+) \; \boxed{9} \; (-) \; \boxed{3} = 17$

13. $\boxed{9}^2 \; (\div) \; (\boxed{6} \; (-) \; \boxed{3}) \; (\times) \; \boxed{5} = 135$

14. $(\boxed{5}^2 \; (+) \; \boxed{6}) \; (-) \; \boxed{7} \; (-) \; \boxed{3} = 21$

15. $\boxed{5} \; (\times) \; \boxed{6} \; (-) \; \boxed{3} \; (-) \; \boxed{7} = 20$

16. $\boxed{3} \; (\times) \; \boxed{6} \; (+) \; \boxed{5} \; (\times) \; \boxed{7} = 53$

Name ___________________________

Fraction Pyramid

Find each sum. Then shade the square containing the greatest value in each row. The shaded squares will form a path to the top of the pyramid.

1.

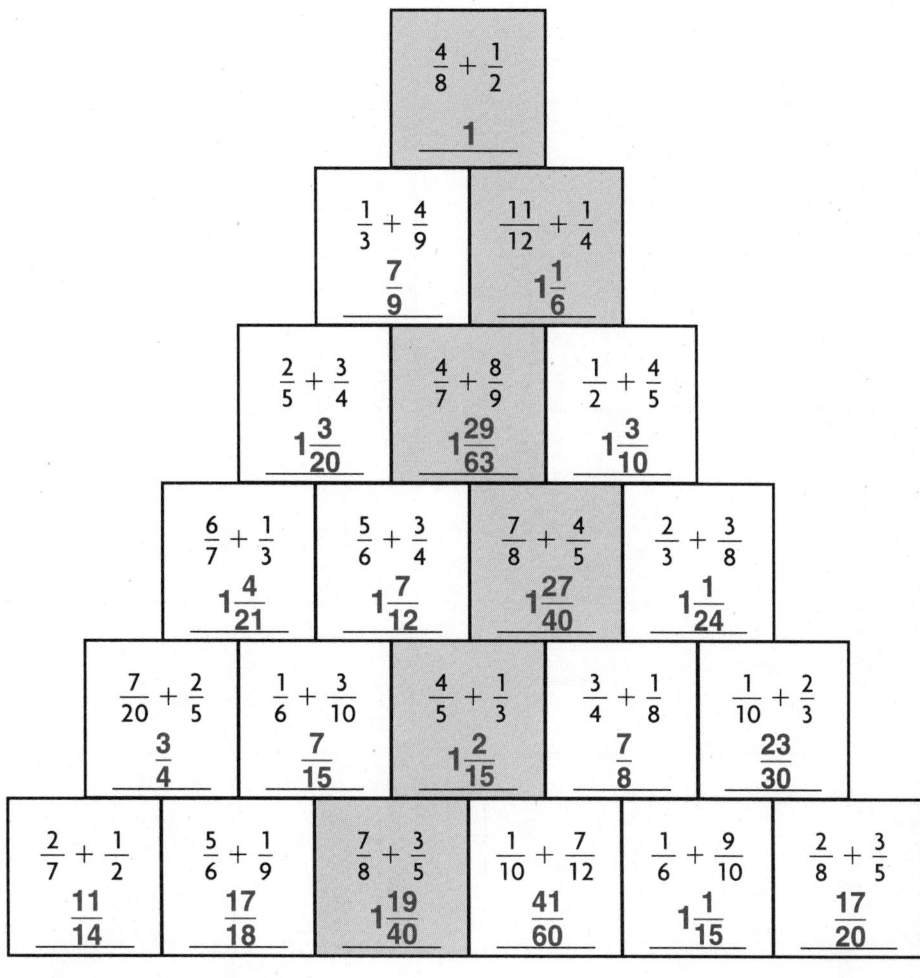

2. Make your own fraction pyramid. Exchange pyramids with a classmate.
Fractions will vary.

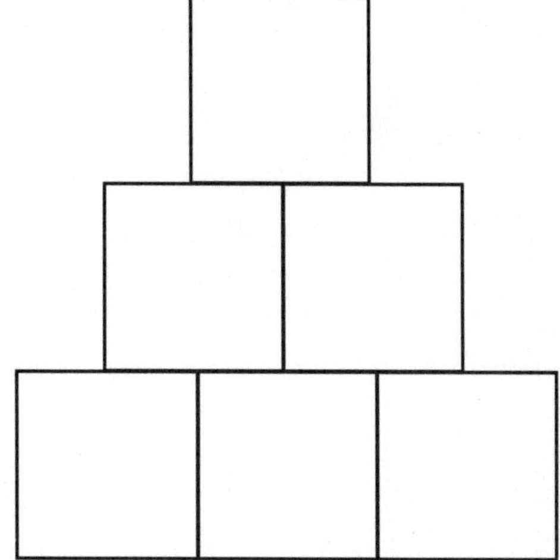

Name ______________________

Fraction Squares

Find the value of each sum or difference. Then shade each outer square that represents a value equal to the amount shown in the center square.

1.

$8\frac{1}{5} - 6\frac{2}{3}$ $1\frac{8}{15}$	$9\frac{18}{24} - 8\frac{5}{10}$ $1\frac{1}{4}$	$5\frac{1}{3} - 4\frac{1}{12}$ $1\frac{1}{4}$
$3\frac{1}{15} - 1\frac{6}{7}$ $1\frac{22}{105}$	$1\frac{1}{4}$	$\frac{4}{5} + \frac{9}{20}$ $1\frac{1}{4}$
$\frac{3}{4} + \frac{7}{14}$ $1\frac{1}{4}$	$2\frac{2}{5} - 1\frac{1}{4}$ $1\frac{3}{20}$	$\frac{15}{20} + \frac{16}{32}$ $1\frac{1}{4}$

2.

$6\frac{1}{4} - 3\frac{5}{12}$ $2\frac{5}{6}$	$5\frac{4}{7} - 3\frac{2}{3}$ $1\frac{19}{21}$	$4\frac{1}{4} - 1\frac{5}{6}$ $2\frac{5}{12}$
$1\frac{2}{3} + 1\frac{1}{6}$ $2\frac{5}{6}$	$2\frac{5}{6}$	$\frac{23}{24} + 1\frac{7}{8}$ $2\frac{5}{6}$
$3\frac{15}{36} - \frac{7}{12}$ $2\frac{5}{6}$	$1\frac{14}{28} + 1\frac{7}{21}$ $2\frac{5}{6}$	$10\frac{3}{8} - 7\frac{3}{4}$ $2\frac{5}{8}$

3.

$1\frac{11}{12} + \frac{54}{72}$ $2\frac{2}{3}$	$7\frac{1}{9} - 3\frac{6}{7}$ $3\frac{16}{63}$	$\frac{13}{14} + 1\frac{5}{7}$ $2\frac{9}{14}$
$1\frac{8}{9} + \frac{16}{30}$ $2\frac{19}{45}$	$2\frac{2}{3}$	$11 - 8\frac{17}{51}$ $2\frac{2}{3}$
$8\frac{11}{12} - 6\frac{1}{4}$ $2\frac{2}{3}$	$3\frac{5}{15} - \frac{6}{9}$ $2\frac{2}{3}$	$1\frac{7}{10} + \frac{19}{20}$ $2\frac{13}{20}$

4.

$\frac{7}{11} + 1\frac{1}{4}$ $1\frac{39}{44}$	$3\frac{1}{16} - 1\frac{14}{32}$ $1\frac{5}{8}$	$5\frac{1}{2} - 2\frac{9}{10}$ $2\frac{3}{5}$
$\frac{21}{24} + \frac{3}{4}$ $1\frac{5}{8}$	$1\frac{5}{8}$	$3\frac{2}{5} - 1\frac{3}{4}$ $1\frac{13}{20}$
$9 - 7\frac{15}{40}$ $1\frac{5}{8}$	$1\frac{1}{10} + \frac{7}{12}$ $1\frac{41}{60}$	$3\frac{3}{4} - 2\frac{1}{8}$ $1\frac{5}{8}$

Name ____________________

Wheels of Estimates

Estimate the sum or difference. Then write the problem on the spoke of the wheel that contains the same value. **Answers may be on different spokes of the same wheel.**

$3\frac{4}{7} - 2\frac{7}{8}$ $\frac{1}{2}$	$5\frac{5}{8} - 4\frac{1}{6}$ $1\frac{1}{2}$	$\frac{14}{15} + \frac{9}{10}$ 2	$5\frac{1}{10} - 4\frac{3}{5}$ $\frac{1}{2}$
$4 - \frac{15}{17}$ 3	$1\frac{4}{9} + 1\frac{5}{10}$ 3	$2\frac{4}{10} - 1\frac{1}{7}$ $1\frac{1}{2}$	$6\frac{1}{7} - 2\frac{2}{3}$ 3
$9\frac{1}{13} - 6\frac{14}{15}$ 2	$6\frac{1}{15} - 3\frac{11}{12}$ 2	$5\frac{1}{12} - 1\frac{13}{14}$ 3	$3\frac{6}{7} - 1\frac{11}{12}$ 2
$1\frac{19}{20} + \frac{6}{7}$ 3	$1\frac{3}{8} + 1\frac{8}{15}$ 3	$\frac{1}{5} + \frac{5}{9}$ $\frac{1}{2}$	$1\frac{11}{12} - \frac{4}{7}$ $1\frac{1}{2}$
$\frac{3}{8} - \frac{1}{7}$ $\frac{1}{2}$	$\frac{15}{28} + \frac{29}{30}$ $1\frac{1}{2}$	$1\frac{7}{9} + \frac{1}{20}$ 2	$\frac{45}{50} + \frac{3}{5}$ $1\frac{1}{2}$
$5\frac{1}{20} - 3\frac{11}{20}$ $1\frac{1}{2}$	$\frac{9}{16} - \frac{1}{100}$ $\frac{1}{2}$	$3 - \frac{5}{6}$ 2	$\frac{15}{16} - \frac{4}{9}$ $\frac{1}{2}$

1.

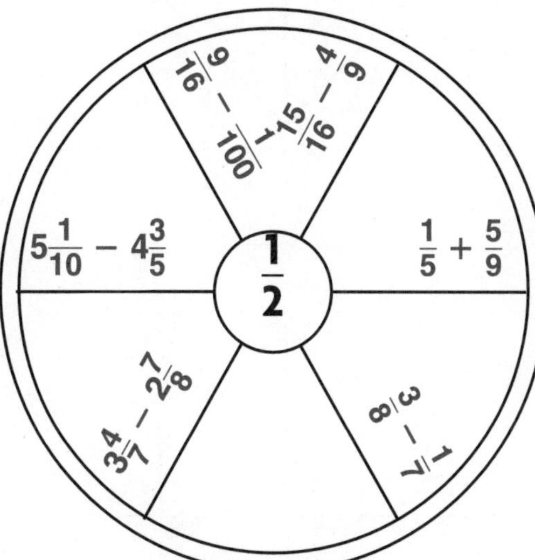

2.

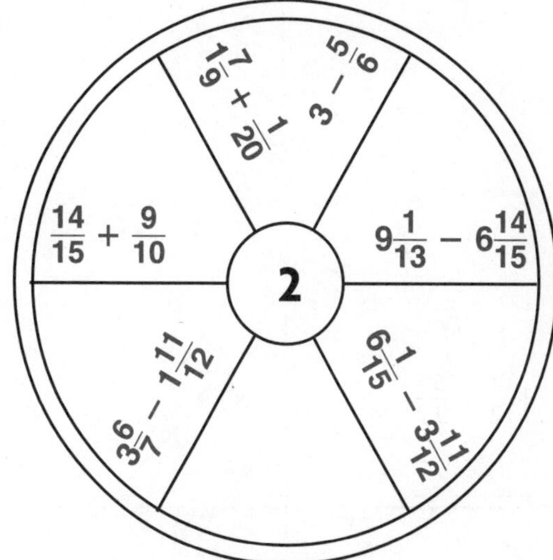

3.

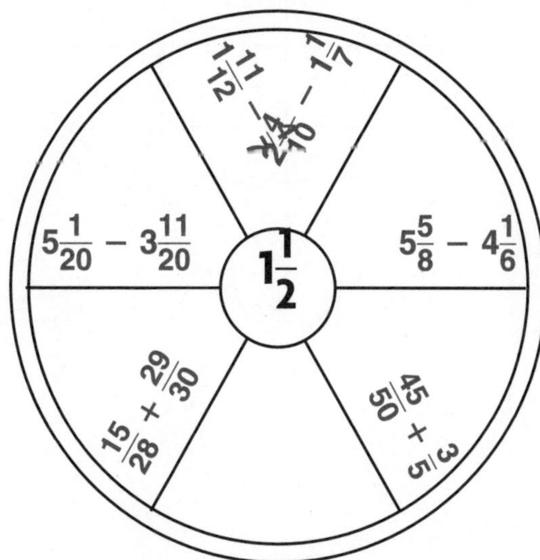

4.

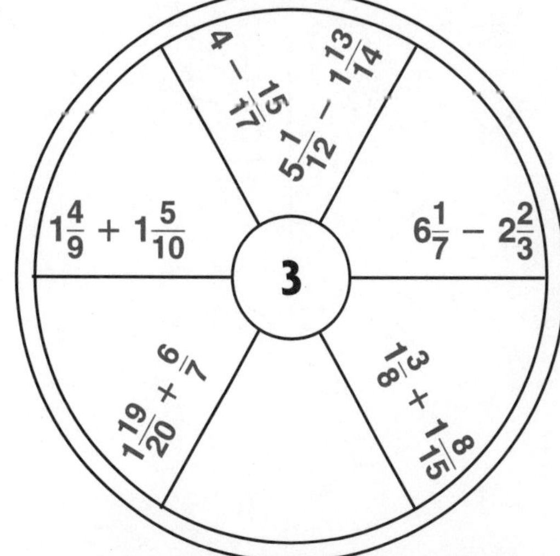

Name ______________________________

Make One Whole

Find each product or quotient. Then shade the two parts of the diamond which contain values whose sum equals one.

1.

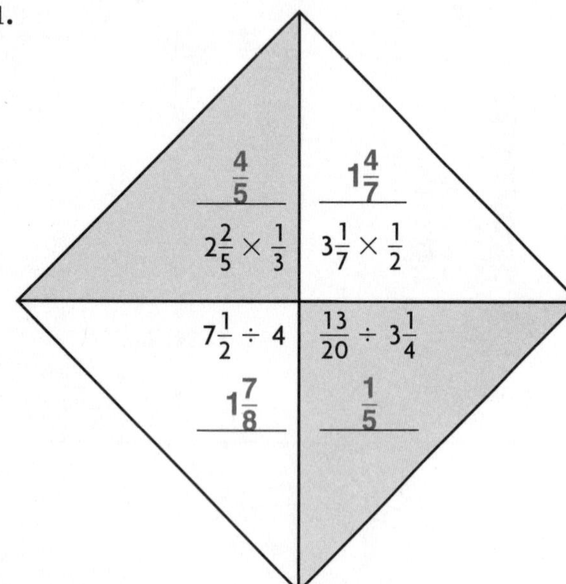

2.

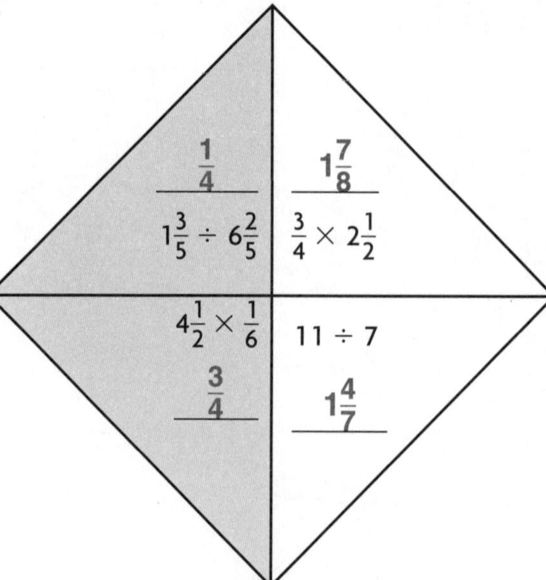

3.

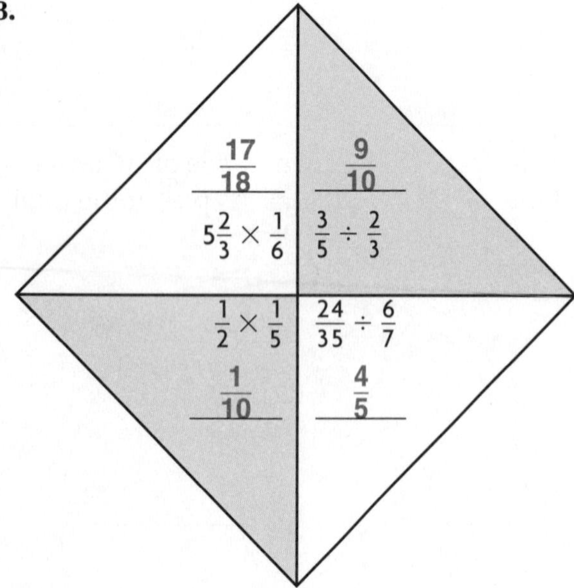

4.

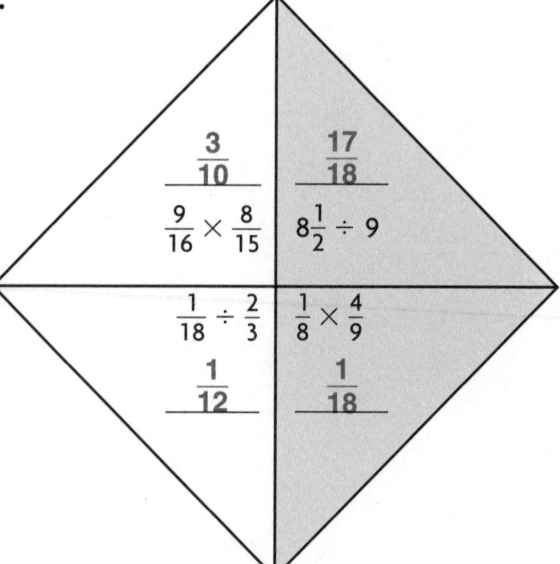

Name ______________________________

LESSON 4.5

Sneaker Study

Tom's Sneaker Haven holds a weekend sale. The bar graph shows the distribution of sales. Use the graph to answer the questions below.

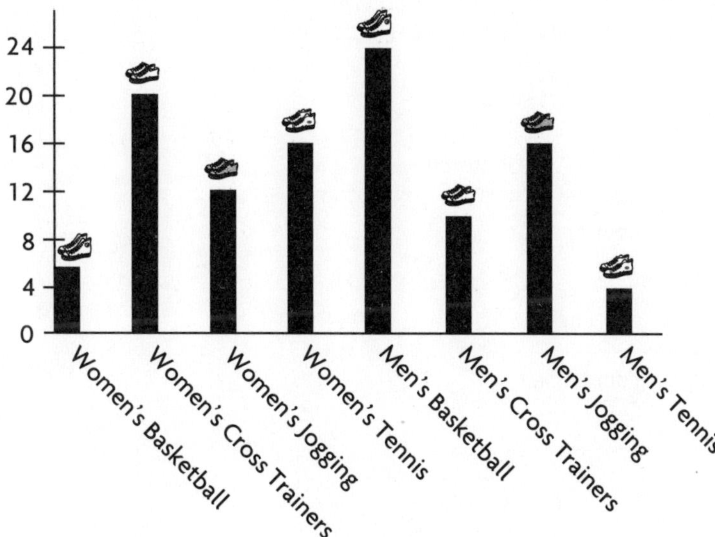

1. How many pairs of shoes are sold during the sale?

   108 pairs

2. Jogging shoes make up what fractional part of the total sales?

   $\frac{7}{27}$

3. Basketball sneakers make up what fractional part of the total sales?

   $\frac{5}{18}$

4. Women's shoes make up what fractional part of the total sales?

   $\frac{1}{2}$

5. Tennis shoes make up what fractional part of the total sales?

   $\frac{5}{27}$

6. What type of sneaker makes up $\frac{1}{18}$ of the total sales?

   Women's Basketball

7. What type of sneaker makes up $\frac{5}{54}$ of the total sales?

   Men's Cross Trainers

8. What type of sneaker makes up $\frac{1}{27}$ of the total sales?

   Men's Tennis Shoes

9. What type of sneakers makes up $\frac{5}{18}$ of the total sales?

   Cross Trainers

10. What two categories of sneakers combined make up $\frac{5}{9}$ of the total sales?

    Basketball and Cross Trainers

11. What two categories of sneakers combined make up $\frac{10}{27}$ of the total sales?

    Basketball and Tennis, or Jogging and Tennis

12. What two categories of sneakers combined make up $\frac{29}{54}$ of the total sales?

    Basketball and Jogging, or Cross Trainers and Jogging

Name ______________________________

Going the Distance

The map below is special. Instead of showing distances, the locations are separated by positive and negative integers. Add the numbers between locations to find the total score for a given route. Remember, different routes between locations have different scores.

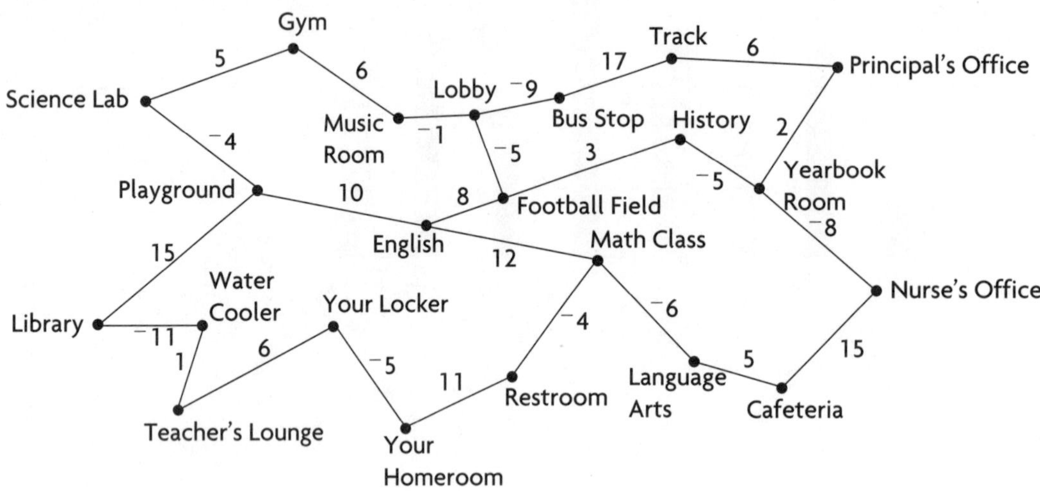

1. What is the score for a trip from the science lab to the cafeteria, through the library, your locker, math class, and language arts?

   8

2. What is the score for a trip from your homeroom to the track, through math class, English, and the lobby?

   30

3. What is the score for a trip from the library to the nurse's office, through your homeroom, math class, and the cafeteria?

   12

4. What is the score for a trip from the nurse's office to the library, through the football field, the gym, and the playground?

   6

5. Find the trip from the cafeteria to the gym with the lowest total score.

   5; through history, the football field, and the lobby

6. Find the trip from language arts to the playground with the lowest total score.

   7; through math class and your homeroom

7. Find the trip from your homeroom to the principal's office with the lowest total score.

   7; through the library, the science lab, the lobby, and the football field

8. Find the trip from the teacher's lounge to the lobby with the lowest total score.

   7; through your homeroom, the cafeteria, the football field, and history

Name ____

You Measure Up

Materials needed: measuring tape

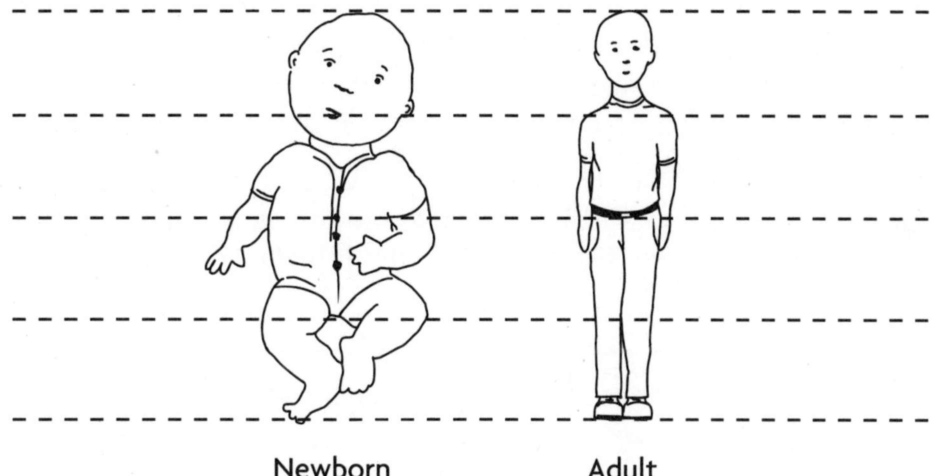

Did you know that at one time your head was as tall as the rest of your body? Look in a mirror. You've changed.

Seven months before you were born, the ratio of your head to your height was approximately 1:2, or 0.5. At birth, that ratio was closer to 1:4, or 0.25. The ratio now is close to what it will remain, approximately 9:58, or ≈0.16.

Use a measuring tape to find the given measurements to the nearest 0.25 inch. Then find the given ratio. **Answers will vary. Check students' work.**

1. Measure around the top of your head. Measure your height. Find the ratio of your height to your head measurement.

   height _____ head _____ ratio _____

2. Measure from your elbow to the end of your longest finger. Find the ratio of your "elbow" measurement to your height.

   elbow _____ height _____ ratio _____

3. Measure your wrist. Find the ratio of your height to your wrist measurement.

   height _____ wrist _____ ratio _____

4. Measure the length of your thumb. Find the ratio of your wrist measurement to your thumb length.

   wrist _____ thumb _____ ratio _____

5. Find the ratio of your thumb length to your wrist measurement.

   thumb _____ wrist _____ ratio _____

6. Measure the length of your arm from the shoulder to the end of your longest finger. Find the ratio of your height to the length of your arm.

   height _____ arm _____ ratio _____

Name ______________________

Are You a Good Guesser?

People often make mistakes entering numbers into calculators and computers. That is why it is important to estimate answers and have ideas about what might have gone wrong if an answer does not look correct.

You have earned \$5.50, \$1.30, and \$3.70 walking your neighbor's dog. You spend \$1.50 for lunch. About how much do you have left to spend?

Will 5.5 + 1.3 + 3.7 − 1.5 be closest to 10, 100, or 1,000?

Using rounding and mental math, you can estimate that the answer is closest to 10. If your answer had been close to 100, you might have forgotten to enter the decimal point in the calculator.

Without calculating, tell which number is closest to the answer.

1. ⁻5 + 15 − ⁻8 − 1 + 2

2, 20, or 200? ___20___

2. 175 − ⁻400 + 12 − 50

5, 50, or 500? ___500___

3. 22 − 9 + 1 + ⁻18

⁻10, 0, or 10? ___0___

4. 24 − 10 + 55 − ⁻3 − 47 + ⁻9

⁻100, 0, or 100? ___0___

5. 203 ÷ 19

10, 100, or 1,000? ___10___

6. ⁻1,035.4 ÷ ⁻21.3

⁻50, 0, or 50? ___50___

7. 8.56 × 23.5

2, 200, or 2,000? ___200___

8. 7.5 × ⁻129.5 − 23.6

⁻1,000, ⁻100, or 10? ___⁻1,000___

9. 56.9 ÷ ⁻5.7

⁻100, ⁻10, or 0? ___⁻10___

10. ⁻407.5 ÷ ⁻397.8

⁻25, 0, or 25? ___0___

11. ⁻65.3 × ⁻0.1

⁻100, 0, or 100? ___0___

12. ⁻29.4 ÷ 2.8

⁻10, 0, or 10? ___⁻10___

13. 5.84 ÷ 0.1

5, 50, or 500? ___50___

14. ⁻7.05 × 19.8

⁻150, ⁻15, or ⁻1.5? ___⁻150___

15. ⁻8.9 × ⁻3.8

⁻36, 0, or 36? ___36___

16. ⁻10 ÷ 0.01

⁻100, ⁻1,000, or ⁻10,000? ___⁻1,000___

17. Mrs. Hudzig worked 8 hours a day for 3 days, earning \$9 per hour. She deposited \$100 of her paycheck in the bank. About how much did she have left, \$10, \$100, or \$300?

___about \$100___

18. Mr. Reuben received a pension check for \$823.45 a month for 10 months. During that time he spent an average of \$718 per month and saved the rest. About how much did he save, \$100, \$1,000, or \$10,000?

___about \$1,000___

Name ______________________

LESSON 5.4

Changing Places

Addition and multiplication are commutative.
So, $3 + 7 = 7 + 3$, and $6 \times 5 = 5 \times 6$.

Some directions are commutative. "Walk 1 mi north. Walk 1 mi south." takes you to the same place as "Walk 1 mi south. Walk 1 mi north."

Subtraction and division are *not* commutative.

Some directions, like "Ready, Aim," and "Aim, Ready," are not commutative. The order makes a difference.

Which of the following directions are commutative? If the directions are not commutative, give the reason.

1. a. Travel north for 8 blocks.
   b. Travel west for 5 blocks.

   commutative

2. a. Mix flour, milk, and eggs.
   b. Put in a frying pan.

   not commutative; need something to put in pan

3. a. Go to the bus station.
   b. Take a bus to Columbus.

   not commutative; can't take bus first

4. a. Take a plane from Cleveland to Los Angeles.
   b. Take a plane from Los Angeles to Cleveland.

   not commutative; end in different places

5. a. Drive 80 miles east.
   b. Drive 45 miles north.

   commutative

6. a. Aim your dart.
   b. Throw your dart at the dartboard.

   not commutative; should aim first

7. a. Withdraw $100 from the bank.
   b. Deposit $200 in the bank.

   commutative

8. a. Deposit $100 in the bank.
   b. Withdraw $100 from the bank.

   commutative

9. a. Measure 2 cups of flour.
   b. Measure 1 cup of milk.

   commutative

10. a. Take the ski lift up the mountain.
    b. Take the ski lift down the mountain.

    not commutative; need to get up the mountain first

11. Make your own set of two directions and exchange them with a classmate. Decide whether or not they are commutative.
    Check students' directions.

Name ______________________

LESSON 5.5

Days and Daze

Some schools schedule classes according to a six-day cycle. The class schedule repeats every six days.

Suppose you have a six-day schedule and have physical education on Days 1 and 4. If this schedule starts on a Monday, when will you again have physical education on a Monday?

The numbers for the schedule show that in three weeks, Day 4 will occur on a Monday. This will be the next physical education class on a Monday.

Sun	Mon	Tue	Wed	Thu	Fri	Sat
	1 (1)	2 (2)	3 (3)	4 (4)	5 (5)	6
7	8 (6)	9 (1)	10 (2)	11 (3)	12 (4)	13
14	15 (5)	16 (6)	17 (1)	18 (2)	19 (3)	20
21	22 (4)	23 (5)	24 (6)	25 (1)	26 (2)	27
28	29 (3)	30 (4)	31 (5)			

For Problems 1–2, use the six-day cycle above.

1. Lu Ann has a study hall on Day 6. She works Tuesdays. What week will she have a study hall on a day she works?

   the third week

2. Dwight works Mondays and Wednesdays and has chess club on Days 2 and 5. On which days of the month will he have work and chess club?

   the 10th, 15th, and 31st

For Problems 3–5, use the calendar given.

3. Norbert has a favorite TV program on Tuesday. He does volunteer work at the library every third night. About how many times a month will he miss his TV program?

   1 or 2 times

4. Mr. Watanabe works nights on the first of the month and every other night after that. Mrs. Watanabe works nights on the first of the month and every third night after. When will they both be working nights?

   the 1st, 7th, 13th, 19th, 25th, 31st

5. Jefferson High schedules classes according to a 7-day cycle. Linda has woodworking on Days 1, 4, and 7. About how many times a month will she have woodworking?

   about 9 or 10 times

6. November 1st is a Wednesday. Louisa does volunteer work on November 1st and every third day after that. What is the next date that she will work on a Wednesday?

   Nov. 22

Sun	Mon	Tue	Wed	Thu	Fri	Sat
	1	2	3	4	5	6
7	8	9	10	11	12	13
14	15	16	17	18	19	20
21	22	23	24	25	26	27
28	29	30	31			

Name ______________________

What Is Reasonable?

If George tells you his car can travel 50 km in 5 min, you have to decide if that is reasonable.

Since 5 min = $\frac{1}{12}$ hr, 50 km in 5 min = 600 km in 1 hr.

A kilometer is less than a mile, but more than one-half mile. If a car travels 50 km in 5 min, then it would travel more than 300 mi per hour. This is too much, so the statement is unreasonable.

Use your knowledge of distance, weight, time, and other measures to decide which of the following statements are reasonable and which are unreasonable. You may need to investigate weights and measures and use your calculator with some of the exercises.

Write *R* for Reasonable and *U* for Unreasonable.

1. The tallest buildings in the world are more than 1,000 ft high. ___R___
2. The tallest mountain in the world is more than 100 mi high. ___U___
3. The world's longest railway tunnel is more than 30 mi long. ___R___
4. The smallest state, Rhode Island, has an area of 150,000 ft^2. ___U___
5. The longest river in the United States is more than 3,000 mi long. ___R___
6. The deepest well in the United States is 31,441 ft deep. ___R___
7. Los Angeles has a population of about 60,000 people. ___U___
8. The Pacific Ocean is more than 10,000 m deep. ___R___
9. A baby elephant weighs about 2,000 g. ___U___
10. A full-grown elephant can weigh as much as 16,000 lb. ___R___
11. A spider's egg sac can hold 3,000 eggs. ___R___
12. An eagle's wing span is about 180 cm. ___R___
13. An elephant might eat 500 lb of food per day. ___R___
14. A whale measures as long as 1,000 m. ___U___
15. There are over 50 billion dogs in the United States. ___U___

Name ______________________

LESSON 6.2

What Is Equal?

Math exercises often use expressions. To find out if two expressions are equivalent, simplify to find the value of each.

Which, if any, are equivalent expressions? **a.** 0.20 **b.** $1 \div \sqrt{4}$ **c.** $\frac{1}{5}$

a. $0.20 = 0.2$ **b.** $1 \div \sqrt{4} = 1 \div 2 = 0.5$ **c.** $\frac{1}{5} = 0.2$

So, the answer is **a** and **c** because 0.20 and $\frac{1}{5}$ are equal.

Which, if any, of the three expressions are equal?

1. **a.** $3^2 - 1$ **b.** 2^3 **c.** $16 \div 2$ **a, b, and c**
2. **a.** $\frac{3}{2}$ **b.** 150% **c.** $5 \div 3$ **a and b**
3. **a.** $2(\frac{5}{2})$ **b.** $\frac{^-10}{2}$ **c.** $\sqrt{25}$ **a and c**
4. **a.** $^-2(4 - 2)^2$ **b.** $^-17 + 28$ **c.** $\frac{1}{2} \times 32$ **none**
5. **a.** $3\frac{1}{3}$ **b.** $\frac{10}{3}$ **c.** $\frac{19}{3}$ **a and b**
6. **a.** $^-0.03$ **b.** $\frac{^-1}{300}$ **c.** $\frac{^-3}{100}$ **a and c**
7. **a.** $(\frac{1}{2})^2$ **b.** 0.0125 **c.** 0.25 **a and c**
8. **a.** $^-3^2$ **b.** $^-9$ **c.** 9 **a and b**
9. **a.** $^-(5 - 2)^3$ **b.** $^-3 \times 3^2$ **c.** 27 **a and b**
10. **a.** $\sqrt{625}$ **b.** 5^2 **c.** $^-50 \div {}^-2$ **a, b, and c**
11. **a.** $(3 \times 3)^2$ **b.** $(^-3 \times {}^-3)^2$ **c.** 9^2 **a, b, and c**
12. **a.** $(1 + 2)^2$ **b.** $2^2 - 1$ **c.** $1^2 + 2$ **b and c**

Write an equivalent number or expression. **Answers will vary. Possible answers are given.**

13. 25 **5^2**
14. $^-3$ **$^-\sqrt{9}$**
15. $(18 - 15)^2 - 1$ **2^3**
16. $^-121$ **$^-11^2$**
17. $649 - (^-3)^2$ **640**
18. $(5 - {}^-4) + 1$ **10**
19. $\frac{1}{3}(241) - 10^2$ **$^-19\frac{2}{3}$**
20. $0.25 \div \frac{4}{6}$ **$\frac{3}{8}$**
21. $(2 - 1)^5$ **1**
22. $(2 + 5) - (3 - 6)^2$ **$^-2$**

Name ____________________

Ancient Egyptian Math

Many ancient cultures represented number values with pictures or tally marks, rather than digits. Ancient Egyptians used pictures for a number system based on the powers of ten.

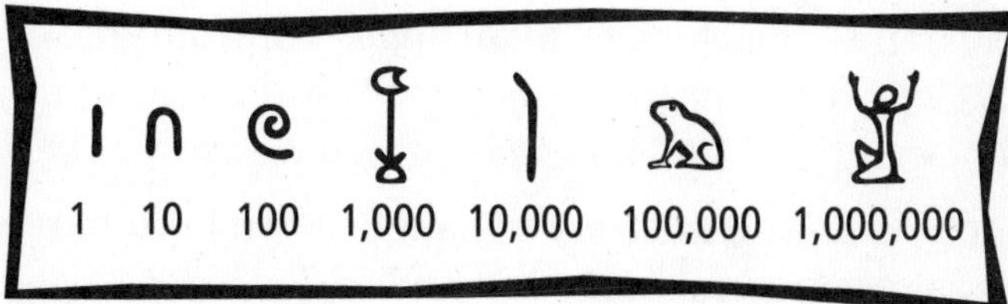

Examples of decimal numbers written using Egyptian symbols:

234 11,035 1,210,320

Write the Egyptian number in the decimal number system.

1. 2,123

2. 20,048

3. 1,031,104

4. 500,300

5. 2,303,201

6. 1,000,077

Draw the decimal number in the Egyptian number system.

7. 364

8. 10,136

9. 4,087

10. 2,331,111

11. 1,040,211

12. 435,007

13. What do you think are some advantages and disadvantages of the Egyptian number system? **Answers will vary.**

14. Make up your own number system using pictures. Write problems that use your number system. Exchange problems with a classmate and solve. **Check students' work.**

Name ______________________________

LESSON 6.4

Clock Angles

The hands of a clock form an angle. For example, at 9 o'clock the hour hand points to 9 and the minute hand points to 12. The angle formed measures 90°.

But how do you measure the angle when both hands are between numbers?

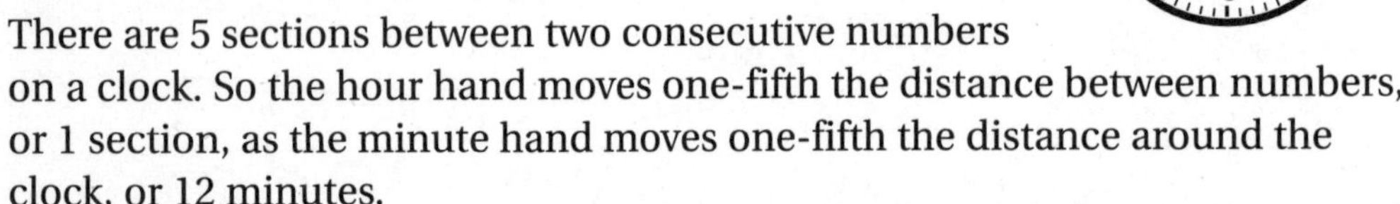

There are 5 sections between two consecutive numbers on a clock. So the hour hand moves one-fifth the distance between numbers, or 1 section, as the minute hand moves one-fifth the distance around the clock, or 12 minutes.

The small hand moves 1 section for every 12 minutes the large hand moves.

What is the angle between the hands at 7:24?

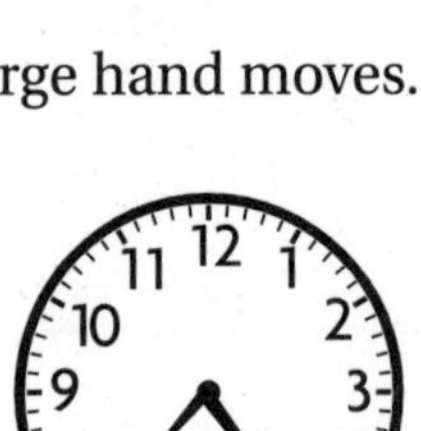

When the minute hand moves 24 minutes, the hour hand moves 2 sections. So, there are $(7 \times 5 + 2) - 24$ or 13 sections between the hands. Each section is $\frac{1}{60}$ of an hour and there are 360° on a clock face.

$13 \times \frac{1}{60} \times 360 = 13 \times 6 = 78$

The angle between the hands measures 78°.

---

1. Draw the clock hands and find the angle between them at 5 o'clock.

150°

2. Draw the clock hands and find the angle between them at 8 o'clock.

120°

3. Find the angle between the hands at 1 o'clock.

30°

4. Find the angle between the hands at 2 o'clock.

60°

5. Find the angle between the hands at 12:24.

132°

6. Find the angle between the hands at 3:48.

174°

7. Find the angle between the hands at 3:12.

24°

8. Find the angle between the hands at 1:36.

168°

Name ______________________________

What's My Equation?

Match each equation with the word problem it represents. Write the equation and corresponding letter with each problem. Then write the letter of the equation in the circle that has the problem number. Discover the message the letters form.

P $2g = 14$	**D** $\frac{p}{3} = 2.50$	**A** $\frac{m}{5} = 8$	**U** $3t = 21$
M $j - 18 = 33$	**S** $w + 7 = 25$	**T** $x + 7 = 22$	**H** $n - 12 = 37$

1. Tom has 7 more CDs than Rick. If Tom has 22 CDs, how many does Rick have?

   $x + 7 = 22$; T

2. Maria is 18 years younger than Joan. If Maria is 33, how old is Joan?

   $j - 18 = 33$; M

3. Five friends went out for dinner. They shared the cost of the meal equally. If each person paid $8, what was the total cost of the meal?

   $\frac{m}{5} = 8$; A

4. Jon paid 3 times as much for a tape as his friend did. If Jon paid $21, how much did his friend pay?

   $3t = 21$; U

5. Marissa and her two friends share a pizza. The cost of the pizza is shared equally among them. If each person pays $2.50, how much does the pizza cost?

   $\frac{p}{3} = 2.50$; D

6. Lee has scored twice as many goals as Jiang. If Lee's goal total is 14, how many goals has Jiang scored?

   $2g = 14$; P

7. Bill sold 7 more magazine subscriptions than Wayne. If Bill sold 25 subscriptions, how many did Wayne sell?

   $w + 7 = 25$; S

8. Shelly delivered 12 fewer newspapers this week than last week. If she delivered 37 papers this week, how many did she deliver last week?

   $n - 12 = 37$; H

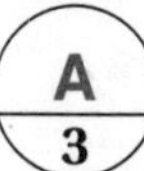

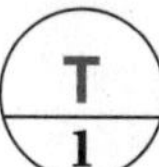

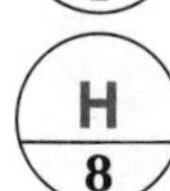

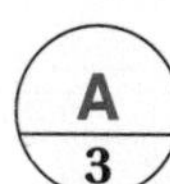

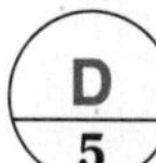

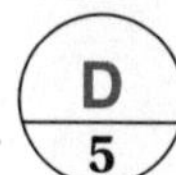

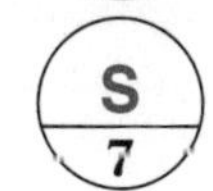

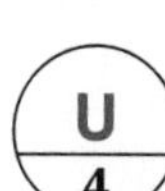

Name ________________________________

Equal Sides

Solve each equation. Then divide the equations into two groups of five. The sum of the solutions in each group should be 150. Write the equations on the scale to make it balance.

1. $m - 13 = 27$ $m = 40$

2. $y + 27 = 60$ $y = 33$

3. $t - 21 = 43$ $t = 64$

4. $p - 13 = 15$ $p = 28$

5. $b + 19 = 40$ $b = 21$

6. $m + 9 = 24$ $m = 15$

7. $r + 6 = 31$ $r = 25$

8. $j + 97 = 117$ $j = 20$

9. $s + 8 = 45$ $s = 37$

10. $c + 6 = 23$ $c = 17$

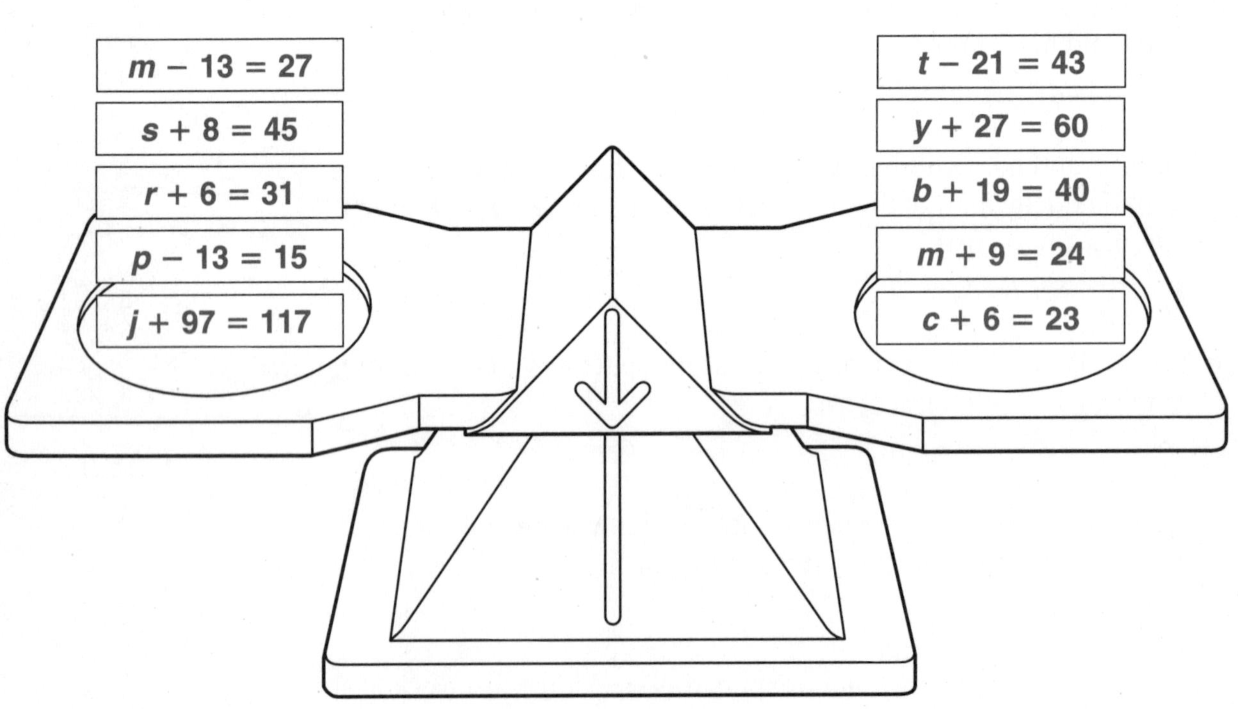

Name ______________________________

A Problem for Every Solution

Work with a classmate.

- Look at what the variable represents.
- On a separate sheet of paper, create a problem that can be solved with the equation given.
- Trade problems with another pair of students.
- Solve each other's problems. **Problems will vary.**

1. Let p = the number of people dining together.

$3.50p = 21.00$

$p = 6$

2. Let s = the number of students in a math class.

$5s = 135$

$s = 27$

3. Let b = the length of a piece of wire.

$14b = 39.2$ cm

$b = 2.8$ cm

4. Let g = the total cost of a gift.

$\frac{g}{8} = \$5.75$

$g = \$46.00$

5. Let j = the cost of a new stereo system.

$\frac{j}{12} = \$456$

$j = \$5{,}472$

6. Let w = the number of banquet guests.

$32w = 3{,}200$

$w = 100$

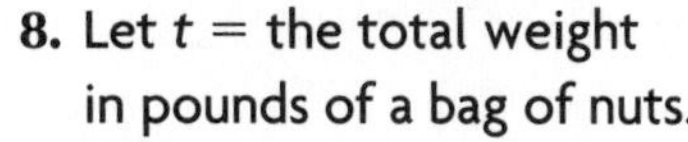

7. Let c = the number of pieces of candy in one box.

$\frac{c}{8} = 6$

$c = 48$

8. Let t = the total weight in pounds of a bag of nuts.

$\frac{t}{2.5} = 45$ lb

$t = 112.5$ lb

9. Let r = the cost of one CD.

$11r = \$142.45$

$r = \$12.95$

10. Let h = the number of honor students.

$35h = 525$

$h = 15$

11. Let x = the number of students on a bus.

$8.50x = 340$

$x = 40$

12. Let d = diameter of a circle.

$3.14d = 628$

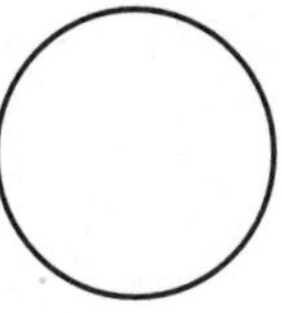

$d = 200$

Name ______________________________

LESSON 7.4

Integer Riddles

1. I am an integer. When you add 5 to me, the result is ⁻6. What integer am I? ⁻11	2. I am an integer. When you subtract 9 from me, the result is ⁻33. What integer am I? ⁻24
3. I am an integer. When you add ⁻8 to me and then subtract ⁻15, the result is 24. What integer am I? 17	4. I am an integer. When you subtract ⁻11 from me and then increase the amount by 6, the result is ⁻3. What integer am I? ⁻20
5. I am an integer. When you add me to myself, the result is ⁻24. What integer am I? ⁻12	6. I am an integer. When you add me to myself, the result is ⁻32. What integer am I? ⁻16
7. I am an integer. When you add 14 to me and then decrease the amount by 21, the result is ⁻9. What integer am I? ⁻2	8. I am an integer. When you add ⁻23 to me and then subtract 5, the result is ⁻25. What integer am I? 3
9. I am an integer. When you double me and then increase the amount by 5, the result is ⁻23. What integer am I? ⁻14	10. I am an integer. When you triple me and then decrease the amount by 8, the result is ⁻14. What integer am I? ⁻2
11. I am an integer. When you increase me by ⁻6 and then subtract ⁻11, the result is 43. What integer am I? 38	12. I am an integer. When you decrease me by 9, then add ⁻3, and subtract ⁻8, the result is ⁻4. What integer am I? 0
13. I am an integer. When you divide me by 5 and then add 6, the result is 9. What integer am I? 15	14. I am an integer. When you divide me by ⁻1 and then subtract 5, the result is 8. What integer am I? ⁻13

Name ______________________________

Size It Up!

Mr. Gonzalez, a builder, purchased the four lots shown below. Mr. Gonzalez needs to know the total area of each lot in square feet. He also needs to know the perimeter of each lot in feet.

You can use proportions to calculate the areas and perimeters for him. For each figure, the scale is 1 in.:60 ft.

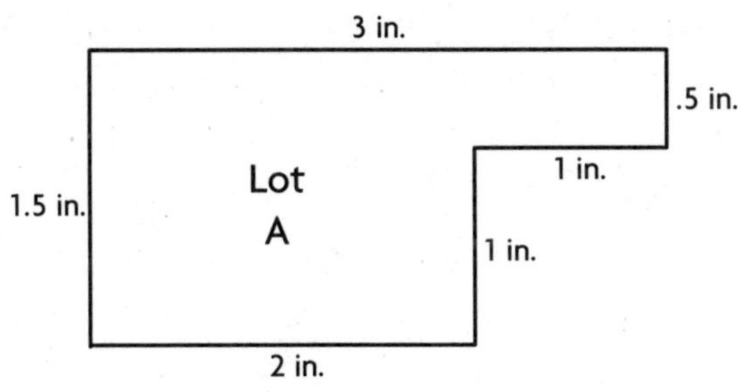

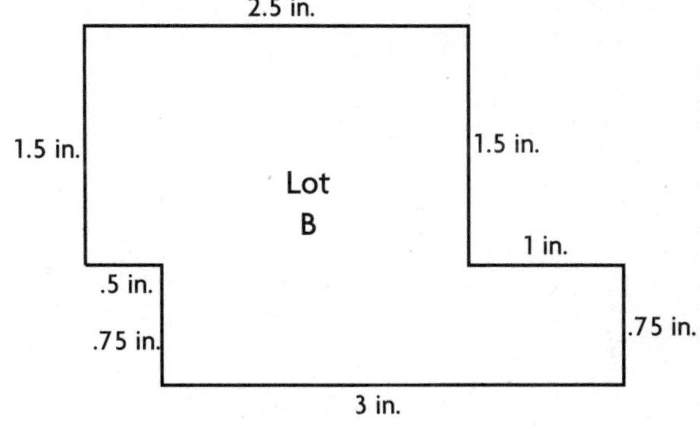

1. total area 12,600 ft^2

   perimeter 540 ft

2. total area 21,600 ft^2

   perimeter 690 ft

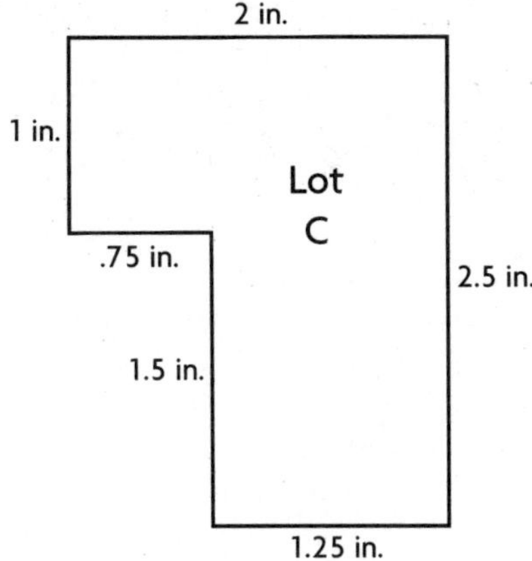

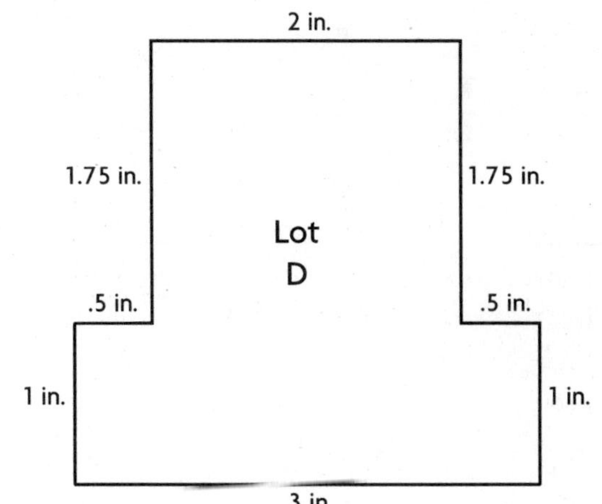

3. total area 13,950 ft^2

   perimeter 540 ft

4. total area 23,400 ft^2

   perimeter 690 ft

5. What is the combined area of all four lots? 71,550 ft^2

6. What length of fencing would be needed to enclose all four lots? 2,460 ft

Name ______________________________

LESSON 8.1

Do You Have a Problem for My Solution?

Below each equation, write a problem that can be solved by the two-step equation. **Problems will vary.**

1. $4n + 3 = 67$ **Sample problem:**

   Steve is 67 years old. He is 3 years older than 4 times Mike's age. How old is Mike? $n = 16$; Mike is 16 yr. old.

2. $5b - 7 = 43$

   $b = 10$

3. $2y + 3.25 = 24.65$

   $y = 10.70$

4. $5b - 1.80 = 8.95$

   $b = 2.15$

5. $4w + 12 = 68$

   $w = 14$

6. $3t - 9 = 75$

   $t = 28$

7. $3m - 1.99 = 7.88$

   $m = 3.29$

8. $2d + 5.15 = 21.99$

   $d = 8.42$

9. $2z - 5 = 13$

   $z = 9$

10. $4r + 2.5 = 18.5$

    $r = 4$

Name ______________________

Equation Wheels

In this activity you will create equations that have the solutions given.

Create two equations by using the terms in each wheel. The symbols needed to form the two equations are shown in the box. Each equation should have three terms on the left side and one term on the right side.

Make sure that the value given is a solution to your equation.

1. Solution: $n = 7$

   $4n - 6 + 3n = 43$

2. Solution: $n = 11$

   $2n + 8 + n = 41$

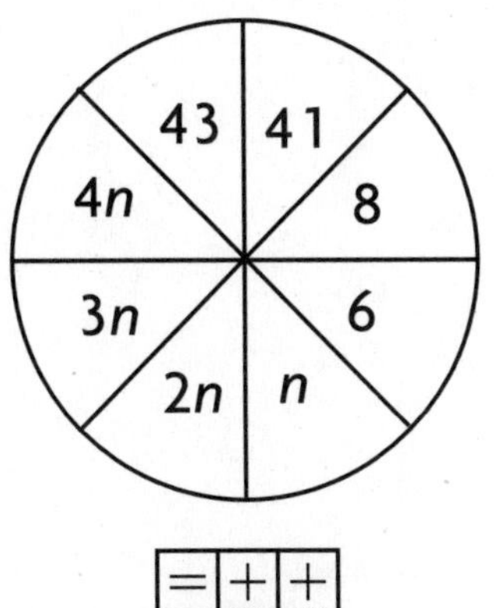

3. Solution: $j = 3$

   $7j - 5 + 3j = 25$

4. Solution: $j = 9$

   $9j - 6 - 5j = 30$

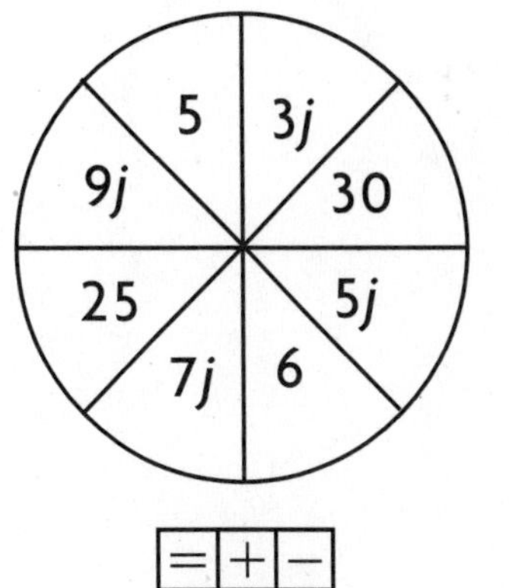

5. Solution: $p = 7$

   $2p + 3^2 + 6p = 65$

6. Solution: $p = 9$

   $8p - 2^2 - 4p = 32$

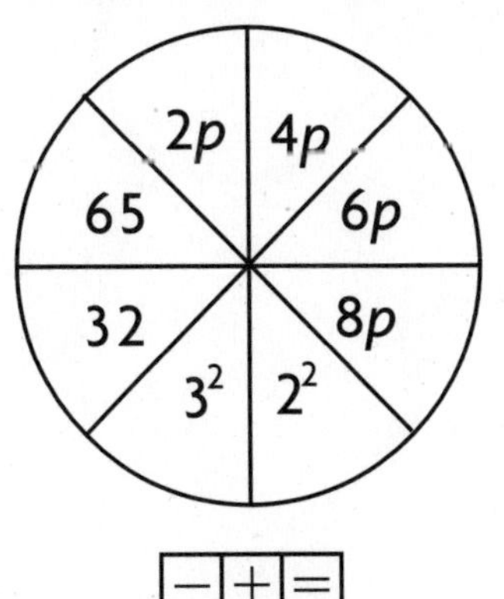

7. Solution: $t = 2$

   $5t + 3 + 3t = 19$

8. Solution: $t = 5$

   $4t - 11 + 6t = 39$

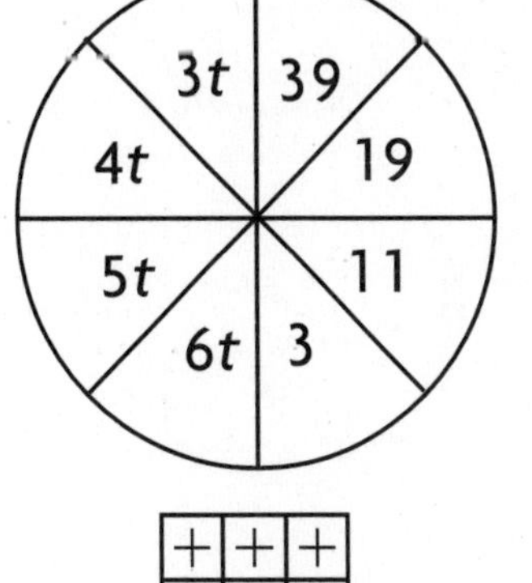

Name ______________________________

LESSON 8.3

Flower Power

Shade the petals of each flower that contain an inequality that is true for the value shown in the center circle.

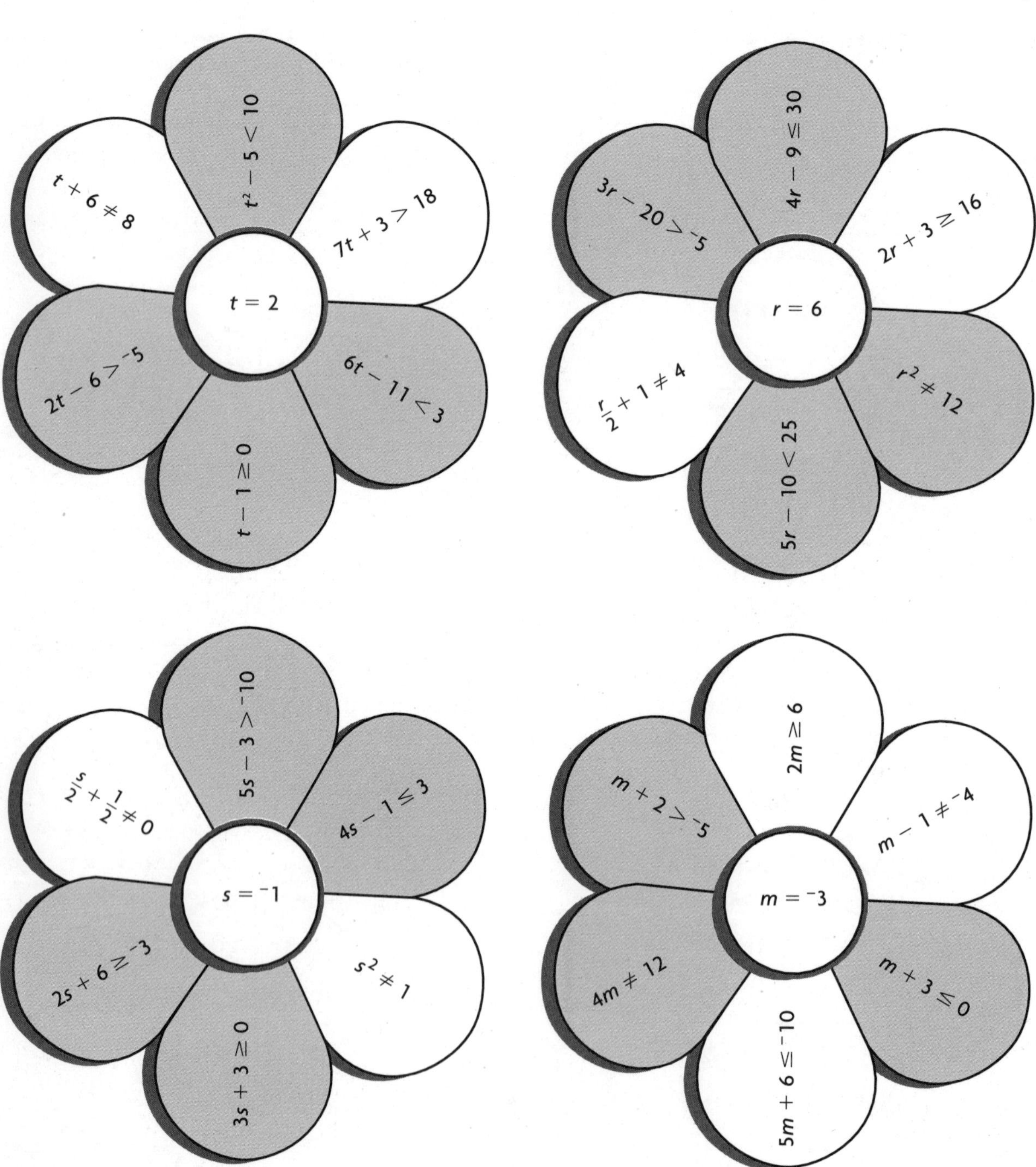

Name ____________________

Match It Up!

Write and solve an inequality for each problem. Match the problem with the graph of its solution.

a. 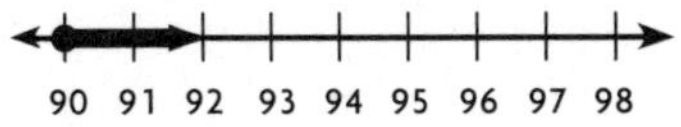

b. 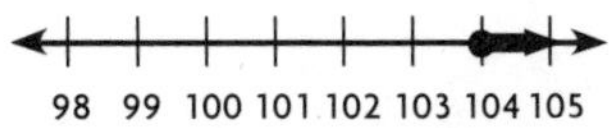

c. 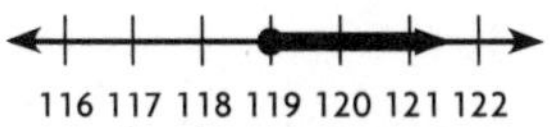

d. 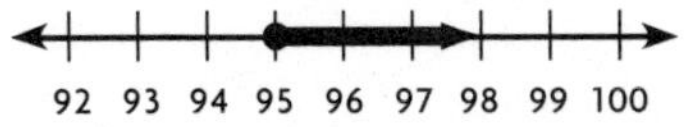

e. 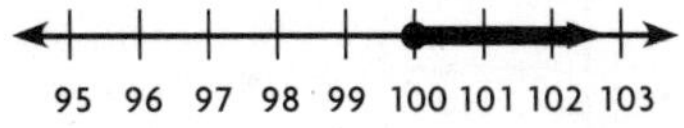

f. 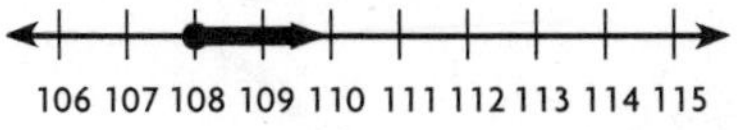

g. 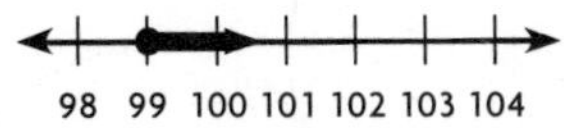

h. 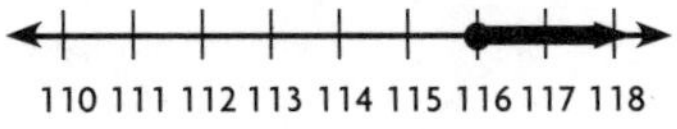

i. 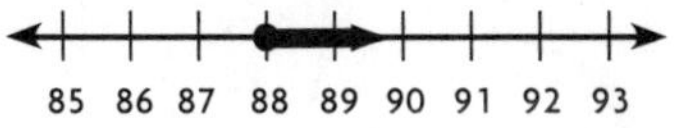

j. 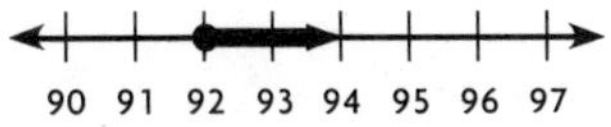

1. Rhea is averaging her grades. On 4 tests she scored 98, 85, 93, and 92. She wants her average to be greater than or equal to 92. What does Rhea's score on her fifth test need to be greater than or equal to?

   $\frac{98 + 85 + 93 + 92 + x}{5} \geq 92$; $x \geq 92$; j

2. Walt is averaging the number of coupons he distributed for 4 days. So far, he has given out 82, 96, 87, and 81 coupons. How many coupons must Walt distribute on the fifth day if he wants to average a minimum of 90 coupons each day?

   $\frac{82 + 96 + 87 + 81 + x}{5} \geq 90$; $x \geq 104$; b

3. Mrs. Bell's homeroom is holding a canned food drive. On the first 3 days of the week, the class brought in 106, 88, and 90 cans. How many cans must be brought in on the fourth day for the class to average at least 100 cans per day?

   $\frac{106 + 88 + 90 + x}{4} \geq 100$; $x \geq 116$; h

4. Max is averaging his language arts grades. On 5 tests, he scored 81, 99, 78, 82, and 100. What must Max score on the sixth test if he wants his average to be 90 or greater?

   $\frac{81 + 99 + 78 + 82 + 100 + x}{6} \geq 90$; $x \geq 100$; e

5. Oak Street School is calculating its daily attendance rate. For the first four days of a school week, the attendance was 87%, 81%, 90%, and 82%. If the school hopes to average 86% for the week, what must the attendance rate be greater than or equal to on the fifth day?

   $\frac{87\% + 81\% + 90\% + 82\% + x}{5} \geq 86\%$; $x \geq 90\%$; a

Name ______________________

Experimenting with Ordered Pairs

1. Graph each of the following ordered pairs. Then connect the points in the order given. (⁻7,⁻1), (⁻3,⁻1), (⁻3,⁻7), (⁻4,⁻7), (⁻4,⁻2), (⁻6,⁻2), (⁻6,⁻3), (⁻7,⁻3),(⁻7,⁻1). Label it figure 1.

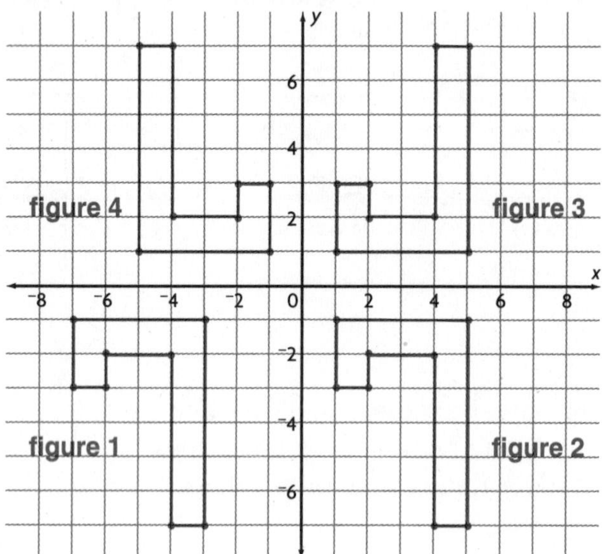

2. What does figure 1 look like? **a number 7**

3. Add 8 to the first number in each ordered pair above. Write the new ordered pairs. **(1,⁻1), (5,⁻1), (5,⁻7), (4,⁻7), (4,⁻2), (2,⁻2), (2,⁻3), (1,⁻3), (1,⁻1)**

4. Graph the ordered pairs in Problem 3, and connect the points in order. Label the new drawing figure 2.

5. How does figure 2 compare with figure 1?

   Same size and shape; shifted 8 units to the right

6. Use the ordered pairs from Problem 3. Replace the second number of each ordered pair with its opposite. Write the new ordered pairs below. Then graph the points, correct them in order, and call it figure 3.

   (1,1), (5,1), (5,7), (4,7), (4,2), (2,2), (2,3), (1,3), (1,1)

7. What does figure 3 look like? **the letter J**

8. Use the ordered pairs from Problem 6. Replace the first number in each ordered pair with its opposite. Graph the new ordered pairs in order, and call it figure 4.

   What does figure 4 look like? **the letter L**

Name ______________________________

Capital Check

Do you know the state capitals of all 50 states? Check your knowledge by completing the mapping diagrams below. Draw an arrow from each state to its capital.

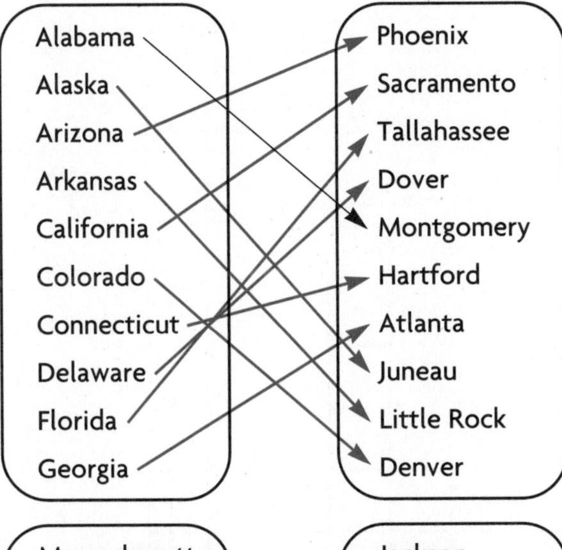

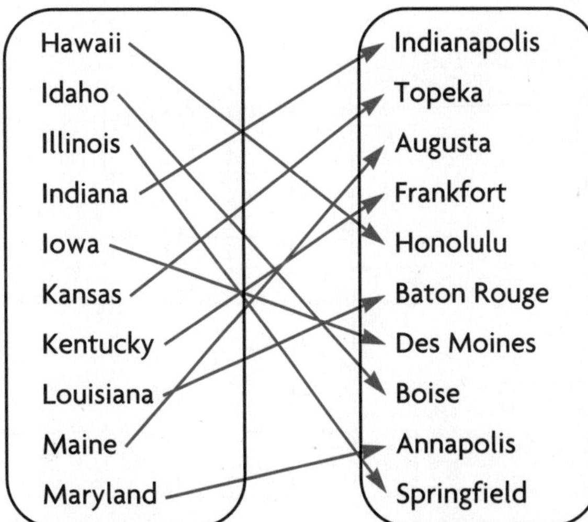

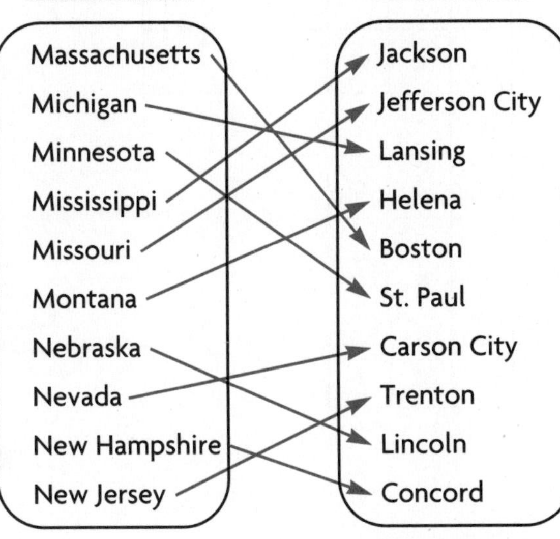

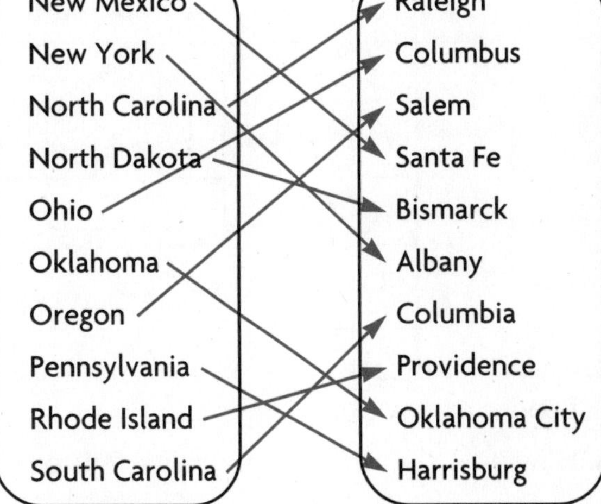

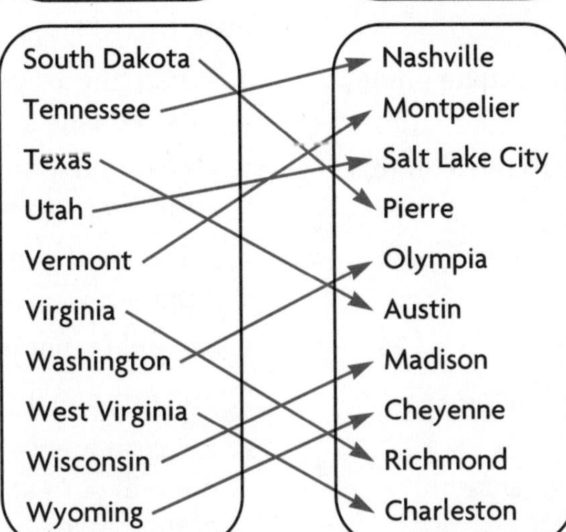

Name ___________________________

LESSON 9.3

Word Relations

Complete the crossword puzzle with important terms that relate to ordered pairs, relations, and functions.

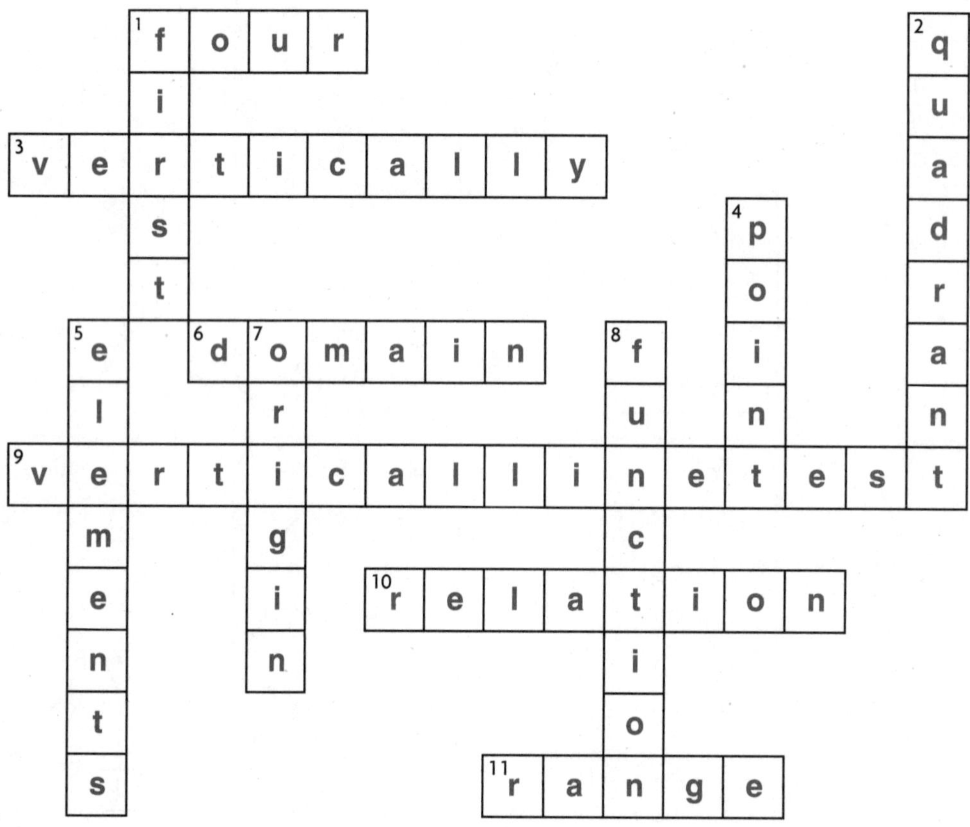

Across

1. Number of quadrants a coordinate plane is divided into
3. The y-coordinate tells you to move in this direction.
6. First set of elements in a relation
9. Use this to find if a relation is a function (3 words).
10. Formed when one set of elements is matched to another set
11. Second set of elements in a relation

Down

1. Where the x-coordinate is placed in an ordered pair
2. One of the four regions that make up a coordinate plane
4. An ordered pair names its position on a plane
5. Members that make up a set
7. The point (0,0)
8. Relation in which each element of the domain corresponds to only one element of the range

Name ______________________________

Patterns, Patterns

Your sister, Mary Etta, is getting married. She planned a small reception, but more and more people are coming. So the cake must have more and more layers.

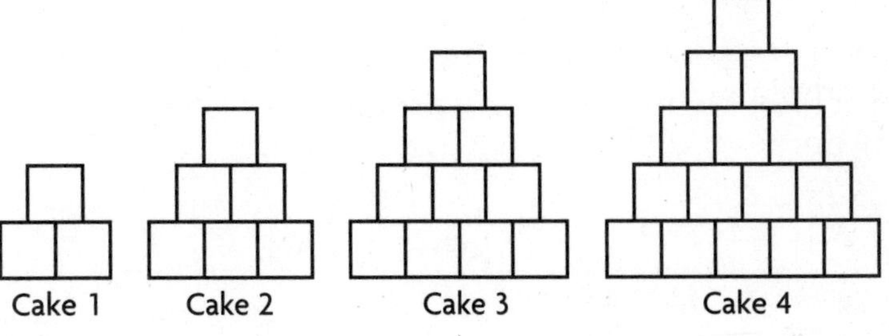

1. The first four wedding cakes selected are shown below. If this pattern continues, how many squares would make up the sixth wedding cake?

   28 squares

2. How many squares would make up the eighth wedding cake?

   45 squares

3. Draw a picture of the eighth wedding cake.

   Check students' drawings; cake should have base of 9 squares.

Marina and Rob are playing a game with house-shaped figures. Two figures can be joined only at the "floors" or at the "roofs."

Move 1 Move 2 Move 3 Move 4 Move 5

4. The first five moves are shown. If this pattern continues, how many small triangles would there be after the seventh move?

   14 triangles

5. Draw a picture after the sixth and seventh moves.

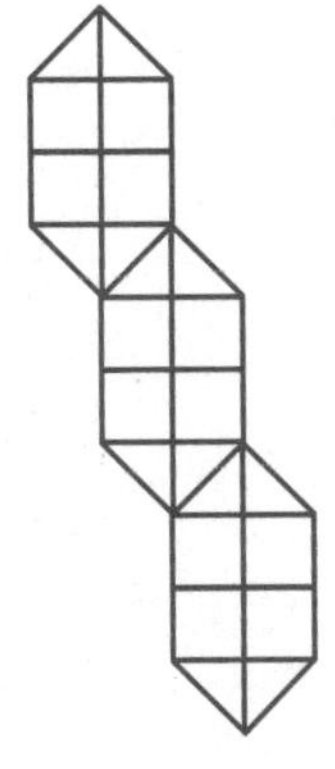

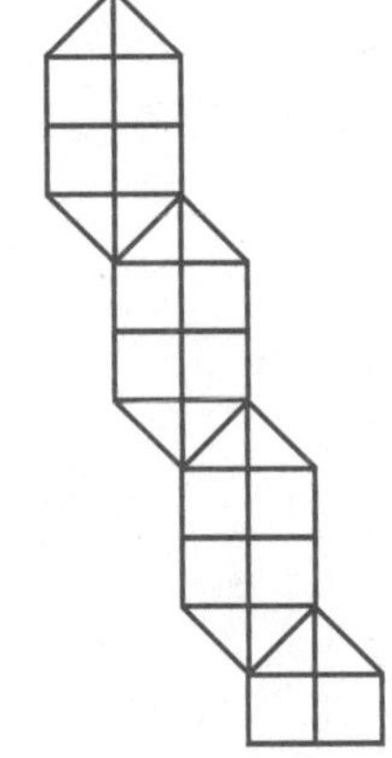

Name ______________________________

Puzzling Angles

Write the correct letter from Column B below. Then write the letter from each problem in the corresponding box labeled with the problem number.

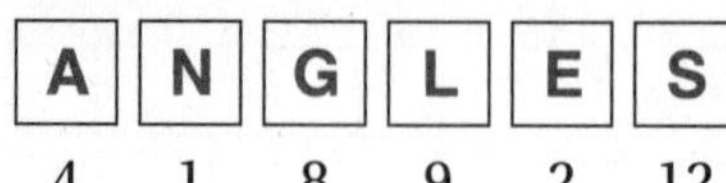

A	N	G	L	E	S		M	A	K	E		A		P	O	I	N	T
4	1	8	9	2	12		6	4	10	2		4		3	11	7	1	5

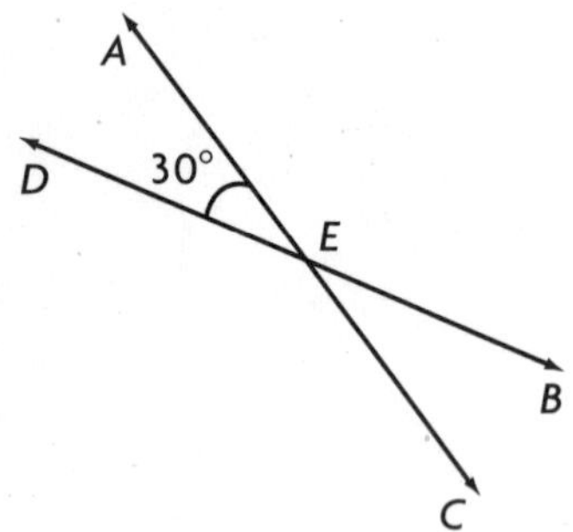

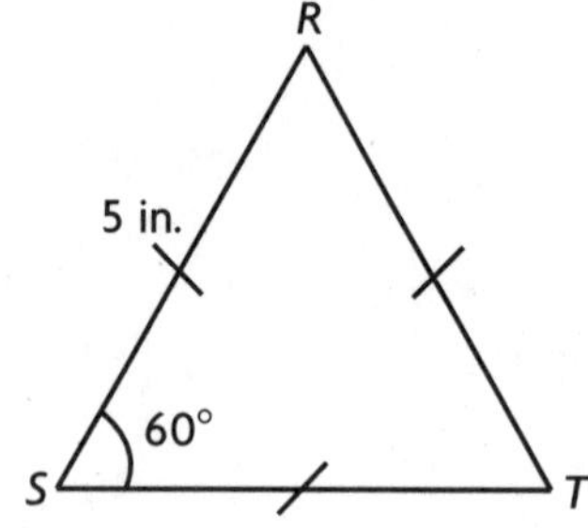

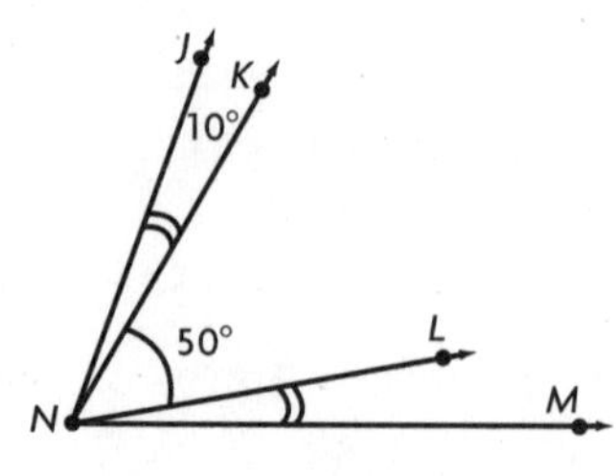

$\angle JNK$ is congruent to $\angle LNM$

	Column A	Column B
1. measure of $\angle CED$	N	A 5 in.
2. measure of $\angle CEB$	E	E 30°
3. measure of $\angle DEA$ + measure of $\angle AEB$	P	G 10°
4. measure of segment *RS*	A	I 15 in.
5. measure of $\angle SRT$	T	K 70°
6. measure of $\angle RST$ + measure of $\angle STR$	M	L 50°
7. perimeter of $\triangle RST$	I	M 120°
8. measure of $\angle LNM$	G	N 150°
9. measure of $\angle KNL$	L	O 20°
10. measure of $\angle JNM$	K	P 180°
11. measure of $\angle JNK$ + measure of $\angle LNM$	O	S 40°
12. measure of $\angle KNL$ − measure of $\angle LNM$	S	T 60°

Name ___________________________

Design Your Own Quilt

This quilt will be a collection of individual squares. In each square, draw a different figure that has the given rotational symmetry.

For example,  has $\frac{1}{2}$-turn or 180° symmetry. **Answers will vary. Check students' work.**

$\frac{1}{4}$ turn, or 90°	$\frac{1}{2}$ turn, or 180°	$\frac{1}{4}$ turn, or 90°
$\frac{1}{3}$ turn, or 120°	$\frac{1}{6}$ turn, or 60°	$\frac{1}{3}$ turn, or 120°
$\frac{1}{4}$ turn, or 90°	$\frac{1}{2}$ turn, or 180°	$\frac{1}{4}$ turn, or 90°
$\frac{1}{3}$ turn, or 120°	$\frac{1}{6}$ turn, or 60°	$\frac{1}{3}$ turn, or 120°

Name ____________________

LESSON 10.3

Transforming a Book Cover

Use the given pattern to create a designer book cover. Your design should use translations, rotations, and reflections. Sketch your designs in the outline of the book cover. Write about which transformations you used. **Check students' work.**

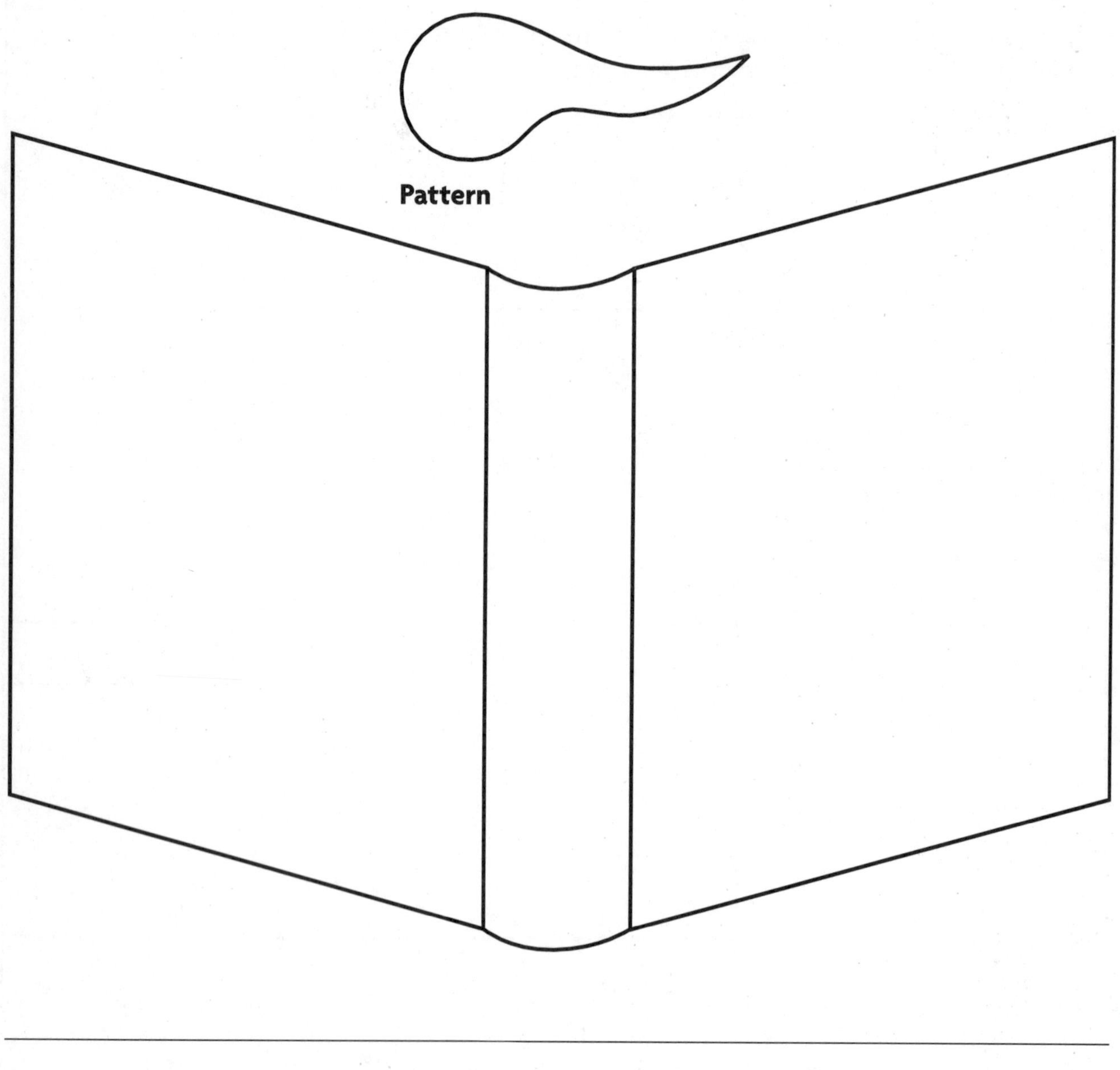

____

____

____

____

Name ______________________________

Follow That Transformation

You know where a treasure chest is buried. You want to direct your friend to the treasure, but you must do so in code. Here is how you will make the code.

Begin by drawing a triangle on the coordinate plane below.

Then list in order 5 transformations that must be done to the original figure. The treasure is located in the image of the transformed triangle.

Exchange papers with a classmate. Follow the directions and draw a triangle to show the location of the treasure. **Check students' work.**

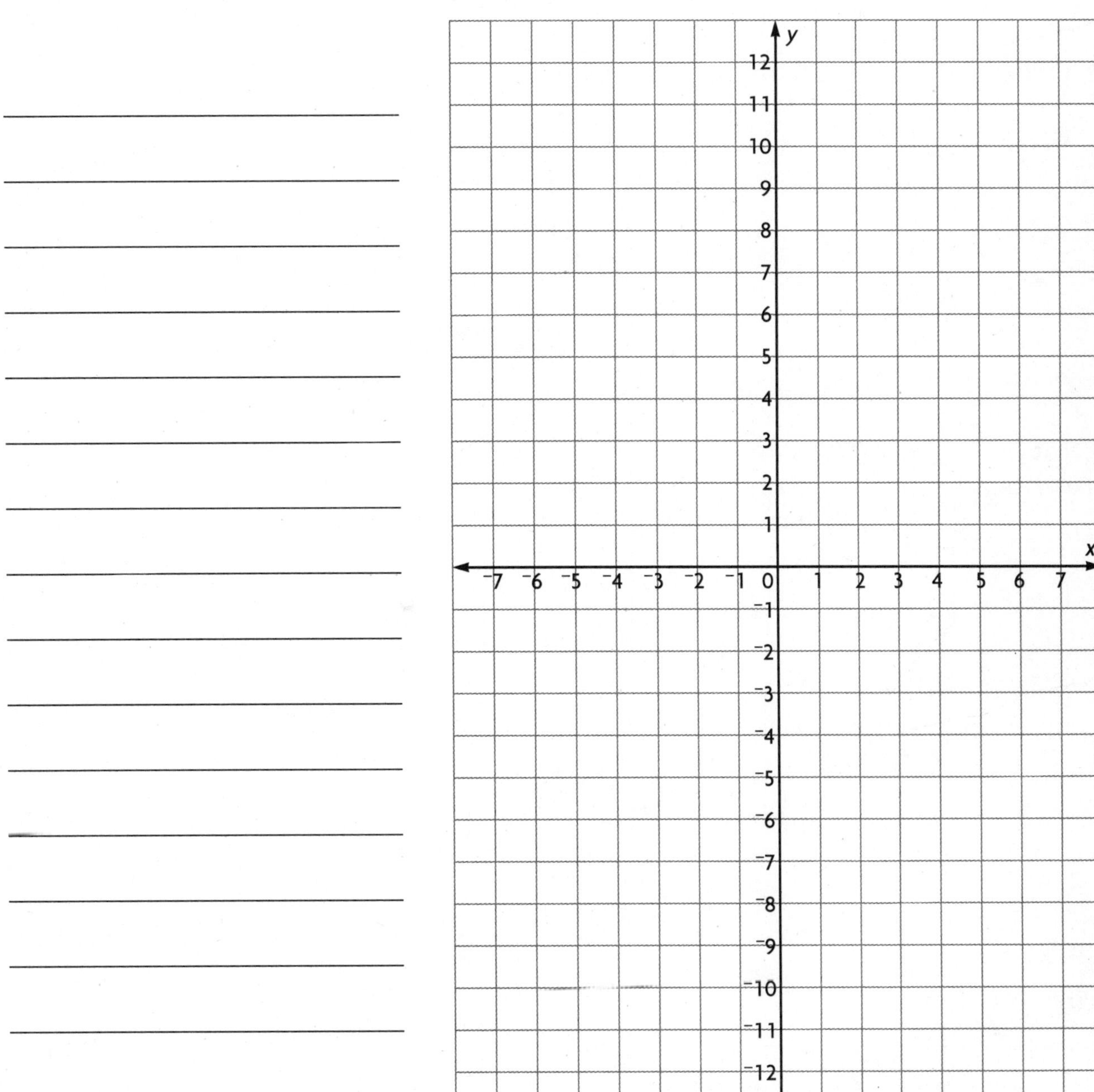

Name ____________________

The Hawaiian Angle

Materials needed: compass and straightedge

The map shows the Hawaiian Island of Oahu.

You will bisect an angle to find where a world-changing event occurred on December 7, 1941. **Exercises 1–3, check students' work.**

1. Draw a ray from Kailua through Honolulu.
2. Draw a ray from Kailua through the Koolau Range and Wahiawa.
3. Bisect the angle formed to find where the event occurred on December 7, 1941.
4. Where did the event occur? **Pearl Harbor**

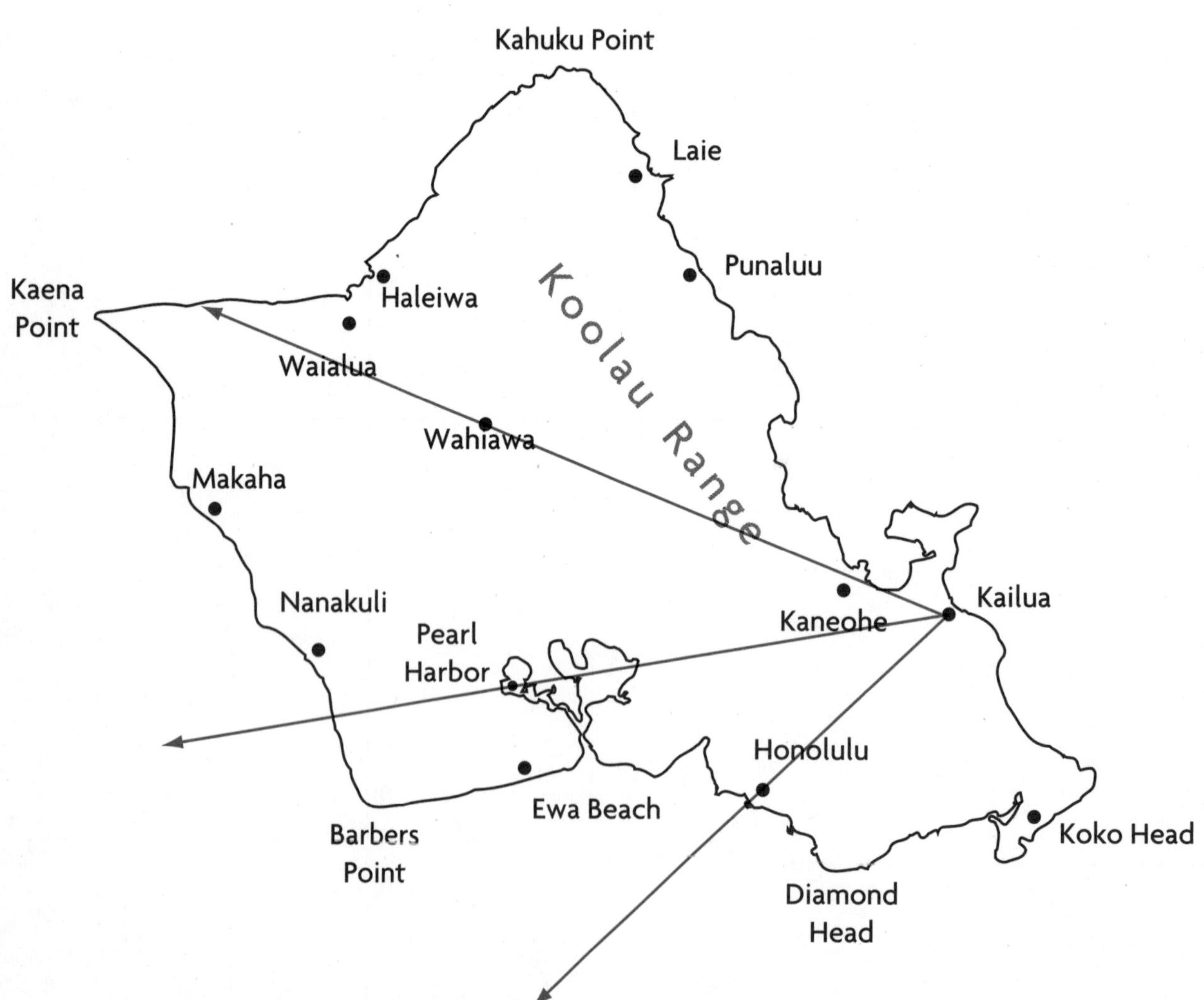

Name ____

Just a Regular Construction

Materials needed: compass, straightedge

Using just a compass and a straightedge, you can construct a regular pentagon inside the circle below. **Check students' work.**

1. Draw a diameter of the circle.
2. Label the center of the circle *O*.
3. Label point *A* where the diameter intersects the circle.
4. Construct a perpendicular bisector of the diameter.
5. Find the midpoint of the radius on the perpendicular bisector. Label it *M*.
6. Construct the angle bisector of $\angle OMA$.
7. Find the intersection of the angle bisector and $\overline{OA}$. Label it *X*.
8. Construct a perpendicular line to $\overline{OA}$ at point *X*.
9. Label the intersections of the perpendicular line and the circle *B* and *E*.
10. Open your compass to the same measure as $\overline{AB}$. Mark off point *C* this same distance from point *B*, and mark off point *D* this same distance from point *C*.
11. Draw $\overline{AB}$, $\overline{BC}$, $\overline{CD}$, $\overline{DE}$, and $\overline{AE}$.

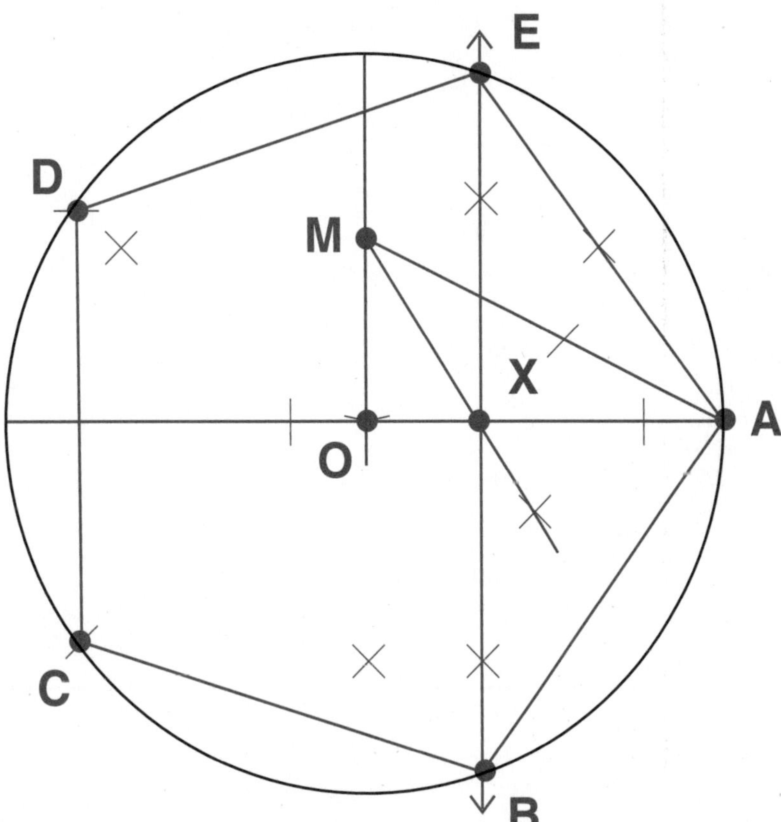

Name ______________________________

LESSON 11.3

Artful Triangle

Materials needed: colored pencils or pens

In the square below, create a pattern for a floor tile made entirely of triangles. Then classify the triangles according to the lengths of their sides. Color scalene triangles one color, isosceles triangles a second color, and equilateral triangles a third color. **Check students' work.**

Name ______________________________

LESSON 11.4

Design Your Own Stained Glass Window

Materials needed: compass, straightedge, colored pencils or pens

You have been selected to design a stained glass window for the lobby of your school. Your guideline is to design the window so that it contains only triangles congruent to those shown.

Construct congruent triangles in the outline of the square. Shade congruent triangles the same color.

Name ______________________________

Polygon Percents

Start with an equilateral triangle. Fold a vertex to the midpoint of the opposite side. Unfold the triangle.

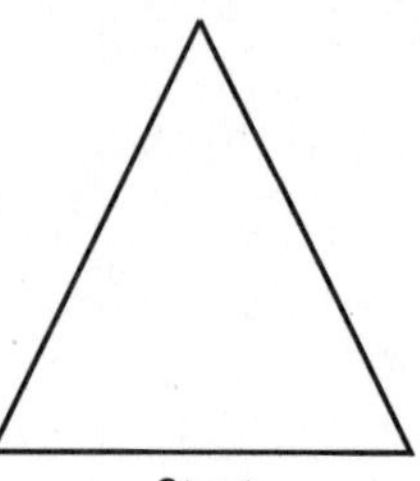
Start

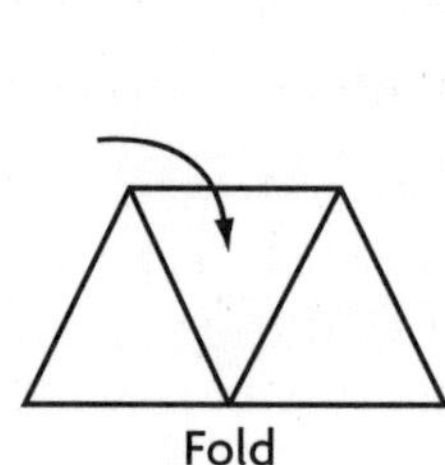
Fold

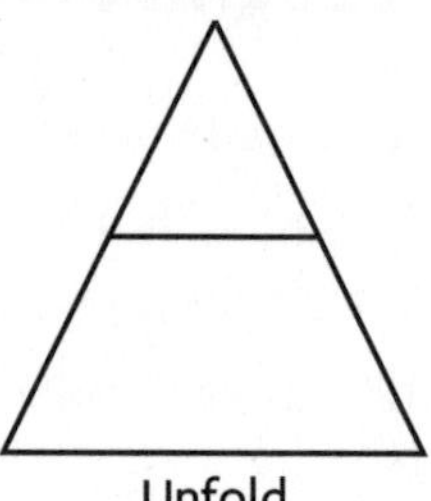
Unfold

1. What two new polygons are formed?

   trapezoid and triangle

2. What percent of the area of the original triangle is the area of each new polygon?

   Area of trapezoid is 75% area of original triangle;

   area of new triangle is 25% area of original triangle.

3. Write a ratio of the area of the smaller polygon to the area of the larger polygon.

   1:3

Start with a square. Fold each vertex to the center. Unfold the square.

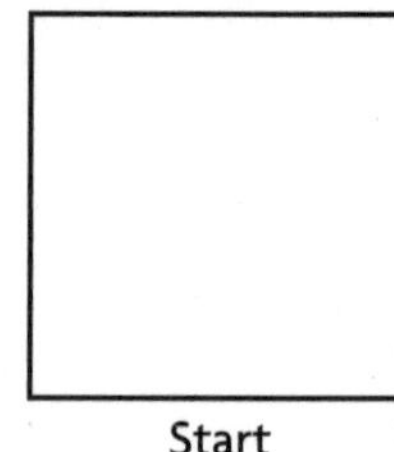
Start

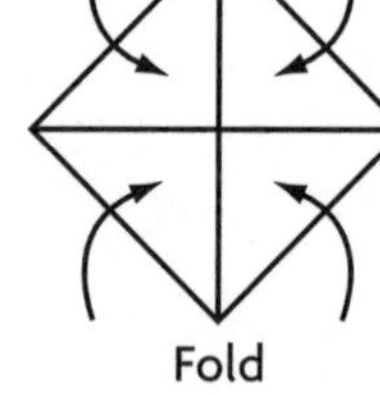
Fold

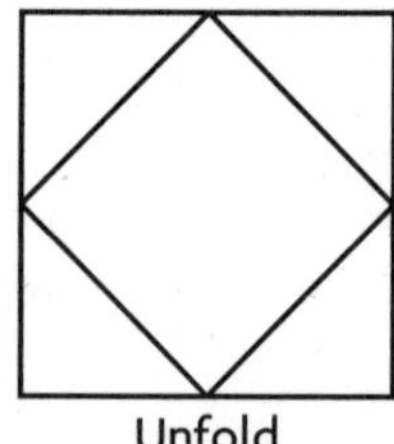
Unfold

4. What new polygons are formed?

   square and 4 triangles

5. What percent of the area of the original square is the area of each new polygon?

   Area of new square is 50% area of original square;

   area of each triangle is 12.5% area of original square.

6. The combined areas of which polygons equal 75% of the area of the original square?

   square and two triangles

7. Write a ratio of the area of the smaller polygon to the area of the larger polygon.

   1:4

Name ______________________

Find the Tile Pattern

Tirado Tile Company designs tile floors. The tables below show the number of tiles used in three new designs.

Find a pattern in the relationship of tiles.

Use the pattern to complete the tables. Then answer the questions. **Equations may vary.**

1.

Red Tiles *(R)*	White Tiles *(W)*	Blue Tiles *(B)*
9	6	11
12	8	16
15	**10**	21
18	12	26
21	14	**31**

2. Write an equation that shows the relationship of red and white tiles to blue tiles.

$R + W - 4 = B$

3.

Black Tiles (*B*)	White Tiles (*W*)	Striped Tiles (*S*)
12	20	40
15	25	50
18	30	**60**
21	35	70
24	**40**	80

4. Write an equation that shows the relationship of black and white tiles to striped tiles.

$1.25\,(B + W) = S$

5.

Triangles	Squares	Rectangles	Total Tiles
4	1	2	7
8	2	4	14
12	**3**	6	**21**
16	4	**8**	28
20	**5**	10	**35**

Let *s* represent the number of square tiles.

6. What is the number of triangles in terms of *s*?

$4s$

7. What is the number of rectangles in terms of *s*?

$2s$

8. Write an equation that relates triangles, squares, and rectangles to total number of tiles.

$s + 2s + 4s = 7s$

Name ______________________________

Wrap It Up

Materials needed: colored pencils or pens, straightedge

You have just been hired to design boxes for a packaging company. Your first assignment is to design a box for each item shown below.

Draw a net for the box. Mark the net with the correct dimensions. Decorate each face of the box using the given theme. **Check students' work.**

1. Theme: Child's Birthday

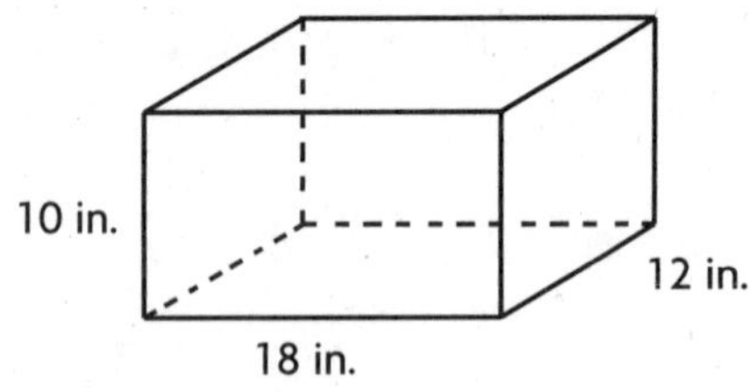

2. Theme: Wedding

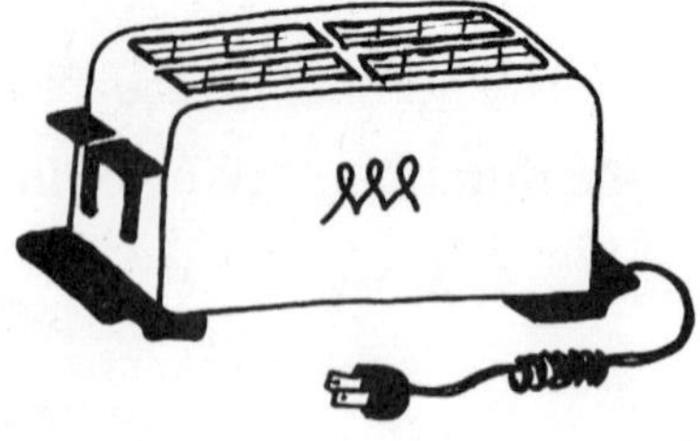

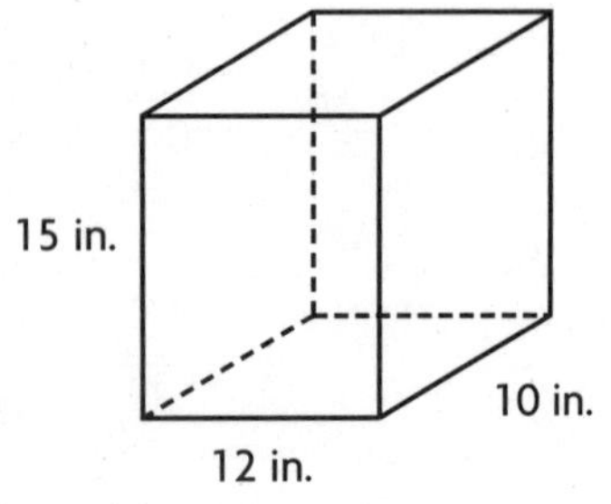

Name ____

A School for the Future

Suppose you are asked to design a school building for the 21st century. What would your building look like?

Draw the front, side, and top views of the school. Label the unique features of your design. **Check students' drawings.**

Name ______________________________

LESSON 13.1

Figure It Out

You can predict if a regular polygon will tessellate or not. Will an equilateral triangle tessellate?

First, find the measure of one interior angle.

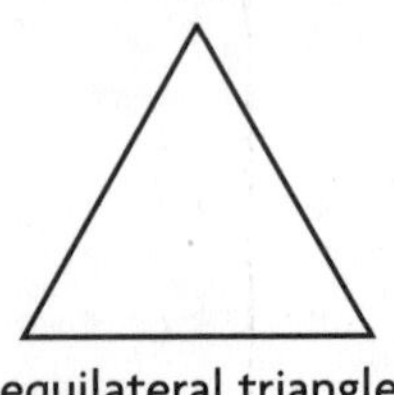
equilateral triangle

- Find the sum of the interior angles. If a regular polygon has n sides, the sum of the interior angles is $(n - 2) \cdot 180°$. So, for an equilateral triangle:

  $(3 - 2) \cdot 180° = 1 \cdot 180° = 180°$.
- Divide by the number of sides.

  $\frac{180°}{3} = 60°$ = measure of one angle

Then, determine if the measure of one angle will divide evenly into 360°.

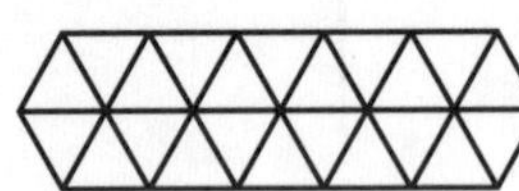

- 60° will divide evenly into 360°, so an equilateral triangle will tessellate.

Complete the table.

	Regular Polygon	Number of Sides	Sum of Angles $(n - 2) \cdot 180°$	One Angle	360° ÷ One Angle	Tessellation Possible?
1.	square	4	360°	90°	4	yes
2.	pentagon	5	540°	108°	$3\frac{1}{3}$	no
3.	hexagon	6	720°	120°	3	yes
4.	heptagon	7	900°	$128\frac{4}{7}°$	$2\frac{4}{5}$	no
5.	octagon	8	1,080°	135°	$2\frac{2}{3}$	no
6.	nonagon	9	1,260°	140°	$2\frac{4}{7}$	no
7.	decagon	10	1,440°	144°	$2\frac{1}{2}$	no

8. If a tessellation was possible in Exercises 1–7, create a tessellation of at least two rows. **Check students' work.**

Name ____________________

Clock Arithmetic

What time is it 3 hours after 10 o'clock? What time is it 6 hours before 3 o'clock?

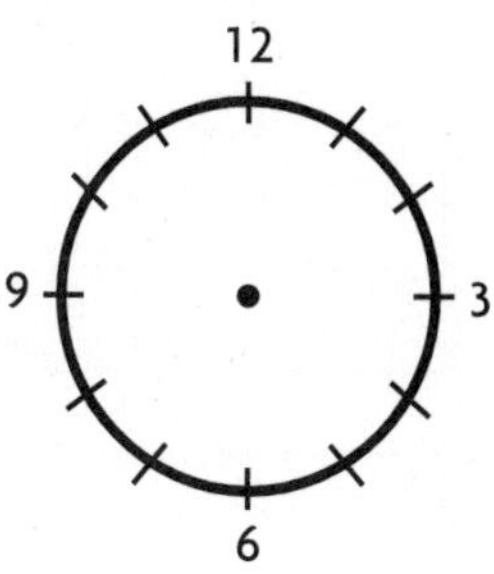

To solve, you can use *clock arithmetic.* Move around a 12-hour clockface to help you.

To find a time after a given hour, add. What time is it 3 hours after 10 o'clock? 10 + 3 = 1 o'clock

To find a time before a given hour, subtract. What time is it 6 hours before 3 o'clock? 3 − 6 = 9 o'clock

1. To find a sum, you move around the clock in what direction?

   clockwise

2. To find a difference, you move around the clock in what direction?

   counterclockwise

Use clock arithmetic. What time is it?

3. 3 hours before 8 o'clock 5 o'clock
4. 8 hours before 3 o'clock 7 o'clock
5. 4 hours after 10 o'clock 2 o'clock
6. 10 hours after 6 o'clock 4 o'clock
7. What number can be added or subtracted without changing the time? 12

When computations are done with a 7-hour clock, the phrase *mod 7* is used. The *mod 7* sum of 3 and 5 is 1. This is also written (3 + 5) *mod 7* = 1.

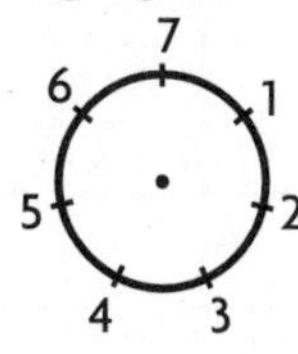

Use the 7-hour clockface to complete Exercises 8–13.

8. (4 + 6) *mod 7* 3
9. (3 − 4) *mod 7* 6
10. (7 + 3) *mod 7* 3
11. (4 − 5) *mod 7* 6
12. (2 − 7) *mod 7* 2
13. (5 + 5) *mod 7* 3
14. What number can be added or subtracted without changing a time in *mod 7*? 7
15. Write and solve addition and subtraction problems using a 5-hour clock. Give your *mod 5* problems to a classmate to solve.

Name ________________________________

LESSON 13.3

I Have a Pattern

This is my pattern. What comes next?

1. 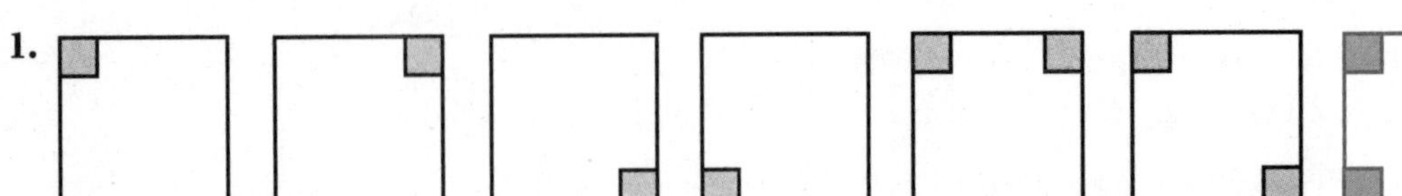

2. 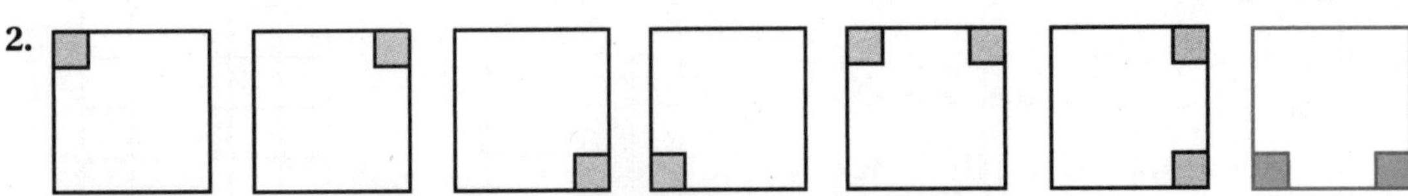

3. 

4. 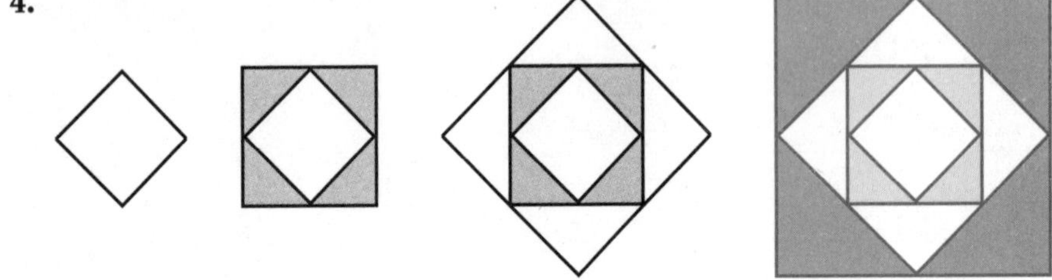

5. 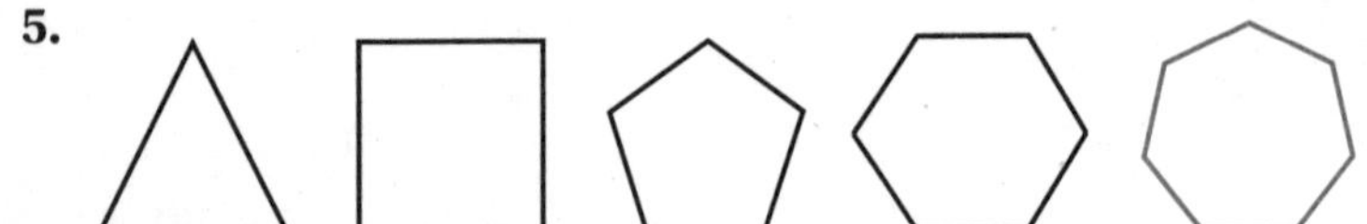

6. 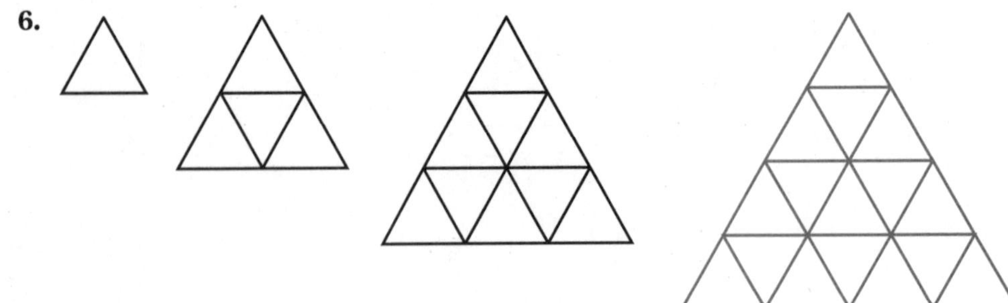

7. 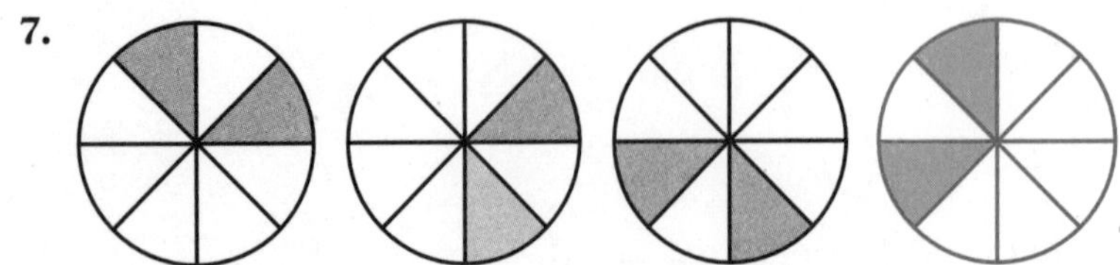

8. 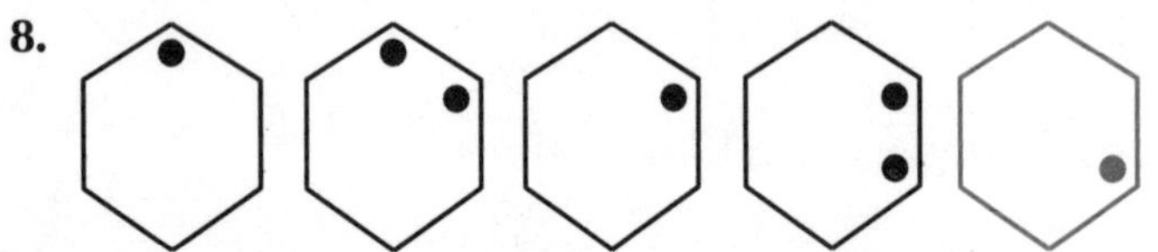

Name ______________________

From Pentominoes to Hexominoes

Materials needed: graph paper

A *pentomino* is formed by five congruent squares. Each square shares at least one side with another square.

Four pentominoes are shown.

A. 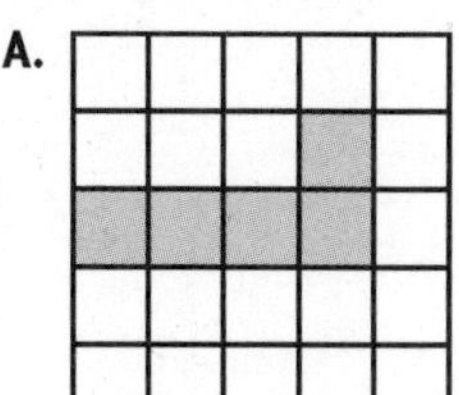

B. 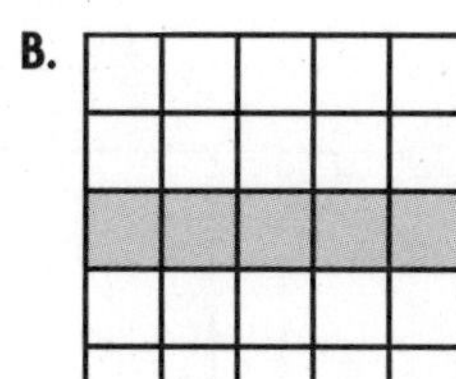

C. 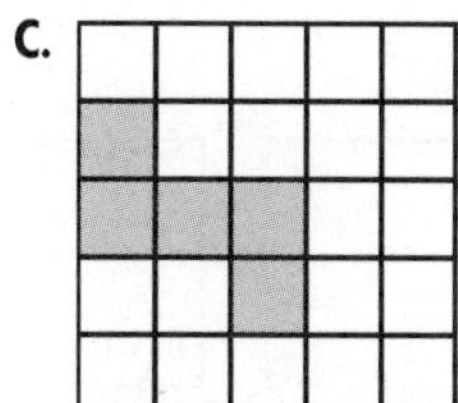

D. 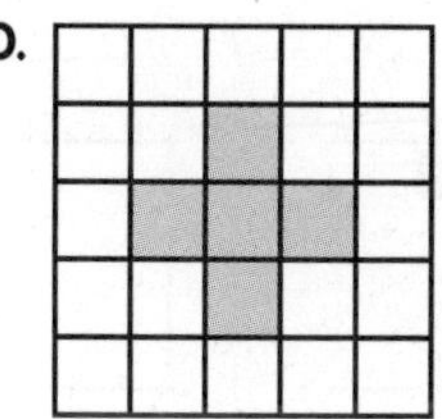

1. There are another 12 different arrangements of the five squares. On graph paper, draw the remaining 12 pentominoes. **Check students' work.**

Some pentominoes can be folded to make an open-top box.

2. Which of the four pentominoes shown above can be folded to make an open-top box? **A, C, and D**

3. How many of your 12 pentominoes can be folded to make an open-top box?

   7 pentominoes

A *hexomino* is formed by six congruent squares. Each square shares at least one side with another square. Some hexominoes can be folded to make a cube.

Four hexominoes are shown.

A. 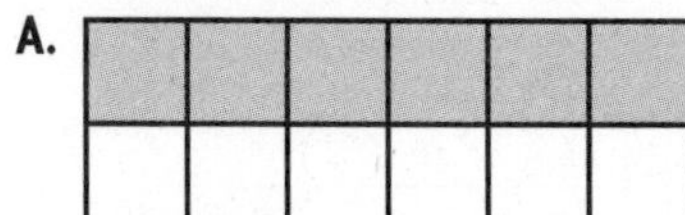

B. 

C. 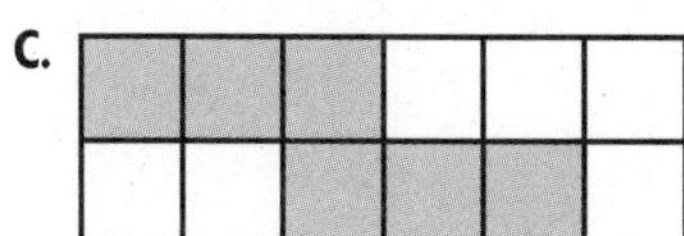

D. 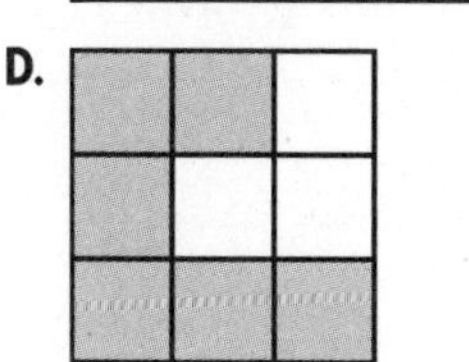

4. Which of the hexominoes shown can be folded to make a cube? **C**

5. There are 35 possible hexominoes. On graph paper, draw as many as you can. **Check students' drawings.**

Name ________________________________

Lattice Fun

A lattice can be an array of dots. The distance between two horizontal or vertical dots is one unit.

The area of a square formed by connecting the four closest points is 1 unit^2. So, the area of a triangle that is half the square is $\frac{1}{2}$ unit^2.

Find the area of each figure drawn on a lattice.

1. 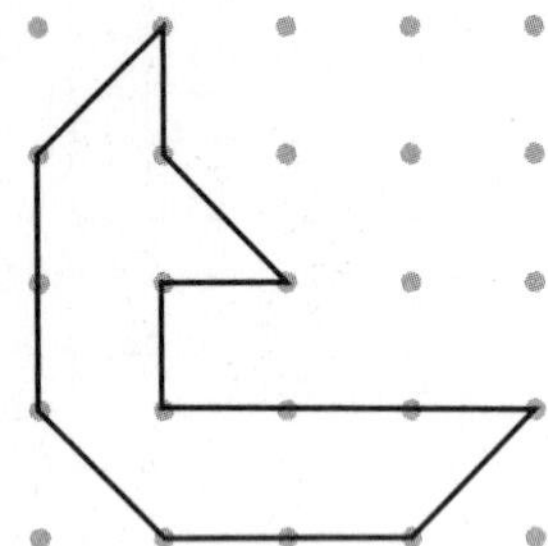

Area **6 unit^2**

2. 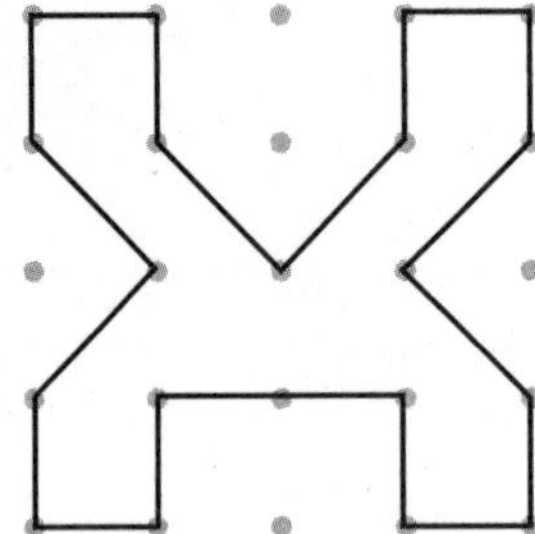

Area **9 unit^2**

3. 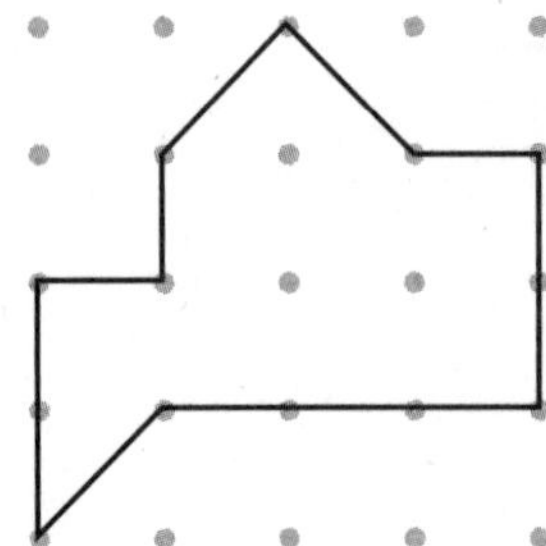

Area **$8\frac{1}{2}$ unit^2**

4. 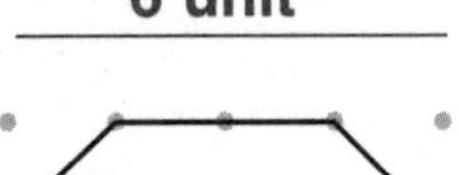

Area 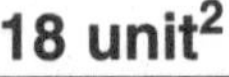 **18 unit^2**

5. 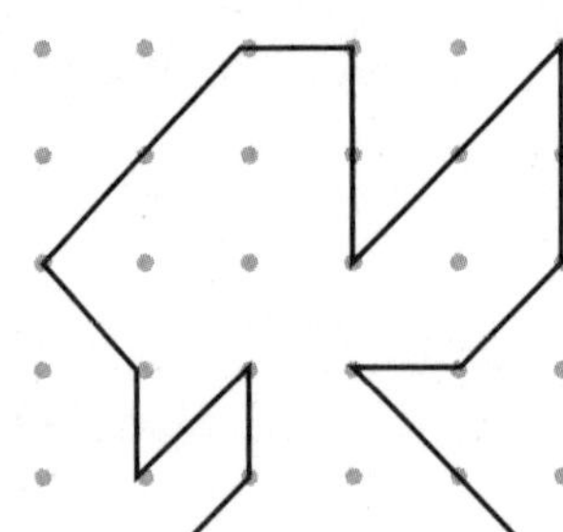

Area **15 unit^2**

6. 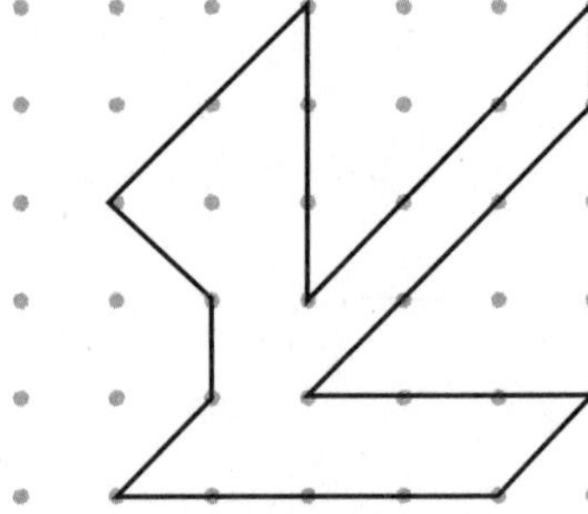

Area 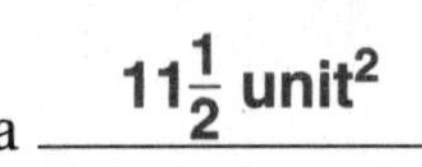 **$11\frac{1}{2}$ unit^2**

7. 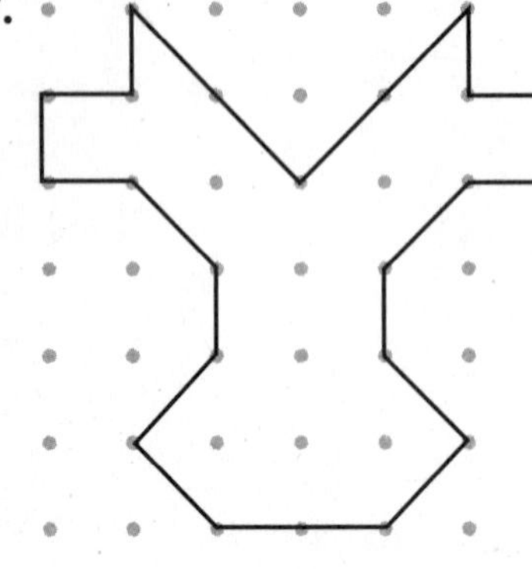

Area **17 unit^2**

8. Draw a lattice with area $17\frac{1}{2}$ unit^2.

Check students' drawings.

9. Draw a lattice with area 11 unit^2.

Check students' drawings.

Name ____

The Rate Maze

Contestants A–H must make their way through the maze to the Winners' Circle. To reach the Winners' Circle, each contestant must find a path from his or her current location through sections containing equivalent unit prices or rates. The contestants can move through sections that share a corner.

Find each unit price or rate. Circle the two contestants that will not be able to get to the Winners' Circle.

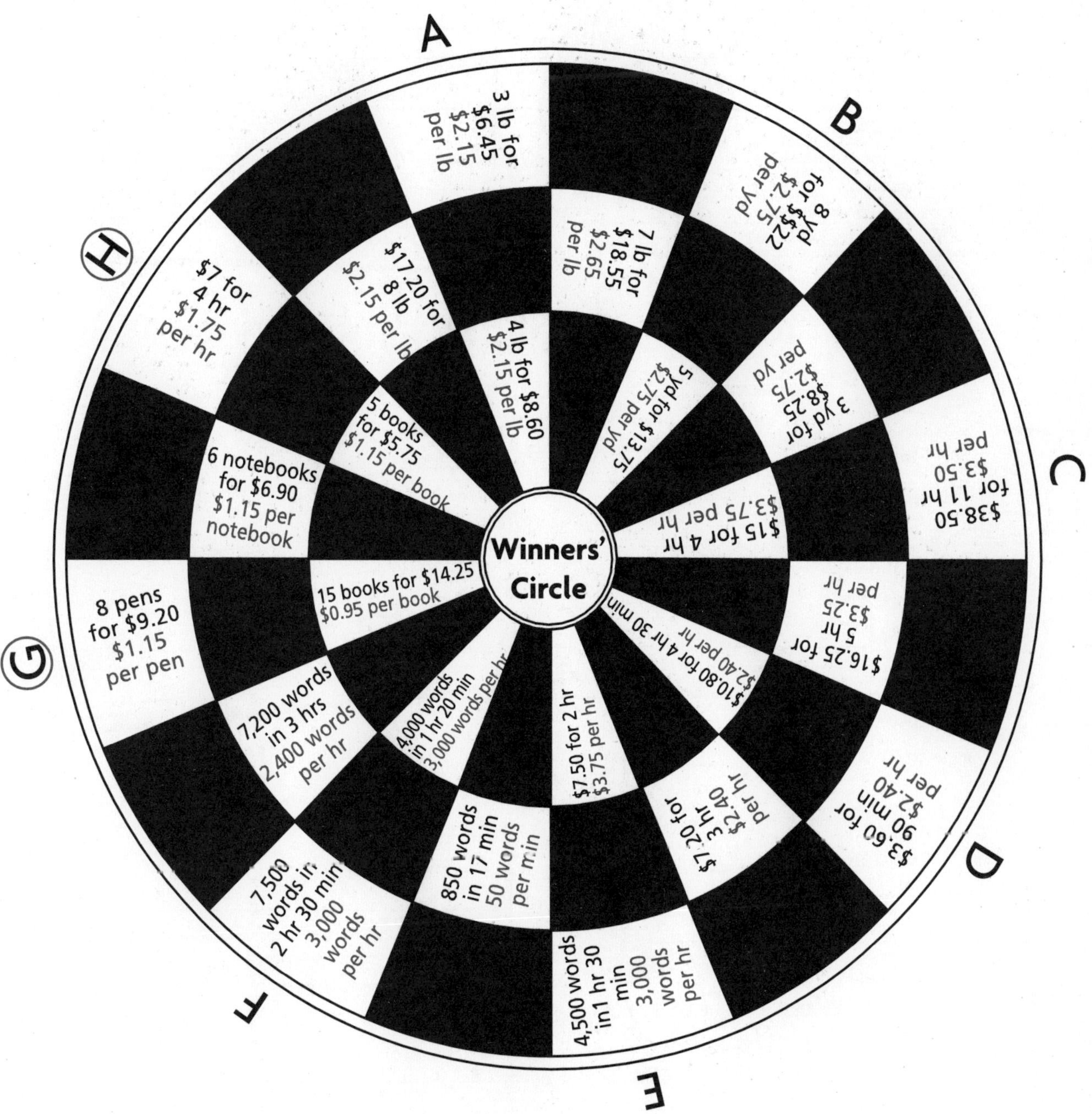

Name ______________________________

You're the Chef!

You are having a dinner party with 11 guests. Change each list of ingredients so the recipe will serve 12 people.

ENTRÉE

Lasagna (Serves 8)

1 lb ground beef
4 oz chopped onion
2 tbsp parsley flakes
16-oz can stewed tomatoes
12 oz tomato sauce
18 oz uncooked lasagna noodles
2 oz grated Parmesan cheese
8 oz shredded mozzarella cheese
24 oz ricotta cheese

Lasagna (Serves 12)

$1\frac{1}{2}$ lb ground beef
6 oz chopped onion
3 tbsp parsley flakes
24-oz can stewed tomatoes
18 oz tomato sauce
27 oz uncooked lasagna noodles
3 oz grated Parmesan cheese
12 oz shredded mozzarella cheese
36 oz ricotta cheese

DESSERT

BEVERAGE

Hot Orange Cider (Serves 12)

16 oz frozen orange juice concentrate
2 qt apple cider
20 orange slices

Name ______________________________

Weather . . . or NOT!

Isotherms are lines on a weather map that show how temperatures are distributed over a region. The map below shows the forecasted high temperatures for select cities in the United States.

You can estimate the temperature for a city by looking at the location of the city in relation to the two closest isotherms.

1. Estimate the high temperature for each city. The first one is done for you. **Possible estimates are given.**

Boston 27°	Chicago **44°**	Dallas **63°**
Kansas City **56°**	Los Angeles **72°**	Miami **75°**
San Francisco **66°**	Salt Lake City **58°**	Seattle **54°**
Orlando **72°**	Washington **50°**	New York **35°**

2. The low temperatures for the next day are given. Draw approximate isotherms for 10°, 20°, 30°, 40°, 50°, and 60°. **Possible isotherms are drawn.**

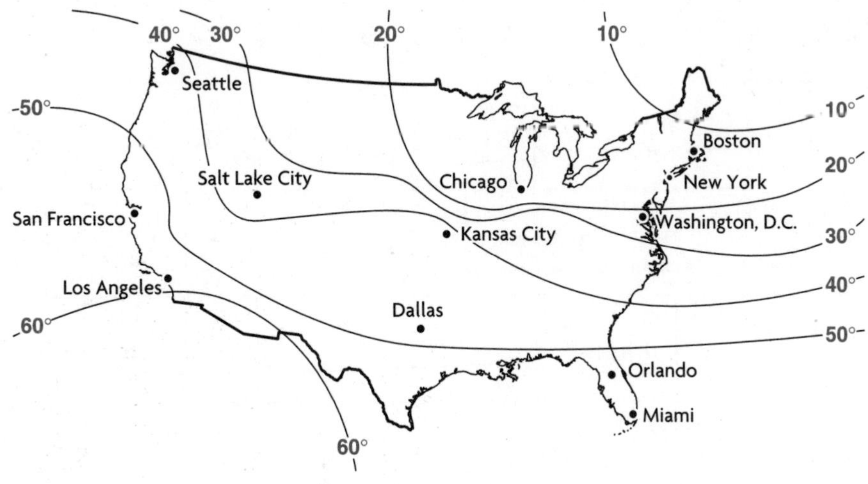

Name ______________________________

LESSON 15.1

Climbing a Percent Pyramid

Begin by changing each ratio in the pyramid to a percent. Then climb to the top by comparing the percents as you go.

The percents must increase as you climb to the top. Each brick on your path must touch the previous brick. Circle the ratios in the path that leads to the top.

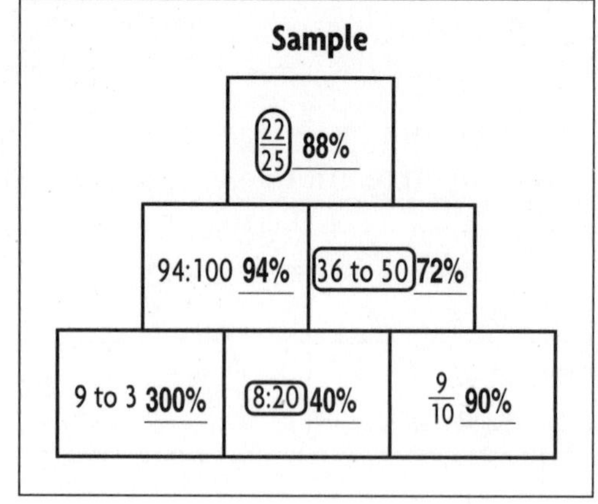

$\frac{19}{20}$ 95%								
83:100 83%	$\frac{920}{1,000}$ 92%							
47 to 50 94%	17 to 20 85%	3 to 10 30%						
49:50 98%	6:10 60%	5:2 250%	16:64 25%					
$\frac{40}{80}$ 50%	$\frac{35}{70}$ 50%	$\frac{2}{5}$ 40%	$\frac{4}{500}$ 0.8%	$\frac{7}{8}$ 87.5%				
24 to 40 60%	5 to 4 125%	9 to 20 45%	$\frac{68}{272}$ 25%	13 to 20 65%	7:1,000 0.7%			
8:200 4%	13:26 50%	3:8 37.5%	28:400 7%	$\frac{18}{10,000}$ 0.18%	9:30 30%	4:5 80%		
10:100 10%	6:200 3%	$\frac{1}{4}$ 25%	45:60 75%	$\frac{9}{3}$ 300%	$\frac{1}{50}$ 2%	$\frac{18}{25}$ 72%	$\frac{2}{16}$ 12.5%	
$\frac{1}{8}$ 12.5%	8:4 200%	12:25 48%	2:10 20%	3:6 50%	1:4 25%	5:8 62.5%	1:5 20%	12:20 60%

Name ____________________

Survey and Tell

The seventh-grade math class at Meyer Middle School took a survey to find which after-school activities students like best. There are 400 students at Meyer Middle School. The results are given in the following table.

Type of Activity	Math Club	Intramurals	Swimming	Yearbook	Band	Total
Percent of students	15%	40%	10%	5%	30%	100%
Number of students	60	160	40	20	120	400

1. To complete the table above, find the number of students who chose each type of activity.
2. Use the table to label the sections of the circle graph. Give the graph a title. **Possible title given.**
3. What is the favorite type of after-school activity?

   intramurals
4. What percent of the students did not choose intramurals or band? **30%**
5. List three popular rock bands. Survey ten students, asking which of the three bands they like best. Draw a circle graph to display the results. Give the graph a title.
   Check students' graphs.

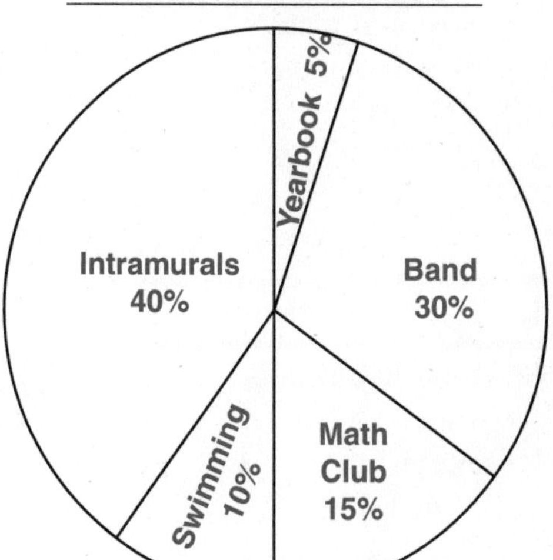

Name ____________________

LESSON 15.3

You Win!

You have just received a check for $108,000 as a winner in the Big Giveaway. After paying 24% of the amount in taxes, you go on a shopping spree. Find the total cost of each item listed. Will you be able to buy all the items listed below? Explain. Yes; the total cost is $79,904.50; $79,904.50 < $82,080.00 (after-tax amount).

CLASSIFIED ADS

120 Home Entertainment

SONY 40″ Stereo Color TV
- picture-in-picture
- great resolution
- cable ready

$2,300 + 7% sales tax

$2,461

130 Household Items

GE Profile Refrigerator
- white
- 26.8 cu ft
- ice maker

$1,800, will discount 15% for cash

$1,530

140 Office Equipment

FAX/COPIER
Hewlett Packard FAX-200
- single cartridge
- 5 pg/min
- great resolution

$500, will sell for 8% cash discount

$460

150 Computers

Power Computing
- PowerPC/166 MHz
- 2.0 GB Hard Drive
- 32 MB RAM
- modem/FAX 33.6 kbps

$2,300 new, will sell for 40% off

$1,380

160 Automotive

FORD 1992 Taurus
- 4-door
- air-conditioning
- power windows/power locks
- AM/FM stereo

$12,500 + 8% license and dealer's fees

$13,500

DODGE 1995
Grand Caravan LE
- V6
- low mileage
- loaded

Was $25,000
Will discount 15%

$21,250

CHEVY 1968 Impala
- a classic
- 2-door
- power steering/brakes

$6,350 + 3% for licensing

$6,540.50

170 Boats

Sailboat
- Ericson 25
- sleeps 4
- 10 hp outboard
- CB, compass

$20,500 + 6% sales tax

$21,730

180 Travel Trailers/RVs

Coleman 1994 pop-up
- sleeps 6
- awning w/screen

$6,400, will discount 3% for cash payment

$6,208

190 Motorcycles

1994 Honda
- like new
- low mileage

$4,750 + 2% for licensing

$4,845

Name ______________________________

It's All in Your Point of View

The box at the right is *not* drawn in perspective. Notice that the edges *AB* and *DC* (also *EF* and *HG*) are drawn parallel to each other.

You can draw a box in perspective by making use of a *vanishing point*. The edges of the box, when extended, meet at the vanishing point. The far side of the box appears smaller, which is what adds depth to the drawing.

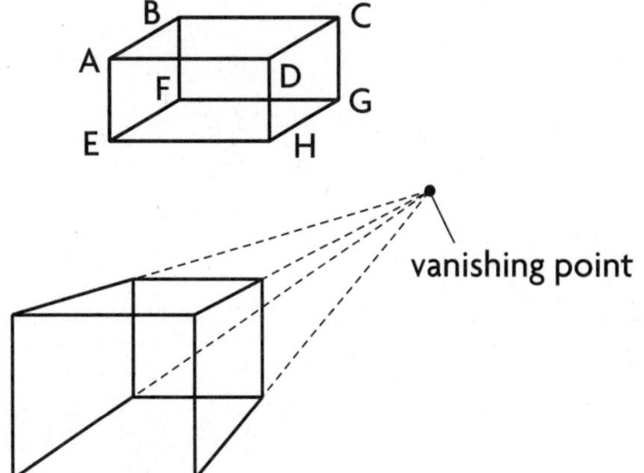

Draw each figure in perspective. A vanishing point and the front side are given. **Check students' work.**

1. 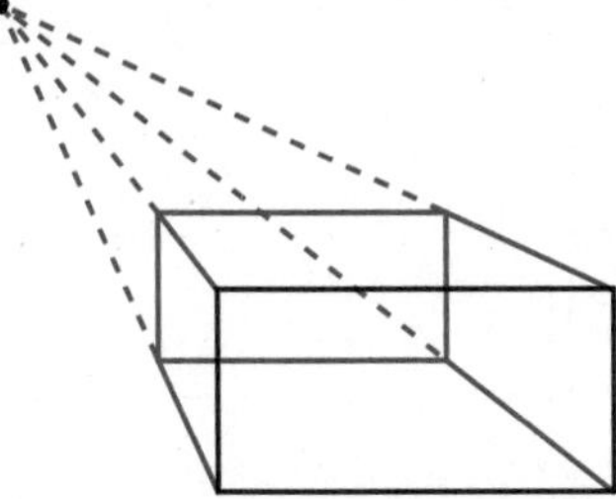

2. 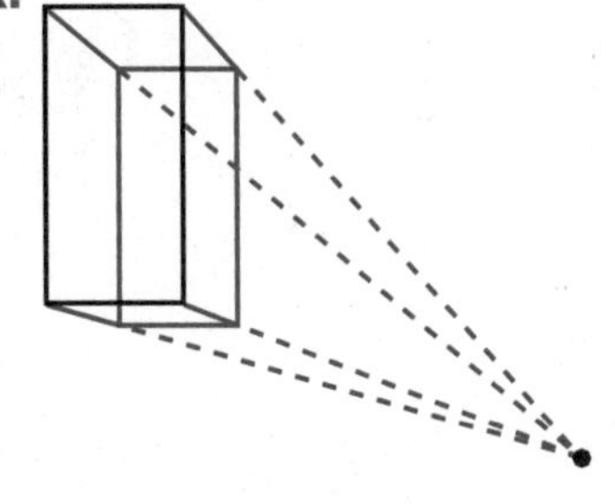

3. 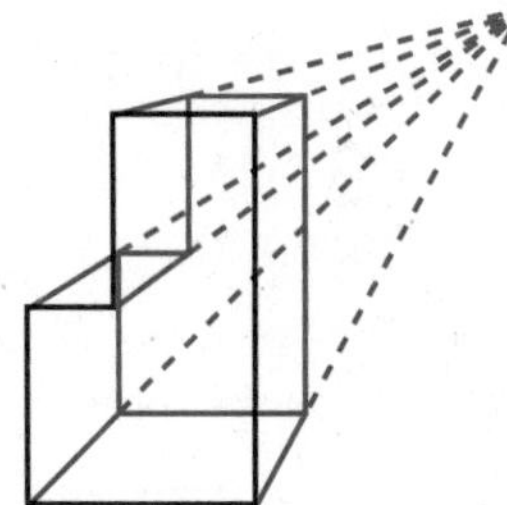

4. The block letter E is drawn in perspective. Find the vanishing point by extending all the edges of the perspective drawing.

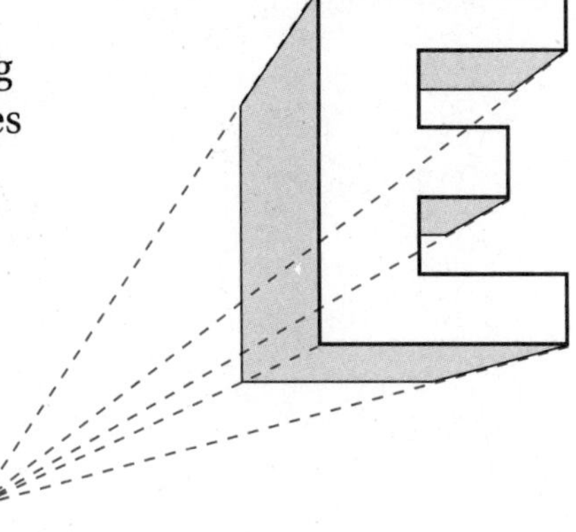

5. Below, draw the letters of your first name as block letters in perspective. Use the same vanishing point for all the letters. **Check students' work.**

Name ______________________________

LESSON 16.1

The Same, Only Bigger

You can sometimes create a similar figure by using copies of the original figure.

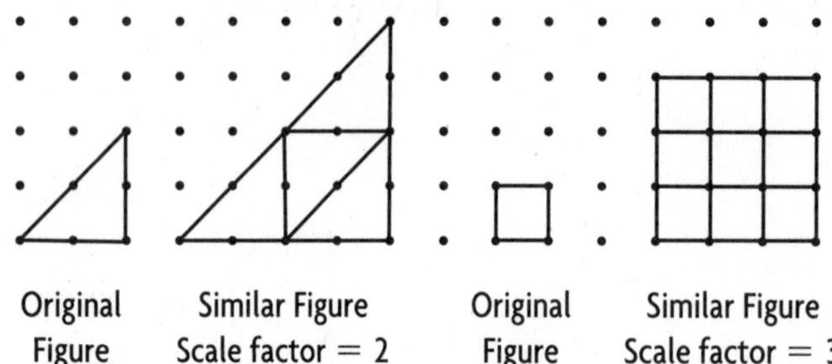

Original Figure | Similar Figure Scale factor = 2 | Original Figure | Similar Figure Scale factor = 3

Notice that the scale factor tells you how many times to repeat the original figure along each side or edge of the similar figure.

Use the given scale factor and copies of the original figure to draw a figure similar to the original figure.

1.

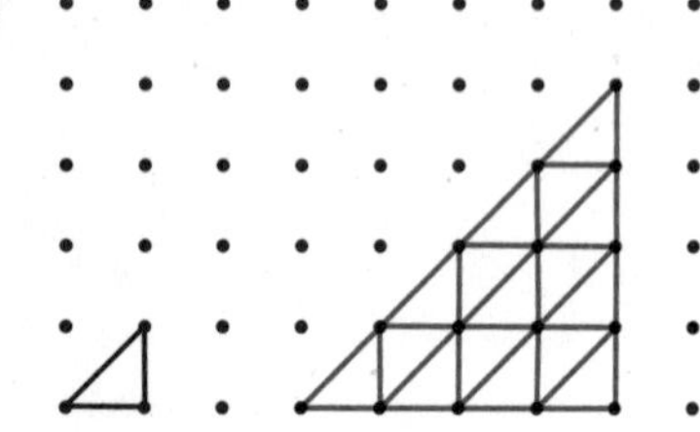

scale factor = 4

2.

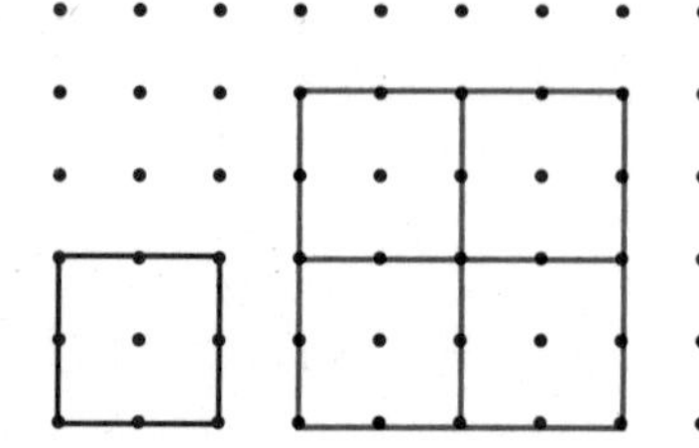

scale factor = 2

3.

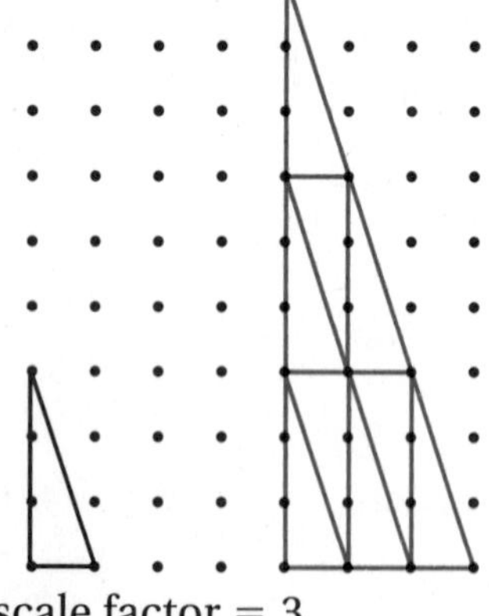

scale factor = 3

4.

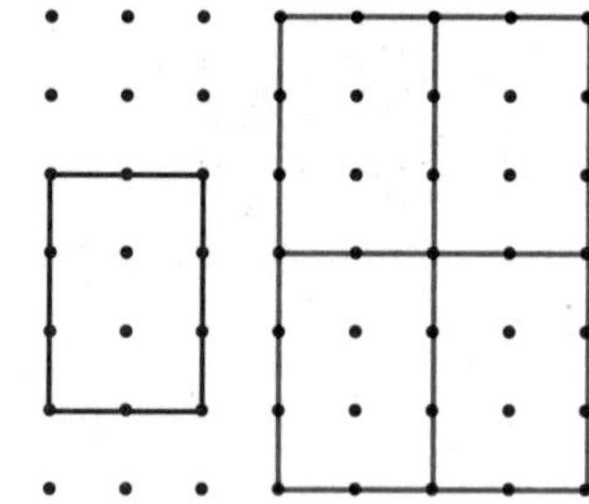

scale factor = 2

5. Draw a figure in the space below. Use a scale factor of 2 to create a similar figure.
Check students' drawings.

Name ______________________________

Scale It!

Juanita, an architect, made this scale drawing of the first floor of a house. Architects always give scale drawings, or blueprints, to builders so the houses will be built correctly. Scale dimensions for each room are shown. The actual dimensions of the garage, for example, are 20 ft × 20 ft.

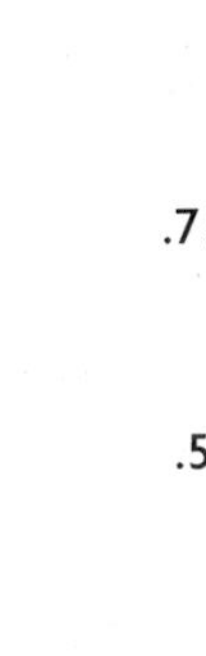

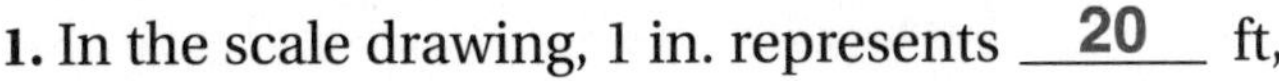

1. In the scale drawing, 1 in. represents __20__ ft, so $\frac{1}{4}$ in. represents __5__ ft. Therefore the scale is __$\frac{1}{4}$__ in. : __5__ ft.

2. Complete the table.

Room	Scale Dimensions	Actual Dimensions
Garage	1 in. × 1 in.	20 ft × 20 ft
Kitchen	1 in. × $\frac{1}{2}$ in.	**20 ft × 10 ft**
Living room	$\frac{3}{4}$ in. × $\frac{3}{4}$ in.	**15 ft × 15 ft**
Family room	$\frac{1}{2}$ in. × $\frac{3}{4}$ in.	**10 ft × 15 ft**
Dining room	$\frac{1}{2}$ in. × $\frac{3}{4}$ in.	**10 ft × 15 ft**

3. The home owner decides to add 5 ft to each side of the garage, making the new dimensions 25 ft × 25 ft. If she uses the same scale of $\frac{1}{4}$ in.:5 ft, what new dimensions will Juanita mark on the sides of the garage in the scale drawing?

$1\frac{1}{4}$ in. × $1\frac{1}{4}$ in.

4. What are the dimensions of a room in your home? What would be the dimensions of a scale drawing of the room, using the scale $\frac{1}{4}$ in.:5 ft?

Possible answer: 10 ft × 12 ft; $\frac{1}{2}$ in. × $\frac{3}{5}$ in.

5. On a separate sheet of paper, sketch a floor plan of your classroom, estimating the length of each wall. Use your floor plan and estimates to draw a blueprint of your classroom. Then check your dimensions by actually measuring them. **Check students' drawings.**

Name ______________________

LESSON 16.3

Connecting Dots

The area of the square formed by connecting the outer dots represents 100%. Why does the area of the inner square represent 25%?

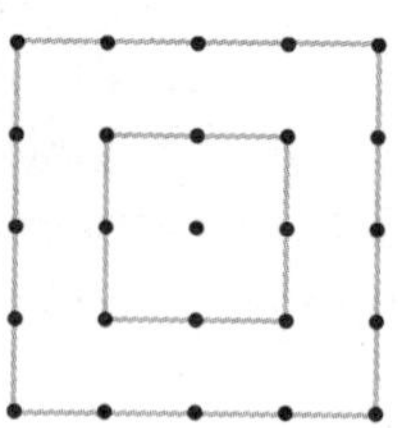

- You can form 16 small squares by connecting 4 dots at a time.
- Each small square is $\frac{1}{16}$ of the large square.
- So, the area of one small square is $\frac{1}{16} = 0.0625 = 6.25\%$, or 6.25% of the entire area.
- The inner square is made up of 4 small squares, so its area is $\frac{4}{16} = \frac{1}{4} = 0.25$ or 25%.

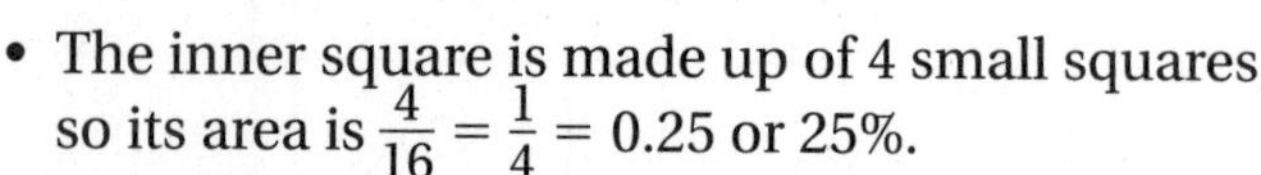

What percent represents the area outside the inner square?

100% − 25% = 75%

---

1. Give another way to show that the area of the inner square above is 25%.

   Possible answer: 4 × 6.25% = 25%

Find the percent of the area inside and outside each inner figure. Be careful! Some of the inner figures are not squares.

2. 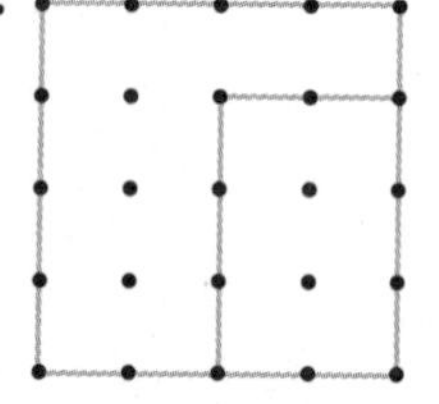

   inside 37.5%

   outside 62.5%

3. 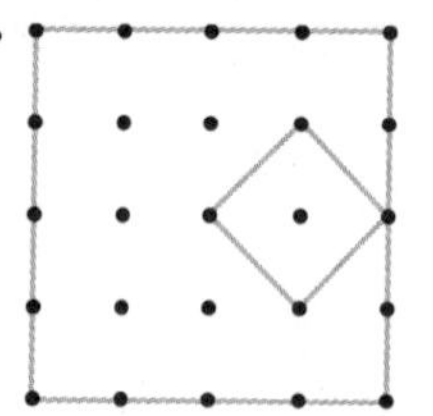

   inside 12.5%

   outside 87.5%

4. 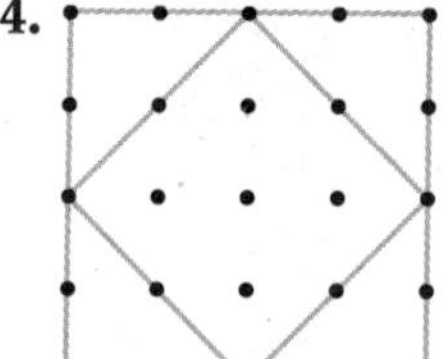

   inside 50%

   outside 50%

5. 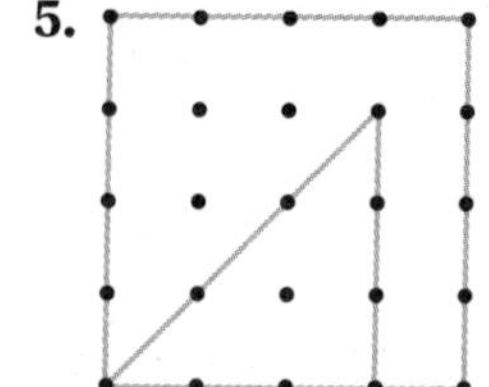

   inside 28.125%

   outside 71.875%

6. In each of Exercises 2–5, the sum of the inside area and outside area should be 100%.

The number of dots has increased. Find the percent of the area inside the inner figure.

7. 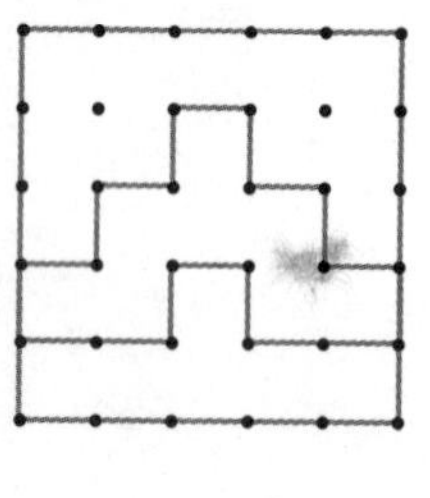

   32%

8. 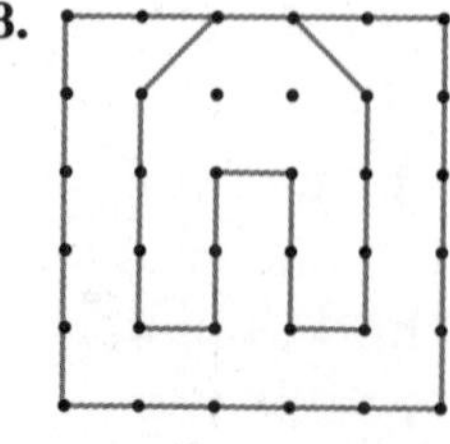

   36%

9. 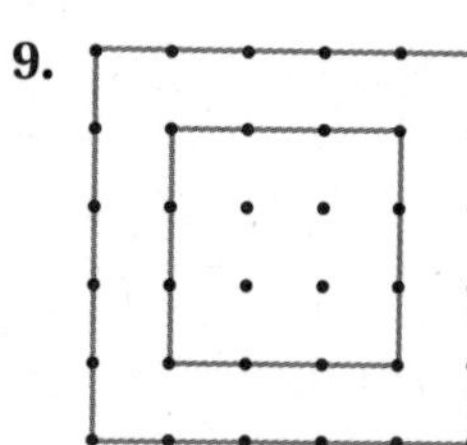

   36%

Name ______________________________

The Value of pi: Beyond 3.14

The ratio of the circumference of a circle to its diameter is always the same number, π, or approximately 3.14. Pi is a Greek letter. Computers have been used to calculate the value of π to hundreds of thousands of decimal places. No one will ever calculate them all!

Solve each proportion. Place the answer on the space above the letter you have solved for. The first one is done for you. As you solve the proportions, you are finding the first 30 decimal places of the number pi.

$\frac{a}{2} = \frac{28}{4}$	$a = 14$	$\frac{27}{h} = \frac{21}{7}$	h = 9	$\frac{r}{2} = \frac{13}{1}$	r = 26
$\frac{5}{b} = \frac{6}{18}$	b = 15	$\frac{10}{j} = \frac{30}{21}$	j = 7	$\frac{15}{1} = \frac{60}{s}$	s = 4
$\frac{3}{2} = \frac{c}{6}$	c = 9	$\frac{k}{3} = \frac{54}{18}$	k = 9	$\frac{3}{t} = \frac{1}{11}$	t = 33
$\frac{78}{6} = \frac{d}{2}$	d = 26	$\frac{3}{6} = \frac{16}{m}$	m = 32	$\frac{240}{60} = \frac{u}{2}$	u = 8
$\frac{11}{e} = \frac{33}{15}$	e = 5	$\frac{n}{228} = \frac{19}{114}$	n = 38	$\frac{16}{v} = \frac{21}{42}$	v = 32
$\frac{10}{7} = \frac{50}{f}$	f = 35	$\frac{48}{p} = \frac{12}{1}$	p = 4	$\frac{11}{w} = \frac{22}{14}$	w = 7
$\frac{2}{14} = \frac{g}{56}$	g = 8	$\frac{q}{21} = \frac{2}{7}$	q = 6	$\frac{5}{x} = \frac{130}{234}$	x = 9

π = 3. 14 (a) 15 (b) 9 (c) 26 (d) 5 (e) 35 (f) 8 (g) 9 (h) 7 (j) 9 (k) 32 (m) 38 (n) 4 (p) 6 (q) 26 (r) 4 (s) 33 (t) 8 (u) 32 (v) 7 (w) 9 (x) . . .

Give the frequency of each digit, 0–9 among the first 30 decimal places for π.

digits	0	1	2	3	4	5	6	7	8	9
frequency	0	2	4	6	3	3	3	2	3	4

Name ____________________

Change My Size

As a designer, you have been asked to enlarge the logo shown.

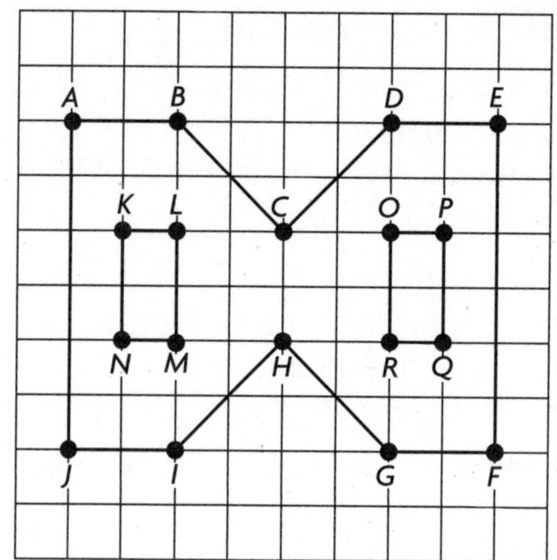

1. On the $\frac{1}{4}$-in. grid below at the left, draw the logo $1\frac{1}{2}$ times its original size. **Check students' drawings.**

What is the new length of the segment?

2. $\overline{AJ}$ $2\frac{1}{4}$ in.
3. $\overline{KL}$ $\frac{3}{8}$ in.
4. $\overline{PQ}$ $\frac{3}{4}$ in.
5. $\overline{DE}$ $\frac{3}{4}$ in.
6. $\overline{AB}$ $\frac{3}{4}$ in.
7. $\overline{KN}$ $\frac{3}{4}$ in.
8. $\overline{GF}$ $\frac{3}{4}$ in.
9. $\overline{EF}$ $2\frac{1}{4}$ in.

Your clients have changed their minds. You are now asked to reduce the original logo by $\frac{1}{2}$. What is the new length of the segment?

10. $\overline{OP}$ $\frac{1}{8}$ in.
11. $\overline{DE}$ $\frac{1}{4}$ in.
12. $\overline{LM}$ $\frac{1}{4}$ in.
13. $\overline{AJ}$ $\frac{3}{4}$ in.
14. $\overline{PQ}$ $\frac{1}{4}$ in.
15. $\overline{EF}$ $\frac{3}{4}$ in.
16. $\overline{JI}$ $\frac{1}{4}$ in.
17. $\overline{NM}$ $\frac{1}{8}$ in.
18. Now design your own logo on the grid below at the right. Ask another student to enlarge or reduce your logo by your scale factor. **Check students' work.**

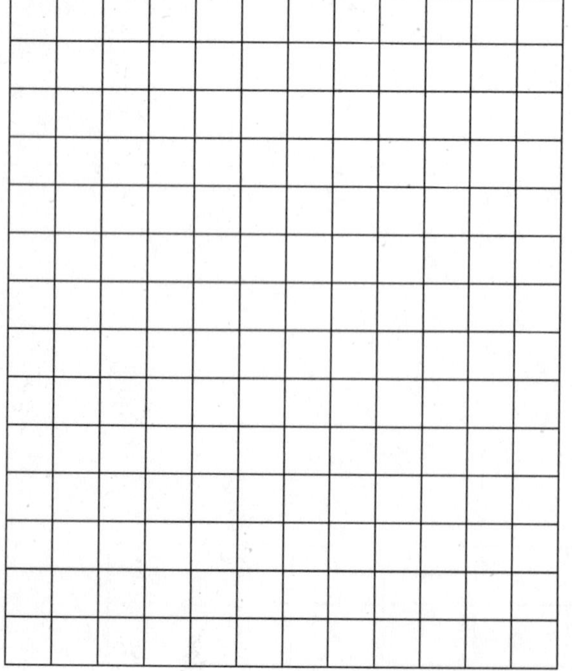

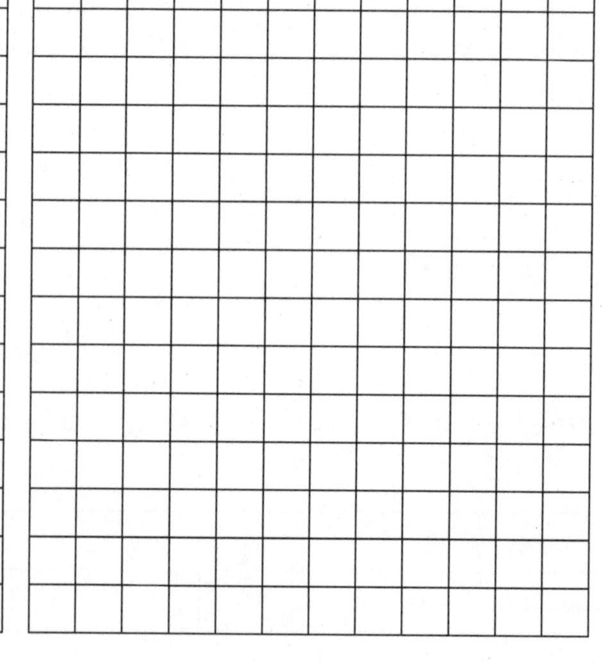

Name ______________________

On the Edge

A polygon drawn on dot paper has *border points* and *interior points.* A border point is a dot on the side of the figure. An interior point is inside the figure.

8 border points
2 interior points

Write the number of border points and interior points for the polygon.

1\. 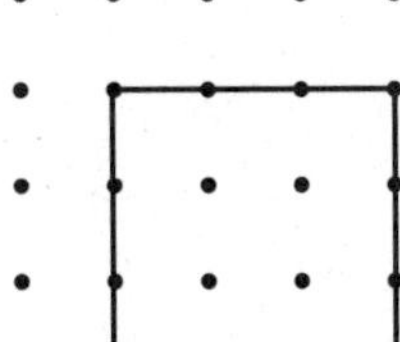

border: 12;
interior: 4

2\. 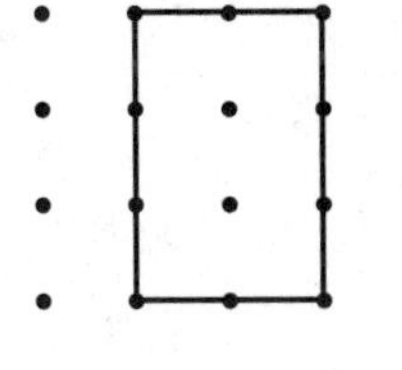

border: 10;
interior: 2

3\.

border: 8;
interior: 3

4\. 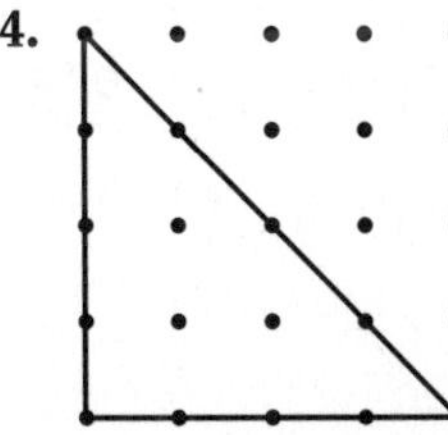

border: 12;
interior: 3

5\. Find the area in square units of each of the polygons in Exercises 1–4.

Ex. 1: 9 sq units | Ex. 2: 6 sq units | Ex. 3: 6 sq units | Ex. 4: 8 sq units

6\. For each of the polygons in Exercises 1–4, find the value of $\frac{1}{2}b + i$, where b represents the number of border points and i represents the number of interior points.

Ex. 1: 10 | Ex. 2: 7 | Ex. 3: 7 | Ex. 4: 9

7\. Compare your answers for Exercises 5 and 6. What pattern do you notice?

The area is 1 less than the value of $\frac{1}{2}b + i$ for each polygon.

This pattern is known as Pick's Formula: $A = \frac{1}{2}b + i - 1$

Use Pick's Formula to find the area of the polygon.

8\. 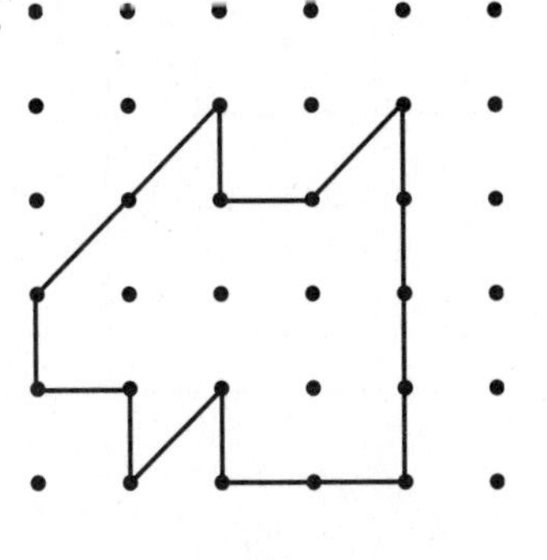

11 sq units

9\. 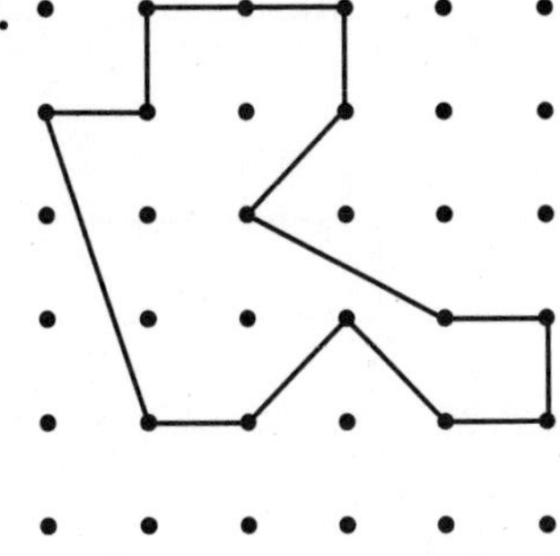

10 sq units

Name ___

Map Out the Land of Wishful Thinking

On the $\frac{1}{4}$-in. grid below, you will make a map of a new state named Wishful Thinking. Use a scale of $\frac{1}{4}$ in.: 30 mi.

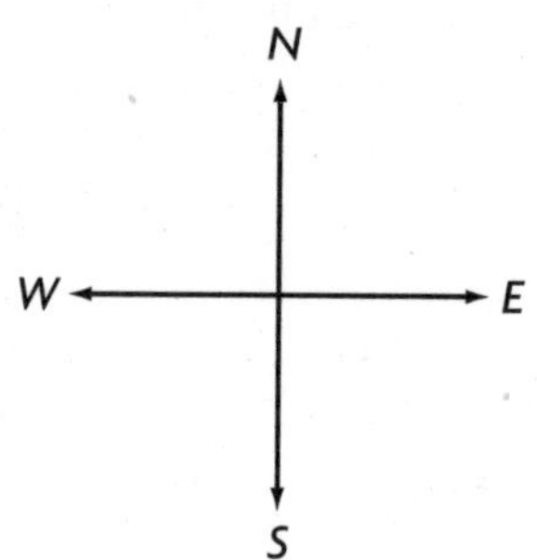

Your state is in the shape of a rectangle. The origin (0,0) is at the bottom left (southwest) corner of the map. Locate these cities on your map by putting a dot on the grid below.

1. Place the city of Pizza at the point (8,9).
2. Popcorn is 60 mi south and 90 mi west of Pizza.
3. Punch is 240 mi east of Pizza.
4. Chips is 150 mi west and 270 mi south of Punch.
5. Cheese is 120 mi east and 45 mi north of Chips.
6. Gum is 165 mi south of Pizza.
7. Pretzels is 105 mi south and 120 mi west of Popcorn.
8. Cereal is 195 mi north of Pretzels.
9. Juice is halfway between Pizza and Punch.
10. Hot Dog is 120 mi north and 210 mi west of Chips.
11. Licorice is 45 mi north and 60 mi east of Gum.

Check students' maps.

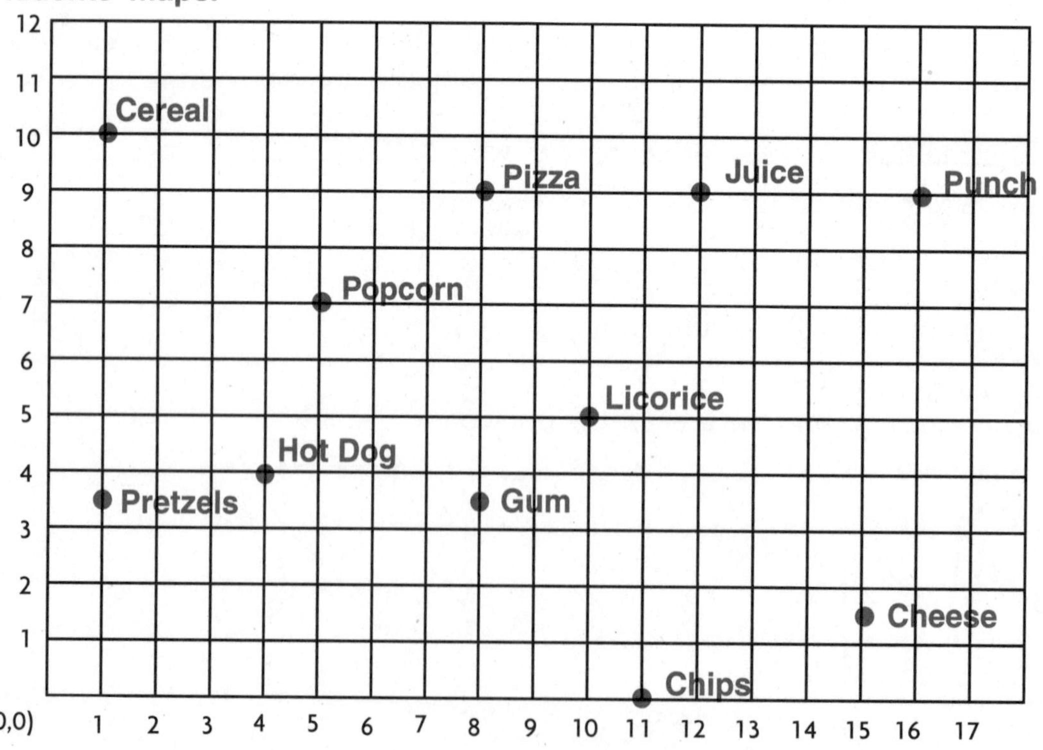

Name ____________________

Puzzling

There are many ways to divide a square into smaller squares.

1	2
4	3

4 squares

6 squares

10 squares

1. There is more than one way to divide a square into 10 squares. Draw another way. **Check students' drawings.**

2. Show ways to divide a square into 7, 8, 9, and 16 smaller squares. **Check students' drawings.**

3. a. In Exercise 2, when all the smaller squares are of equal size, how many smaller squares do you have? **9 squares; 16 squares**

   b. In the three figures at the top of the page, when all the smaller squares are of equal size, how many smaller squares do you see? **4 squares**

   c. What do you notice about the numbers of equal-size smaller squares?

   The numbers are perfect squares.

4. Try to find more than one way to make each division in Exercise 2. For which number is only one division possible? **7**

5. What do you notice about the sum of the areas of the smaller squares within a larger square? **The sum is a perfect square.**

HINT: Divide into 4 squares: $4 \times 1^2 = 4$
Divide into 6 squares: $5 \times 1^2 + 1 \times 2^2 = 9$
Divide into 10 squares: $2 \times 2^2 + 8 \times 1^2 = 16$

Name ____

The A-*maze*-ing Golden Rectangle

Travel in this Golden Rectangle from top to bottom. Find a path by entering only those squares that contain a Golden Ratio. You can move from square to square if they share a common side or corner.

10 cm:8 cm 1.25	$\frac{8}{5}$ 1.6	1:0.8 1.25	$\frac{27}{12}$ 2.25	23 to 15 $1.5\overline{3}$
16 to 9 $1.\overline{7}$	95 in.:85 in. 1.12	26 cm:16 cm 1.625	10 in. to $6\frac{1}{4}$ in. 1.6	$\frac{12}{6.5}$ 1.85
44 to 20 2.2	$\frac{35}{18}$ $1.9\overline{4}$	10 m:4 m 2.5	$\frac{18}{8}$ 2.25	24:15 1.6
$\frac{100}{55}$ $1.\overline{81}$	25 m:50 m 0.5	$\frac{40}{30}$ $1.\overline{3}$	8 ft:7 ft 1.14	100 to 62.5 1.6
3 ft to 2 ft 1.5	$\frac{84}{72}$ $1.1\overline{6}$	14 ft:7.2 ft $1.9\overline{4}$	18 in. to $11\frac{1}{4}$ in. 1.6	$\frac{6}{4}$ 1.5
1.5 m:0.8 m 1.875	$\frac{93.75}{50}$ 1.875	8 ft to 10 ft 0.8	162 cm:100 cm 1.62	$\frac{17}{12}$ $1.41\overline{6}$
87 ft:51 ft 1.71	$\frac{34}{18}$ $1.\overline{8}$	4 to 2.5 1.6	50 cm:25 cm 2	0.4 to 0.3 $1.\overline{3}$
13 in.:6 in. $2.1\overline{6}$	$\frac{80 \text{ ft}}{64 \text{ ft}}$ 1.25	35 in. to 35 in. 1	$\frac{20}{12.5}$ 1.6	9:7 1.29

Name ______________________________

Digit Fun

Use the digits 2, 3, 4, 6, and 9 to find the largest or smallest answer. Use each digit only once. **For Exercises 1–2, possible answers are given.**

1. largest sum

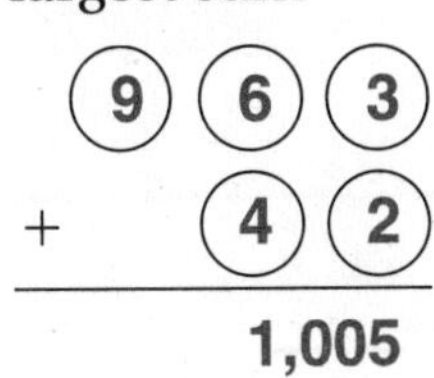

1,005

2. smallest sum

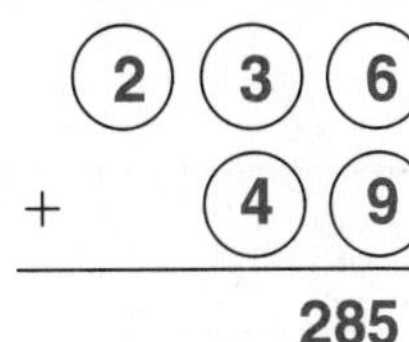

285

3. largest difference

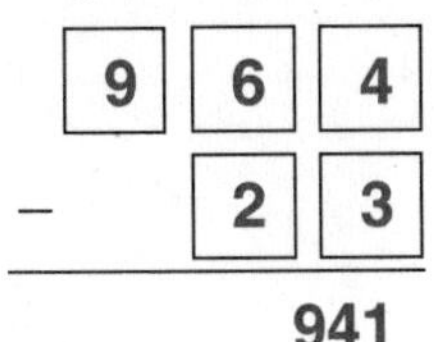

941

4. smallest difference

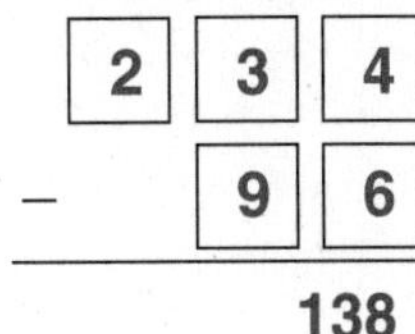

138

5. largest product

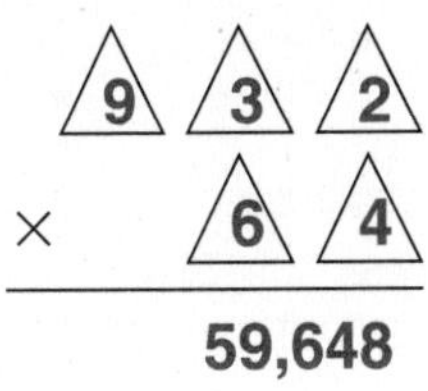

59,648

6. smallest product

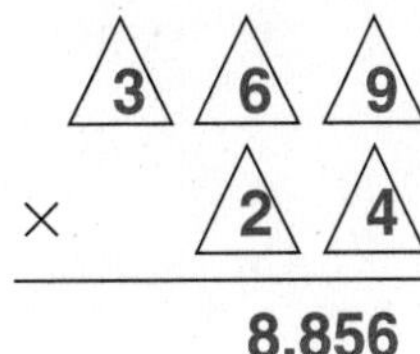

8,856

7. largest product

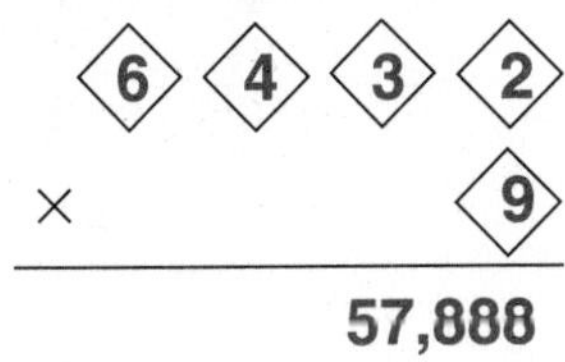

57,888

8. smallest product

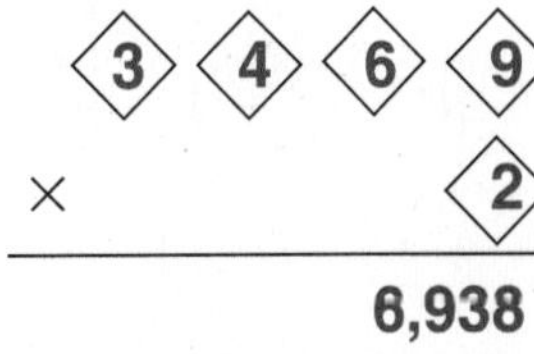

6,938

9. Try Exercises 1–8 with five other digits. **Check students' work.**

Name ____________________

LESSON 18.2

So Many Choices: Using Pascal's Triangle

You have 5 friends, and you can invite 2 of them to join you at a concert. How many choices do you have? Pascal's triangle will help you answer the question. In the table the diagonals of Pascal's triangle are arranged in columns. Find 5 at the left and 2 at the top. The arrows meet at 10. You have 10 choices.

Column Number

Row of Pascal's Triangle	0	1	2	3	4	5	6	7	8	9	10
0	1										
1	1	1									
2	1	2	1								
3	1	3	3	1							
4	1	4	6	4	1						
5	1	5	10	10	5	1					
6	1	6	15	20	15	6	1				
7	1	7	21	35	35	21	7	1			
8	1	8	28	56	70	56	28	8	1		
9	1	9	36	84	126	126	84	36	9	1	
10	1	10	45	120	210	252	210	120	45	10	1

1. Arnie's friends are Bob, Carl, Don, Ed, and Frank. List the 10 different pairs of friends Arnie could invite to the concert.

   Bob and Carl; Bob and Don; Bob and Ed; Bob and Frank;
   Carl and Don; Carl and Ed; Carl and Frank; Don and Ed;
   Don and Frank; Ed and Frank

2. You own 6 pairs of shorts and are taking 2 pairs on vacation. In how many ways can you choose 2 pairs of shorts? There is a total of 6 pairs of shorts to choose from and 2 pairs to take. You have 15 different ways to choose 2 pairs of shorts.

3. Frank's Diner has 7 fillings for sandwiches. It is having a special on sandwiches with 4 fillings. How many different sandwiches with 4 fillings are possible? 35 sandwiches

Name ______________________________

Prove It

Pat, Chris, and Jean are in the kitchen. One of them ate all the cookies. If you can prove Chris did not and Jean did not, what have you proved?

Pat ate the cookies. You used indirect reasoning.

Here are some other examples that require indirect reasoning.

1. Sam, Mike, and Philip are soccer players. One plays for San Diego, one for Minneapolis, and one for Philadelphia.
Clue 1: No player's city starts with the same letter as his name.
Clue 2: Philip has never been to San Diego.

Who plays for Philadelphia? You can use a table and indirect reasoning to help you solve this problem.

	Sam	Mike	Philip
San Diego	X		X
Minneapolis	XX	X	
Philadelphia		XX	X

- Use Clue 1 and Clue 2 to put *X*'s in the boxes that can be ruled out.
- Use indirect reasoning. Mike must play for San Diego, so mark an *XX* to show that he does not play for Philadelphia. Philip must play for Minneapolis, so mark an *XX* to show that Sam does not.

Who plays for Philadelphia? **Sam**

2. Pam, Pete, Paul, and Penelope each favor a different flavor of pudding: chocolate, vanilla, strawberry, or lemon. Paul does not like fruit-flavored pudding. Chocolate is neither boy's favorite. Lemon is one girl's favorite. Penelope is allergic to chocolate. What is each student's favorite flavor? Use the table below to help you solve.

Pam: chocolate; Pete: strawberry;

Paul: vanilla; Penelope: lemon

	Pam	Pete	Paul	Penelope
Chocolate		X	X	X
Vanilla	XX	XX		XX
Strawberry	XX		X	XX
Lemon	XX	X	X	

Name ________________________________

LESSON 18.4

What's My Pattern?

1. Complete the tables below.

Powers of 2	
2^1	2
2^2	4
2^3	8
2^4	16
2^5	32
2^6	64
2^7	128
2^8	256

Powers of 3	
3^1	3
3^2	9
3^3	27
3^4	81
3^5	243
3^6	729
3^7	2,187
3^8	6,561

Powers of 4	
4^1	4
4^2	16
4^3	64
4^4	256
4^5	1,024

2. Find a pattern for the units digits of the powers of 2 values.

2, 4, 8, 6 repeating

3. What is the units digit of 2^9? of 2^{13}? of 2^{38}? 2; 2; 4

4. Describe the pattern of the units digits of the powers of 3 values.

3, 9, 7, 1 repeating

5. What is the units digit of 3^{10}? of 3^{22}? of 3^{31}? 9; 9; 7

6. Do the units digits for the values of the powers of all whole numbers follow a pattern of *four* repeating digits? Explain.

No. The powers of 4 have only two repeating digits.

7. What is the units digit of 8^3? of 8^4? of 8^5? of 8^6? 2; 6; 8; 4

8. The units digits of the values of the powers of 8 are the same as the units digits of the powers of 2.

9. Describe the patterns shown by the powers of 5. The last 2 digits always form 25.

10. Describe the pattern shown by the powers of 1. They are all 1s.

Name ___________________________________

LESSON 19.1

Order, Please!

Your stock market club invests in some blue chip stocks. Does your stock increase more if it increases by 0.375 or by $\frac{5}{16}$?

Here is how to compare a decimal and a fraction.

- Rewrite the fraction as a decimal.
- Add zeros so that the decimals have the same number of decimal places.
- Compare each digit from left to right.

$\frac{5}{16} = 0.3125$

$0.375 = 0.3750$

The stock increases more if it increases by 0.375.

Order from least to greatest.

1. $\frac{1}{100}, \frac{1}{10}, 0.011, 0.\overline{11}, 0.\overline{101}$

2. $\frac{72}{100}, \frac{3}{4}, 0.\overline{72}, \frac{7}{10}, \frac{12}{25}$

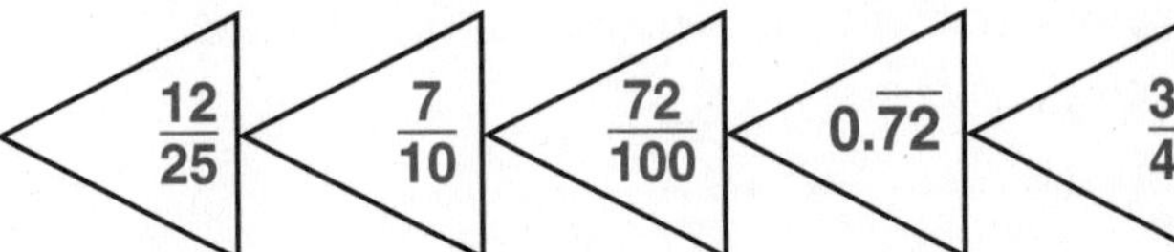

3. $0.\overline{334}, \frac{3}{10}, \frac{2}{3}, \frac{33}{100}, 0.\overline{3}$

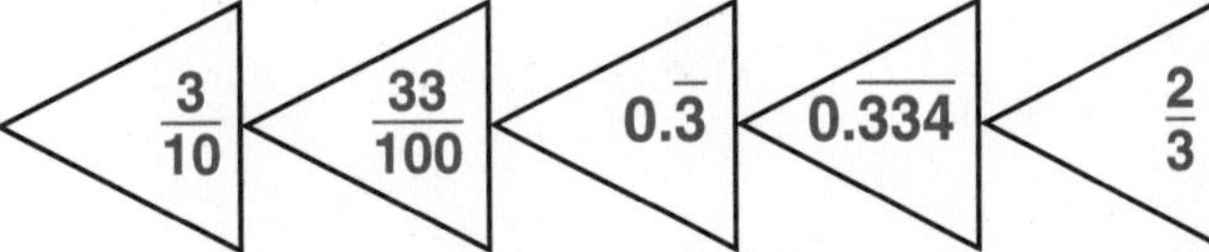

4. $1.\overline{6}, 0.\overline{85}, \frac{5}{8}, 1\frac{7}{10}, \frac{23}{45}$

Order from greatest to least.

5. $0.\overline{25}, \frac{1}{8}, 0.17, \frac{2}{9}, \frac{1}{4}$

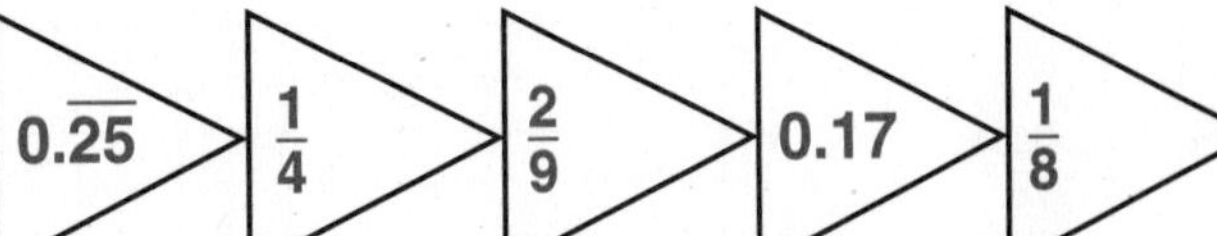

6. $0.\overline{0528}, \frac{1}{20}, \frac{4}{17}, \frac{1}{25}, 0.0\overline{528}$

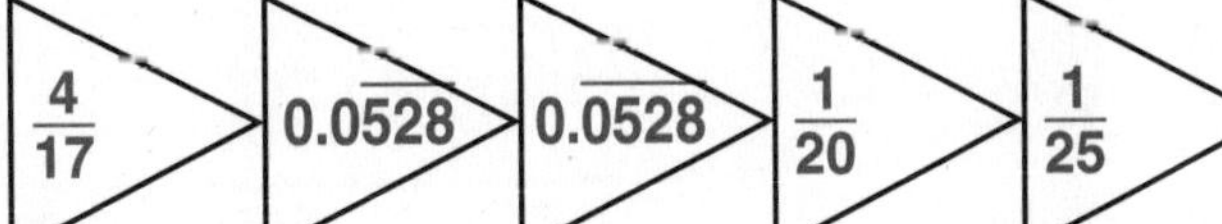

7. $\frac{1}{9}, 0.1\overline{8}, \frac{2}{13}, 0.\overline{18}, 0.15$

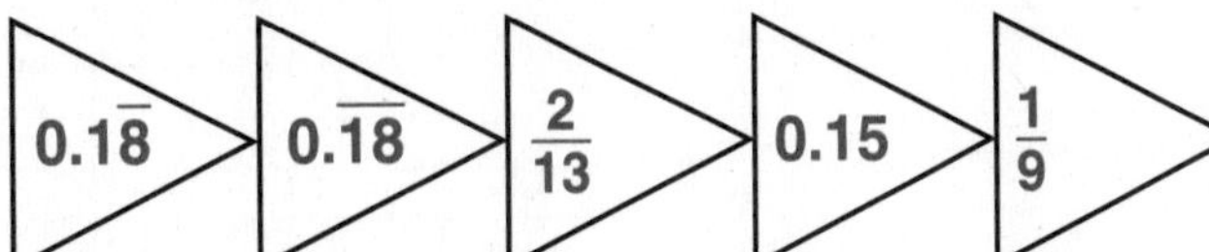

8. $\frac{-1}{3}, {}^{-}0.\overline{35}, \frac{-3}{11}, \frac{-10}{33}, {}^{-}0.3\overline{5}$

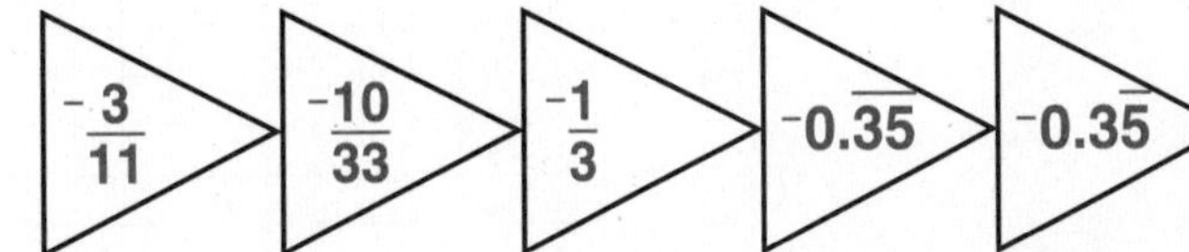

Name ____________________

Midpoint Mystery

The point halfway between two points is called the *midpoint.*

To find the *x*-coordinate of a midpoint, average the *x*-coordinates of the two given points. To find the *y*-coordinate, average the *y*-coordinates of the two given points.

Find the coordinates (*x*,*y*) of the midpoint of the segment joining points (4,⁻6) and (2,⁻2). Then graph the three points.

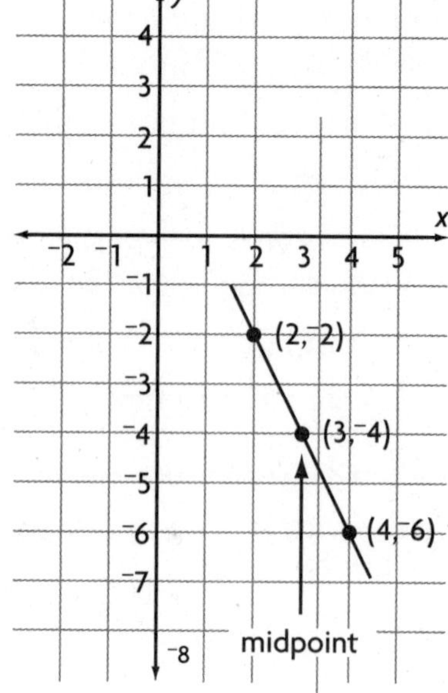

$$(x,y) = \left(\frac{4+2}{2}, \frac{^-6+(^-2)}{2}\right)$$

$$= \left(\frac{6}{2}, \frac{^-8}{2}\right)$$

$$= (3,^-4)$$

Solve the mystery. Find the midpoint of the segment joining the two given points. Graph all the midpoints below. Then connect the midpoints to find out where Justin left his math book.

Check students' graphs; connected midpoints should form a car.

1. (⁻13,4); (⁻11,2) **(⁻12,3)**
2. (⁻7,3); (⁻3,3) **(⁻5,3)**
3. (⁻1,4); (⁻5,8) **(⁻3,6)**
4. (3,3); (3,9) **(3,6)**
5. (4,2); (6,4) **(5,3)**
6. (10,1); (14,5) **(12,3)**
7. (14,⁻1); (10,⁻1) **(12,⁻1)**
8. (7,2); (7,⁻4) **(7,⁻1)**
9. (6,2); (4,0) **(5,1)**
10. (3,2); (3,⁻4) **(3,⁻1)**
11. (6,⁻1); (4,⁻5) **(5,⁻3)**
12. (8,⁻2); (6,0) **(7,⁻1)**
13. (1,0); (5,⁻2) **(3,⁻1)**
14. (⁻5,5); (⁻5,⁻7) **(⁻5,⁻1)**
15. (⁻1,7); (⁻13,⁻5) **(⁻7,1)**
16. (⁻8,1); (⁻10,⁻3) **(⁻9,⁻1)**
17. (⁻11,⁻3); (⁻3,⁻3) **(⁻7,⁻3)**
18. (⁻8,⁻4); (⁻2,2) **(⁻5,⁻1)**
19. (⁻5,1); (⁻13,⁻3) **(⁻9,⁻1)**
20. (⁻9,2); (⁻15,⁻4) **(⁻12,⁻1)**
21. (⁻10,9); (⁻14,⁻3) **(⁻12,3)**

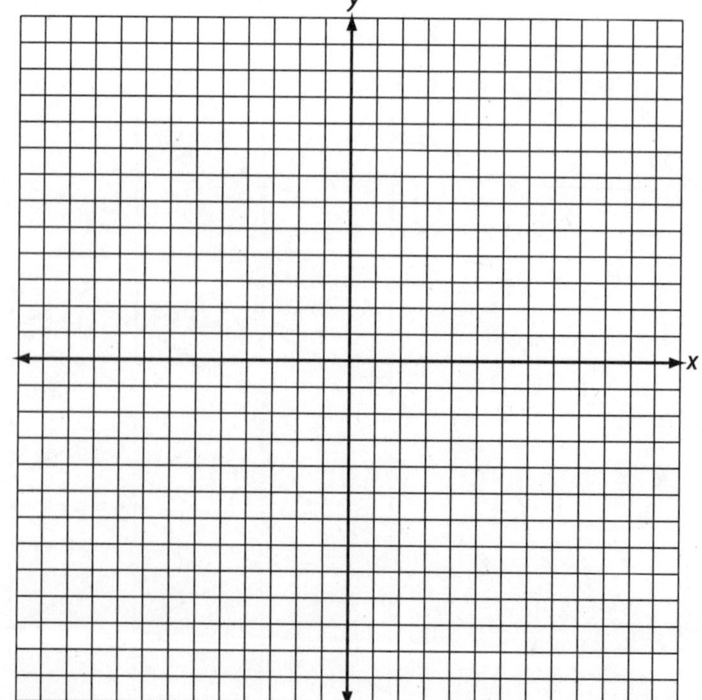

Name ______________________________

Crossword Craze

Solve, rename, simplify, or fill in the pattern to complete the puzzle.

Across

2. 2^6 **64**

4. 15% of 2,000 **300**

5. $4 \times (9 \div 3)$ **12**

7. $\frac{n}{40} = 24$; $n =$ **960**

8. 74,865 − 13,879 **60,986**

11. 8, 16, 32, 64, **128**, . . .

12. $^-3 \times {}^-91$ **273**

14. Round 362.358 to the nearest one. **362**

15. Write 2.50 as **250** %.

17. 25% of 2,008 **502**

18. Write 3.25×10^3 in standard form. **3,250**

Down

1. $6^2 \times 10$ **360**

3. 8^4 **4,096**

5. 30% of 560 **168**

6. $4 \times 12 - 3 - 5^2$ **20**

9. Round 90,182 to the nearest hundred. **90,200**

10. $\frac{4}{7} = \frac{n}{238}$; $n =$ **136**

11. 1, 1, 2, 6, 24, **120**

13. $\frac{5}{8} = \frac{n}{56}$; $n =$ **35**

14. 20, 23, 26, 29, **32**, . . .

16. $8 \div 2 + 3 \times 5^2 - 7$ **72**

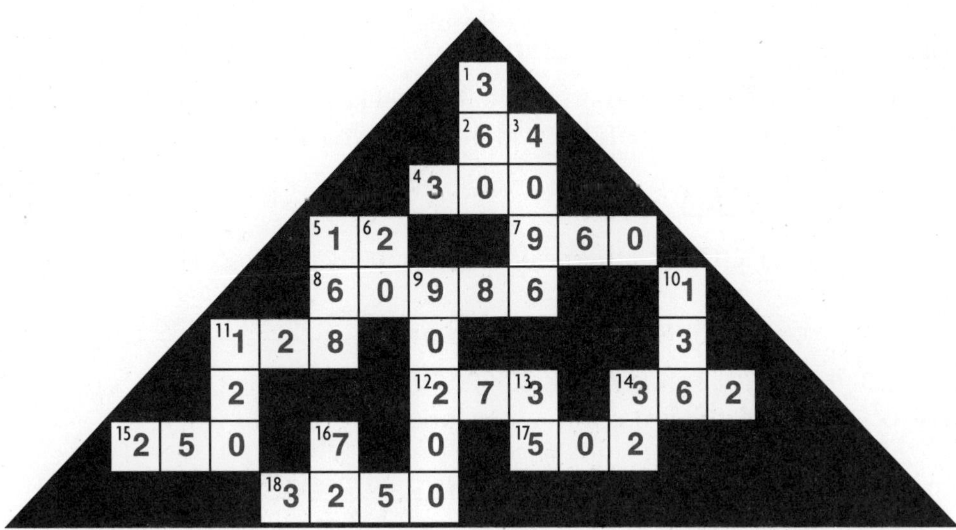

Name ______________________________

LESSON 19.4

The Science of Scientific Notation

You have used exponents to express numbers in scientific notation.

$9{,}500{,}000 = 9.5 \times 10^6$ The exponent is positive because the number is greater than 1.

$0.00125 = 1.25 \times 10^{-3}$ Notice that the exponent is negative because the number is less than 1.

You can use scientific notation to calculate operations with very large and very small numbers.

$\frac{(93{,}000{,}000)\,(0.005)}{0.0015} = \frac{(9.3 \times 10^7)\,(5 \times 10^{-3})}{1.5 \times 10^{-3}}$ ← First write each number in scientific notation.

$= \frac{(9.3 \times 5)(10^7 \times 10^{-3})}{(1.5 \times 10^{-3})}$ ← Regroup the factors.

$= \frac{46.5 \times 10^4}{1.5 \times 10^{-3}}$ ← *Add* the exponents to *multiply* the powers of 10.

$= 31 \times 10^7$ ← *Subtract* the exponents to *divide* the powers of (4 − ⁻3 = 7) 10.

$= (3.1 \times 10^1) \times 10^7$ ← Rename the first number in scientific notation.

$= 3.1 \times 10^8$ ← Add the exponents to multiply the powers of 10.

Do your calculations in scientific notation. Express each answer in scientific notation.

1. $\frac{0.0000426}{200}$ 2.13×10^{-7}

2. $\frac{(0.000012)\,(400{,}000)}{600}$ 8×10^{-3}

3. $\frac{(0.006)\,(0.008)}{0.0012}$ 4×10^{-2}

4. $\frac{(4{,}000)(30{,}000)}{0.0006}$ 2×10^{11}

Solve. Express the answer in scientific notation.

5. Each year, a planet travels approximately 940,000,000 km around its sun. About how far does the planet travel in 30,000 years?

   about 2.82×10^{13} km

6. Joan's computer can do a trillion (10^{12}) calculations in 400,000 sec. How long will it take the computer to do one calculation? 4×10^{-7} sec

7. The distance to the sun is approximately 93,000,000 mi. If a space probe travels at a speed of 3,100 miles per hour, how long will it take to reach the sun? (HINT: rate × time = distance) approximately 3×10^4 hr

Name ____________________

LESSON 20.1

A Sample Investigation

Look through newspapers at home or in the library to find an article that describes the results of a survey. Then complete the following to describe the article and the survey. **Check students' work.**

Title of article: ____________________

Summary of article: ____________________

____

____

____

____

Question(s) the survey asked: ____________________

____

____

Description of the sample group: ____________________

____

____

____

Type of sampling method used: ____________________

What the survey concluded about the population: ____________________

____

____

____

____

____

____

Name ________________________________

Bias in Advertising

Some advertisements use the results of a biased sample that did not represent all members of a population.

Other advertisements use the results of a survey that used biased questions.

In order to make good choices, you need to be aware of bias in advertising.

You want to sell a new product. Describe, name, and draw a sketch of your product in the space below. **Check students' work.**

____

____

____

Now advertise your product. You want millions of people to buy it. In the space below, design an advertisement for your product that is unbiased. **Check students' work.**

Name ______________________________

Survey Evaluation

Obtain a copy of a survey from a magazine, market research firm, local library, or municipal building. Examine the questions asked in the survey. Then answer these questions. **Check students' work.**

1. What organization sponsored the survey?

____

2. What was the purpose of the survey?

____

____

____

3. What questioning format was used?

____

____

4. Did the survey contain any biased questions? If so, give an example of one.

____

____

5. Write two questions you would add to the survey.

____

____

____

____

6. How would you rate the overall effectiveness of the survey? Explain.

____

____

____

____

____

Name ____________________

Survey The Community

Some communities are debating a proposal to lengthen the school year.

Supporters believe that students would learn more by spending more time in the classroom. They claim that American students spend too much time vacationing and not enough time studying.

Opponents insist that students need a long break from the rigors of school. They argue that a shorter vacation would cause student stress and burnout.

1. Use what you have learned about samples, bias, and survey questions to write a survey about lengthening the school year. Write five questions for your survey. **Check students' questions.**

   - ____________________
   - ____________________
   - ____________________
   - ____________________
   - ____________________

2. Survey a sample of 20 members of your community. Be sure that your sample represents all members of the community. Select the community members by random sampling, stratified sampling, or systematic sampling. Record your data on another sheet of paper. **Check students' data.**

3. Analyze your results. Based on your survey, what does your community think about this issue? **Answers will vary.**

Name ______________________________

Organizing by Venn

A survey at Happy Hamburger Haven asks 100 customers what they eat on their hamburgers.

The survey shows:

40 eat onions.	15 eat onions and mustard.
35 eat mustard.	20 eat mustard and catsup.
50 eat catsup.	25 eat onions and catsup.
5 eat onions, mustard, and catsup.	

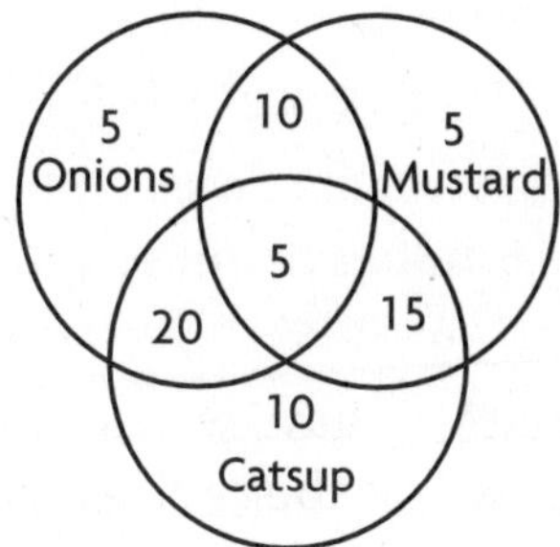

You can answer many questions quickly when you organize the data in a Venn diagram.

Step 1 Draw a Venn diagram with 3 overlapping circles.

Step 2 Write "5" where onions, mustard, and catsup overlap.

Step 3 Write 15 − 5, or "10," where only onions and mustard overlap.
Write 20 − 5, or "15," where only mustard and catsup overlap.
Write 25 − 5, or "20," where only onions and catsup overlap.

Step 4 Write 40 − 20 − 5 − 10, or "5," in the remaining onion circle.
Write 35 − 10 − 5 − 15, or "5," in the remaining mustard circle.
Write 50 − 15 − 5 − 20, or "10," in the remaining catsup circle.

Notice that the sum of the numbers in the Venn diagram is less than 100, which means some customers eat nothing on their hamburgers.

For Exercises 1–3, find the number of customers who eat the following on their hamburgers.

1. only onions

5 customers

2. nothing

30 customers

3. one item

20 customers

A survey asks 1,000 people what they recycle.

The survey shows:

200 recycle glass.	15 recycle paper and glass.
450 recycle cans.	50 recycle cans and glass.
300 recycle paper.	60 recycle cans and paper.
10 recycle glass, cans, and paper.	

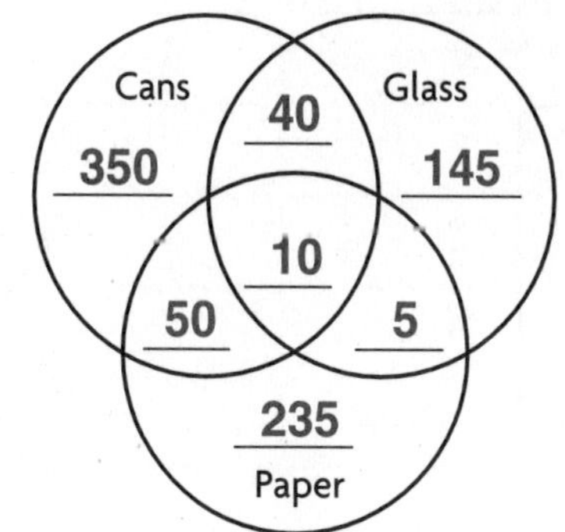

4. Complete the Venn diagram.

For Exercises 5–7, find the number of people who recycle the following.

5. nothing

165 people

6. only one item

730 people

7. only paper

235 people

Name ______________________

Can I Get a Scholarship?

You can find your grade point average if you know the numerical value of each letter grade:

A = 4   B = 3   C = 2   D = 1   F = 0

You also need to know the number of *credit hours* of each subject. This is usually the number of hours per week a class meets.

Credit Hours	Grade	Grade Value	Credit × Grade Value
4	B	3	12
2	A	4	8
5	C	2	10
1	F	0	0
3	B	3	9
15	Sum		39

Step 1 Multiply the Credit Hours by the Grade Value.

Step 2 Find the sum of the Credit Hours.

Step 3 Find the sum of the Credit × Grade Value column.

Step 4 Grade Point Average (GPA) equals the sum of the Credit × Grade Value column divided by the sum of the Credit Hours column.
GPA = 39 ÷ 15 = 2.6

Tanya, Barry, and Samuel need a GPA of at least 3.0 to be eligible for scholarship aid. Complete each table.

1. Tanya

Credit Hours	Grade	Grade Value	Credit × Grade Value
3	A	4	12
3	B	3	9
4	B	3	12
2	C	2	4
4	D	1	4
16	Sum		41

2. Barry

Credit Hours	Grade	Grade Value	Credit × Grade Value
3	C	2	6
4	B	3	12
4	A	4	16
2	D	1	2
2	C	2	4
15	Sum		40

3. Samuel

Credit Hours	Grade	Grade Value	Credit × Grade Value
3	A	4	12
3	C	2	6
1	A	4	4
4	B	3	12
4	A	4	16
15	Sum		50

Round the GPA to the nearest tenth.

4. What is Tanya's GPA? 2.6

5. What is Barry's GPA? 2.7

6. What is Samuel's GPA? 3.3

7. Who is eligible for scholarship aid? Samuel

Name ______________________

LESSON 21.3

Strike a Hit

The Super Strikers Bowling Team bowled 3 games. Use the scores in the table to answer the questions.

Circle the letter of the correct answer choice. Put the letter on the numbered line below. Solve the riddle. The first Exercise is done for you.

	Game 1	Game 2	Game 3	Players Total
Allie	142	136	157	435
Bob	173	131	209	513
Cathy	169	171	180	520
Dan	216	154	172	542
Edith	153	167	161	481
Team Score	853	759	879	2,491

1. Who has the greatest range of scores?

S. Dan **(O.)** Bob

2. Who has the lowest mean score?

R. Edith **(E.)** Allie

3. What is the approximate mean score of all the scores in all 3 games?

(R.) 166 **P.** 172

4. Who bowled the median total score?

J. Cathy **(R.)** Bob

5. What is the approximate mean of the scores in Game 1?

(Y.) 171 **G.** 181

6. Whose mean score is higher?

C. Bob **(U.)** Cathy

7. Whose mean score is higher than the team's overall mean score?

(F.) Dan **K.** Allie

8. In Game 3, who bowled nearer the team's mean score for that game?

V. Edith **(U.)** Cathy

9. For which game was the team's mean score the lowest?

(U.) Game 2 **V.** Game 1

10. Is the team's overall mean score above or below its overall median score?

(T.) below **F.** above

Riddle: What is it that you cannot see but is always before you?

Y O U R   F U T U R E

5 1 9 3   7 6 10 8 4 2

Name ________________

LESSON 21.4

Scrooge, the Sea, and Statistics

"Scrooge resumed his labors with an improved opinion of himself and in a more facetious temper than was usual with him." Charles Dickens, *A Christmas Carol*

1. Complete the cumulative frequency table of the number of letters in each word.
2. Find the approximate mean, median, and mode for the number of letters per word. Round to tenths if necessary.

   4.6; 4; 3, 4, and 7
3. Do you think the approximate mean, median, and mode for the number of letters per word in today's English literature would be the same? Why or why not?

   Answers may vary.

Number of Letters per Word	Tally	Frequency	Cumulative Frequency
1	/	1	1
2	///	3	4
3	////	4	8
4	////	4	12
5	/	1	13
6	//	2	15
7	////	4	19
8	/	1	20
9	/	1	21

"Everything about him was old except his eyes and they were the same color as the sea and were cheerful and undefeated." Ernest Hemingway, *The Old Man and the Sea*

4. Complete the cumulative frequency table of the number of letters in each word.
5. Find the approximate mean, median, and mode for the number of letters per word. Round to tenths if necessary.

   4.4; 3.5; 3
6. Which measures of central tendency best represent the number of letters per word in this passage?

   median and mode
7. How do the extreme values of more than 7 letters in a word affect the mean?

   They increase it.

Number of Letters per Word	Tally	Frequency	Cumulative Frequency
1			0
2	/	1	1
3	~~////~~ ~~////~~	10	11
4	~~////~~	5	16
5	//	2	18
6	/	1	19
7			19
8	/	1	20
9			20
10	//	2	22

8. Choose a sample of 30 words or less from your favorite book or poem. Find the mean, median, and mode for the number of letters per word. Compare them with the means, medians, and modes of the above passages.

   Answers may vary.

Name ______________________

Probability with Pascal

In how many ways can you toss heads with 3 coin tosses?

- You can toss 0 heads in 1 way, TTT.
- You can toss 1 head in 3 ways, HTT, THT, or TTH.
- You can toss 2 heads in 3 ways, HHT, HTH, or THH.
- You can toss 3 heads in 1 way, HHH.

1. The *total* number of outcomes when tossing 3 coins is 1 + 3 + 3 + 1 = __8__.

2. Complete to find the probability of tossing 2 heads when tossing 3 coins.

$$P(2 \text{ heads}) = \frac{\boxed{3}}{\boxed{8}}$$ ←number of outcomes with 2 heads / ←total possible outcomes

The probability is $\frac{3}{8}$.

3. Complete the table. The number of ways to toss 0, 1, 2, and 3 heads with 3 coin tosses are entered for you.

NUMBER OF WAYS TO TOSS 0, 1, 2, 3, 4, AND 5 HEADS					
Number of Heads	**1 Toss**	**2 Tosses**	**3 Tosses**	**4 Tosses**	**5 Tosses**
0	1	1	1	1	1
1	1	2	3	4	5
2		1	3	6	10
3			1	4	10
4				1	5
5					1

Notice that if you turn the page $\frac{1}{4}$-turn clockwise, this array is Pascal's triangle.

For Exercises 4–8, use the table (Pascal's triangle). Suppose you toss a coin 4 times.

4. How many outcomes are possible? __16 outcomes__

5. P(1 head) = $\frac{4}{16}$, or $\frac{1}{4}$

6. P(all tails) = $\frac{1}{16}$

7. P(more than 2 heads) = $\frac{5}{16}$

8. P(at least 1 tail) = $\frac{15}{16}$

9. Suppose you toss a coin 5 times. How many outcomes are possible? __32 outcomes__

Name ______________________

LESSON 22.2

Probabilities with Number Cubes

Materials needed: two number cubes labeled 1–6

1. Toss two number cubes 50 times. After each toss, find the sum of the values on the cubes. Put a tally mark in the table for each sum you toss. **Check students' work.**

Sum of Cubes	2	3	4	5	6	7	8	9	10	11	12
Tally of numbers of times tossed											

Using your table, find the probability of getting each sum. **Answers will vary but should be close to answers given.**

2. P(sum of 4) = $\frac{1}{12}$ **3.** P(sum of 8) = $\frac{5}{36}$ **4.** P(sum < 6) = $\frac{5}{18}$

5. Complete by filling in the sums if two number cubes are tossed.

Number Cube 1 (columns) / **Number Cube 2** (rows)

	1	2	3	4	5	6
1	2	3	4	5	6	7
2	3	4	5	6	7	8
3	4	5	6	7	8	9
4	5	6	7	8	9	10
5	6	7	8	9	10	11
6	7	8	9	10	11	12

6. Complete the table, using the chart of sums in Exercise 5.

Sum of Cubes	2	3	4	5	6	7	8	9	10	11	12
Number of ways to get the sum	1	2	3	4	5	6	5	4	3	2	1

7. How many possible outcomes are there if you roll 2 number cubes with 6 different faces? **36 outcomes**

Find the probability of getting each sum, using the table in Exercise 6.

8. P(sum of 4) = $\frac{1}{12}$ **9.** P(sum of 8) = $\frac{5}{36}$ **10.** P(sum < 6) $\frac{5}{18}$

11. Compare your answers to Exercises 2–4 with your answers to Exercises 8–10.

Answers should be close.

Name ______________________

Symbols Matter

Using order of operations and the symbols +, −, ×, and ÷, and parentheses, you can make three 3's equal 2, equal 3, or equal 4.

3 3 3 → (3 + 3) ÷ 3 = 2

→ 3 + 3 − 3 = 3

→ 3 + 3 ÷ 3 = 4

Write the given number using exactly four 4's and the symbols +, −, ×, and ÷, or parentheses. **Possible answers are given.**

1. 1 = 4 − 4 + 4 ÷ 4

2. 2 = 4 ÷ 4 + 4 ÷ 4

3. 3 = (4 + 4 + 4) ÷ 4

4. 4 = (4 − 4) × 4 + 4

5. 5 = (4 × 4 + 4) ÷ 4

6. 6 = (4 + 4) ÷ 4 + 4

7. 7 = 4 + 4 − 4 ÷ 4

8. 8 = 4 × 4 ÷ 4 + 4

9. 9 = 4 + 4 + (4 ÷ 4)

10. 24 = 4 × 4 + 4 + 4

11. 20 = 4 × (4 ÷ 4 + 4)

12. 17 = 4 × 4 + 4 ÷ 4

13. Find two ways to make five 5's equal 5.

5 + 5 − 5 + 5 − 5

5 + 5 × 5 ÷ 5 − 5

Name ______________________

Top Spin

	Number Of Symbols On Top		
Symbol	**Top A**	**Top B**	**Top C**
Apple	1	3	1
Banana	1	3	3
Cherry	7	7	0
Lemon	3	0	4
Orange	3	6	7
Plum	5	1	5

Probability tells you your chances of winning some games.

You are playing a game in which you spin three 20-sided tops. You win if you spin the same symbol on all three tops.

Each top has a symbol on each of the 20 sides. The table shows the number of each symbol on each top.

1. What is the total number of possible outcomes if you spin the three tops?

20 (number of choices for Top A) × 20 (number of choices for Top B) × 20 (number of choices for Top C) = 8,000 possible outcomes

2. What is the probability of spinning 3 apples?

1 (number of apples on Top A) × 3 (number of apples on Top B) × 1 (number of apples on Top C) = 3 ways to get 3 apples

$$P(3 \text{ apples}) = \frac{\text{number of favorable outcomes}}{\text{number of possible outcomes}} = \frac{3}{8{,}000}$$

What is the probability of spinning each of the following?

3. 3 bananas $\frac{9}{8{,}000}$

4. 3 cherries 0

5. 3 lemons 0

6. 3 oranges $\frac{126}{8{,}000} = \frac{63}{4{,}000}$

7. 3 plums $\frac{25}{8{,}000} = \frac{1}{320}$

8. Which symbol—the banana, the apple, the orange, or the plum—has the least chance of being spun on all three tops? the greatest chance?

the apple; the orange

9. Which symbols can never be spun on all three tops?

the cherry and the lemon

Name ______________________________

Pondering Probability

Materials needed: paper plate, construction paper, metal fastener

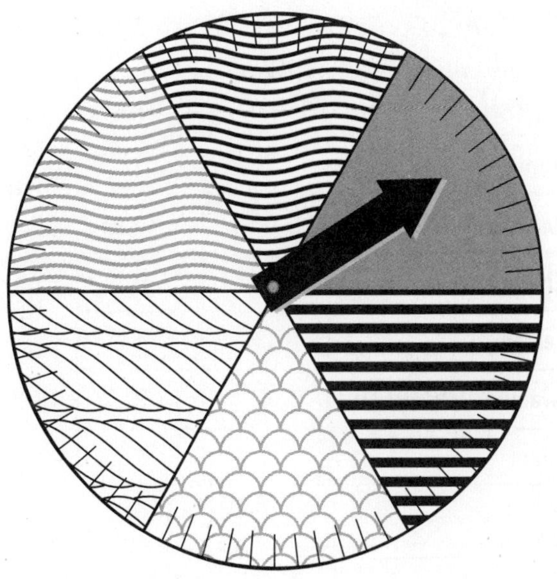

Sample Spinner

Use a paper plate, construction paper arrow, and metal fastener to construct a spinner. Your spinner should have 6–8 congruent sections. Draw a different design in each section.

Spin the pointer 50 times and record your results in the table.

Section								
Times spun								

1. What is the mathematical probability that the pointer will stop on each section of the spinner?

   Possible answers: $\frac{1}{6}$ for 6 sections; $\frac{1}{7}$ for 7 sections; $\frac{1}{8}$ for 8 sections

2. What is your experimental probability of landing on each section?

   Answers will vary.

3. Was your experimental probability of landing on any section close to the mathematical probability? Explain.

   Answers will vary; the experimental probability should be close to the mathematical probability.

4. Were any of your results surprising? Explain.

   Answers will vary.

Name ___________________________

Investigate the Arrangement

There are 24 possible ways to arrange the 4 letters in the word *four.* They are listed in alphabetical order.

foru	four	frou	fruo	fuor	furo
ofru	ofur	orfu	oruf	oufr	ourf
rfou	rfuo	rofu	rouf	rufo	ruof
ufor	ufro	uofr	uorf	urfo	urof

1. What is the probability of randomly selecting an English word from the 24 arrangements? $\frac{1}{24}$

2. a. Write all the possible ways to arrange the 4 letters in the word *nine.* Use all 4 letters.

   einn, enin, enni, ienn, inen, inne, nein, neni,

   nien, nine, nnei, nnie

   b. How many different arrangements are possible?

   12 arrangements

3. Both words *four* and *nine* have 4 letters, but each word has a different number of possible letter arrangements. Explain.

   Four contains 4 different letters and *nine* contains

   3 different letters.

4. What is the probability of randomly selecting an English word from the arrangements in Exercise 2? $\frac{1}{12}$

5. a. Write all possible ways to arrange the 3 letters in the word *ten.*

   6 ways: ent, etn, net, nte, ten, tne

   b. What is the probability of randomly selecting an English word from the arrangements? $\frac{2}{6}$, or $\frac{1}{3}$

6. a. Write all possible ways to arrange the 3 letters in the word *pet.*

   6 ways: ept, etp, pet, pte, tep, tpe

   b. What is the probability of randomly selecting an English word from the arrangements? $\frac{1}{6}$

Name ____________________

Be a Natural Scientist

Circle the proportion that you would use to estimate the given animal population in each national park.

1.

$$\frac{\text{total tagged bears}}{\text{tagged bears caught 2}^{\text{nd}}\text{ day}} = \frac{\text{total bears caught 2}^{\text{nd}}\text{ day}}{\text{total bears in park}}$$

$$\frac{\text{tagged bears caught 2}^{\text{nd}}\text{ day}}{\text{total tagged bears}} = \frac{\text{total bears in park}}{\text{total bears caught 2}^{\text{nd}}\text{ day}}$$

$$\frac{\text{tagged bears caught 2}^{\text{nd}}\text{ day}}{\text{total bears caught 2}^{\text{nd}}\text{ day}} = \frac{\text{total tagged bears}}{\text{total bears in park}}$$

Grizzly Bears in Banff National Park

2.

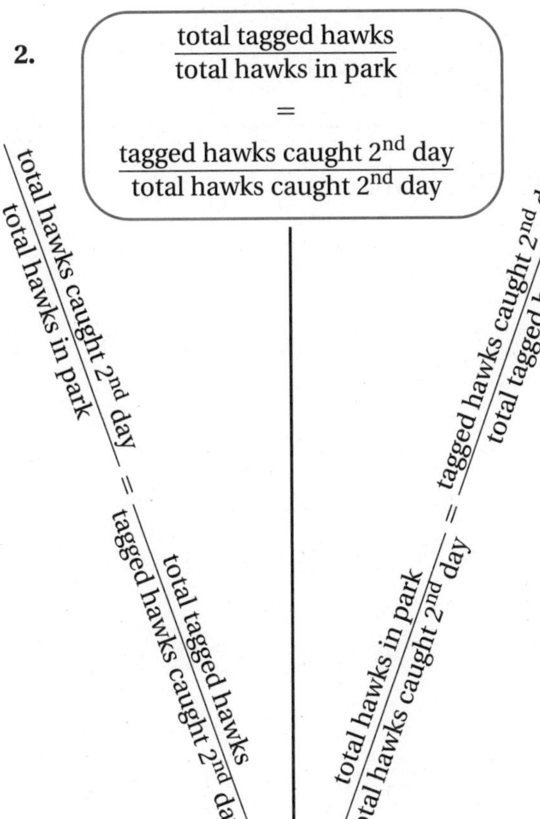

Hawks in Yellowstone National Park

3.

$$\frac{\text{tagged eagles caught 2}^{\text{nd}}\text{ day}}{\text{total eagles caught 2}^{\text{nd}}\text{ day}} = \frac{\text{total eagles in park}}{\text{total tagged eagles}}$$

$$\frac{\text{tagged eagles caught 2}^{\text{nd}}\text{ day}}{\text{total eagles caught 2}^{\text{nd}}\text{ day}} = \frac{\text{total tagged eagles}}{\text{total eagles in park}}$$

$$\frac{\text{total eagles caught 2}^{\text{nd}}\text{ day}}{\text{tagged eagles caught 2}^{\text{nd}}\text{ day}} = \frac{\text{total tagged eagles}}{\text{total eagles in park}}$$

Eagles in Mt. Ranier National Park

Name ______________________________

It's Your Game

area of a circle = πr^2

The area of the blue region is $\pi(2)^2 - \pi(1)^2 = 4\pi - \pi = 3\pi$.

The geometric probability that a dart that hits the target will land in the blue region is $\frac{\text{area of blue region}}{\text{total area}} = \frac{3\pi}{\pi(3)^2} = \frac{3}{9}$, or $\frac{1}{3}$.

yellow
blue
red
1 in.
2 in.
3 in.

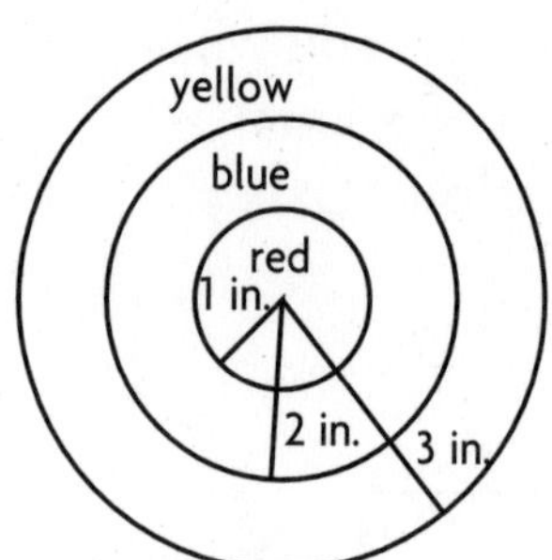

Complete the target below by assigning a radius to each circle. Then find the probability P that a dart that hits the target will land in each region. **Answers will vary. Possible answers are given.**

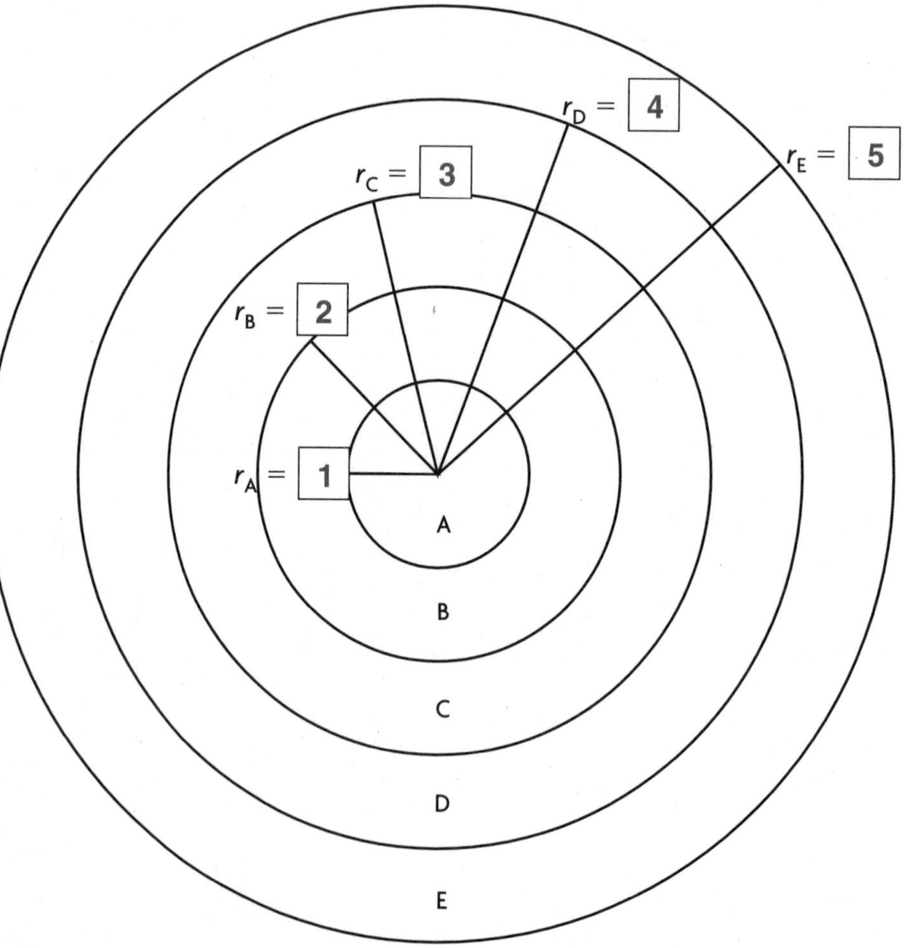

r_A = 1
r_B = 2
r_C = 3
r_D = 4
r_E = 5
A
B
C
D
E

P(A) = $\frac{1}{25}$

P(B) = $\frac{3}{25}$

P(C) = $\frac{5}{25}$

P(D) = $\frac{7}{25}$

P(E) = $\frac{9}{25}$

Name ______________________

Finding Shapes

1. How many triangles can you find?

   12 triangles

2. How many parallelograms can you find?

   20 parallelograms

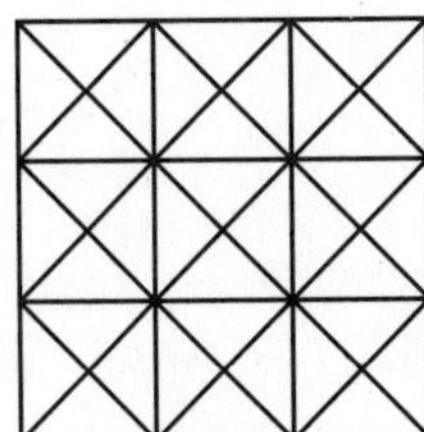

3. How many squares can you find?

   31 squares

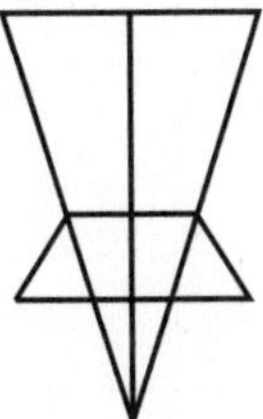

4. How many trapezoids can you find?

   10 trapezoids

Name a shape in the diagram as described. **Answers will vary; possible answers are given.**

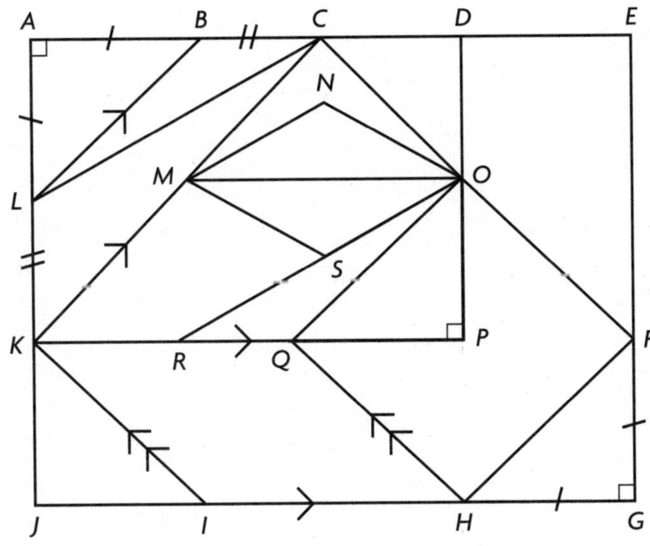

5. a square **square *FHQO***
6. a rectangle that is not a square

   rectangle *ADPK*
7. a parallelogram that is not a rectangle

   parallelogram *KQHI*
8. an isosceles right triangle

   △*LAB*
9. a right scalene triangle

   △*CAL*
10. a trapezoid that is not isosceles

    trapezoid *DEFO*
11. an isosceles trapezoid

    trapezoid *BCKL*

Name ___________________________

LESSON 24.2

Picture This

Plot each of the ordered pairs on the coordinate plan. Connect the points in order.

1. (0,13)	**2.** (⁻2,11)	**3.** (⁻3,9)	**4.** (⁻3,4)
5. (⁻8,⁻5)	**6.** (⁻5,⁻5)	**7.** (⁻5,⁻8)	**8.** (⁻8,⁻11)
9. (⁻5,⁻10)	**10.** (⁻4,⁻14)	**11.** (⁻3,⁻10)	**12.** (0,⁻11)
13. (⁻2,⁻8)	**14.** (⁻2,⁻5)	**15.** (2,⁻5)	**16.** (2,⁻8)
17. (0,⁻11)	**18.** (2,⁻10)	**19.** (4,⁻14)	**20.** (5,⁻10)
21. (8,⁻11)	**22.** (5,⁻8)	**23.** (5,⁻5)	**24.** (8,⁻5)
25. (3,4)	**26.** (3,9)	**27.** (2,11)	**28.** (0,13)

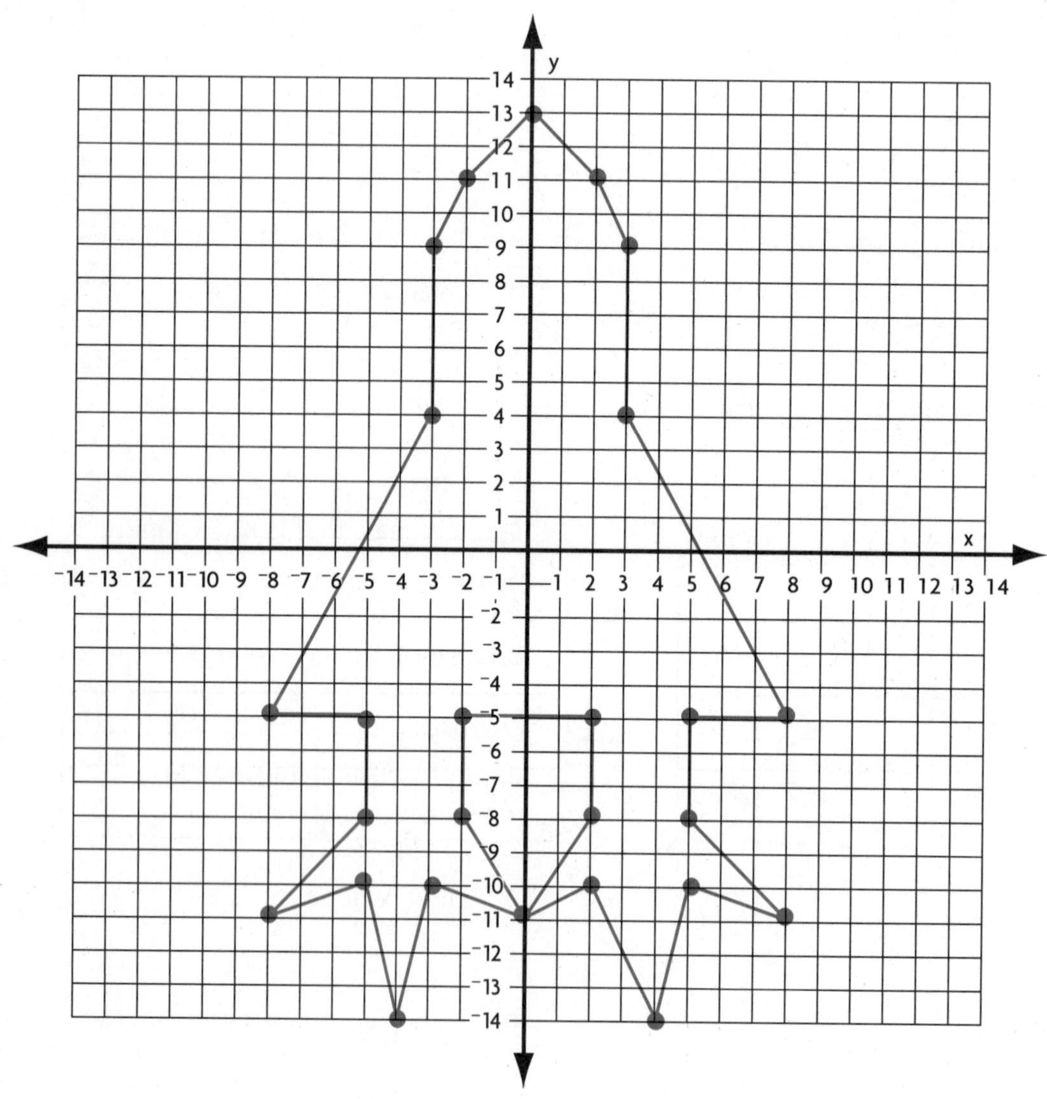

29. What property does the graph show? symmetry

30. I am a picture of a R O C K E T.

Name ____________________

Families of Right Triangles

Any three numbers that satisfy the formula $a^2 + b^2 = c^2$ form a *Pythagorean triple.*

$3^2 + 4^2 = 5^2$

$9 + 16 = 25$

(3, 4, 5) is a Pythagorean triple.

When you multiply or divide a Pythagorean triple by the same number, you still have a Pythagorean triple.

So, $(3 \times 2, 4 \times 2, 5 \times 2)$ or (6, 8, 10) is a Pythagorean triple.

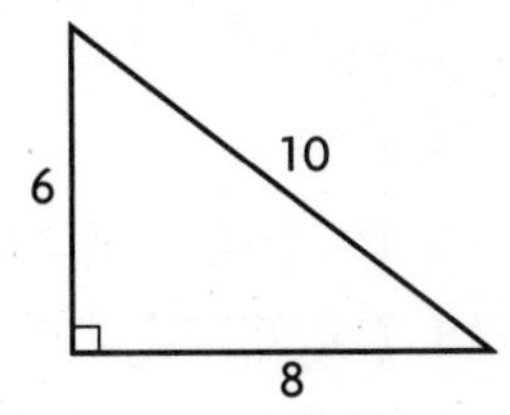

Check it out: $6^2 + 8^2 = 10^2$.

$36 + 64 = 100$

Complete each table to find new Pythagorean triples.

1. The (3, 4, 5) Family

Multiply by 3.	(9, 12, 15)
Multiply by 5.	(15, 20, 25)
Multiply by 10.	(30, 40, 50)
Divide by 2.	$\left(\frac{3}{2}, 2, \frac{5}{2}\right)$
Divide by 5.	$\left(\frac{3}{5}, \frac{4}{5}, 1\right)$

2. The (5, 12, 13) Family

Multiply by 2.	(10, 24, 26)
Multiply by 3.	(15, 36, 39)
Divide by 2.	$\left(\frac{5}{2}, 6, \frac{13}{2}\right)$
Divide by 10.	$\left(\frac{1}{2}, \frac{6}{5}, \frac{13}{10}\right)$

3. The (7, 24, 25) Family

Divide by 4.	$\left(\frac{7}{4}, 6, \frac{25}{4}\right)$
Divide by 10.	$\left(\frac{7}{10}, \frac{12}{5}, \frac{5}{2}\right)$
Multiply by 2.	(14, 48, 50)
Multiply by 4.	(28, 96, 100)

4. The (8, 15, 17) Family

Divide by 2.	$\left(4, \frac{15}{2}, \frac{17}{2}\right)$
Divide by 5.	$\left(\frac{8}{5}, 3, \frac{17}{5}\right)$
Multiply by 3.	(24, 45, 51)
Multiply by 4.	(32, 60, 68)

5. Check one of the (3, 4, 5) family.
Answers may vary.
$9^2 + 12^2 =$ 15^2

$81 + 144 = 225$

6. Check one of the (5, 12, 13) family.
Answers may vary.
$10^2 + 24^2 = 26^2$

$100 + 576 = 676$

7. Check one of the (7, 24, 25) family.
Answers may vary.
$14^2 + 48^2 = 50^2$

$196 + 2{,}304 = 2{,}500$

8. Check one of the (8, 15, 17) family.
Answers may vary.
$24^2 + 45^2 = 51^2$

$576 + 2{,}025 = 2{,}601$

Name ____________________

Out of the Big Picture

You can add and subtract areas to find the area of a shaded region.

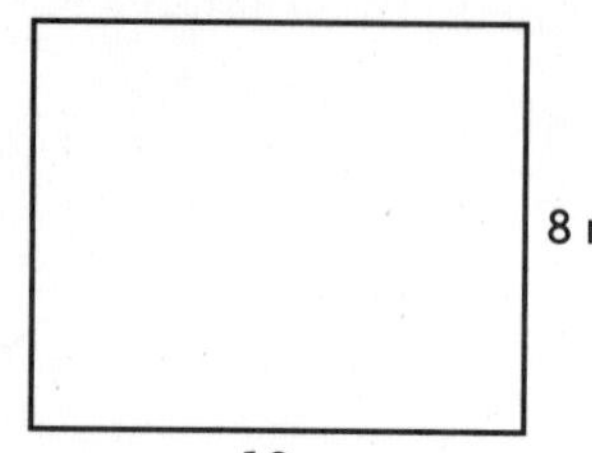

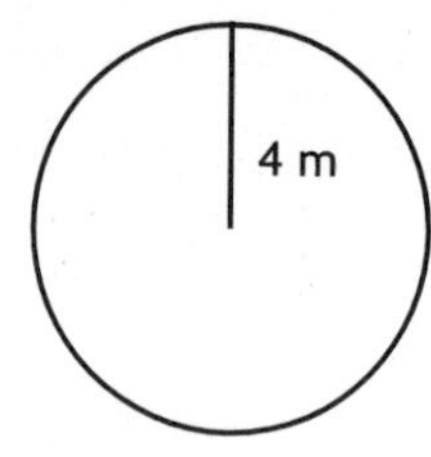

- Find the area of the rectangle.
  $A = lw = 10 \times 8 = 80$
- Find the area of the circle.
  $A = \pi r^2 = \pi \times 4^2 \approx 50.24$
- shaded area $\approx 80 \text{ m}^2 - 50.24 \text{ m}^2 \approx 29.76 \text{ m}^2$

Add or subtract to find the area of the shaded region.

1.

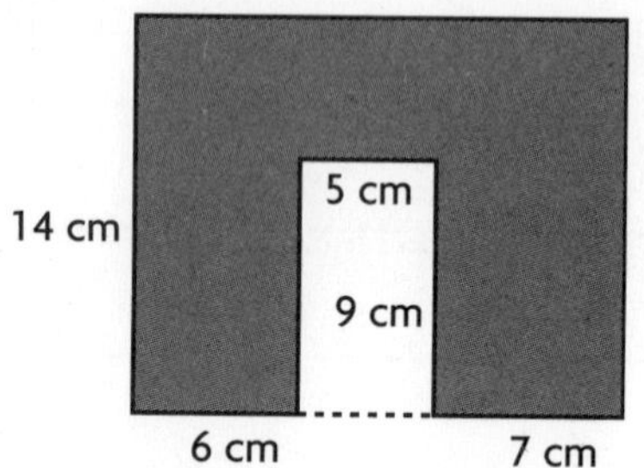

207 cm²

2.

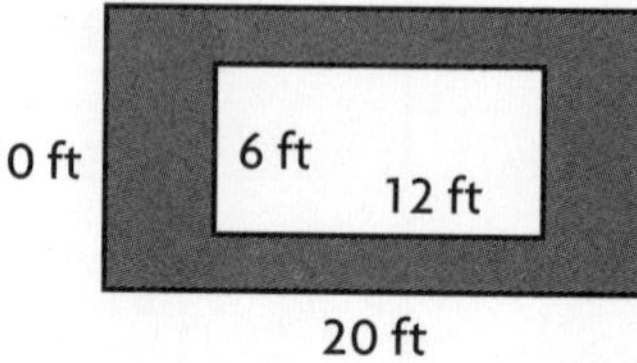

128 ft²

3.

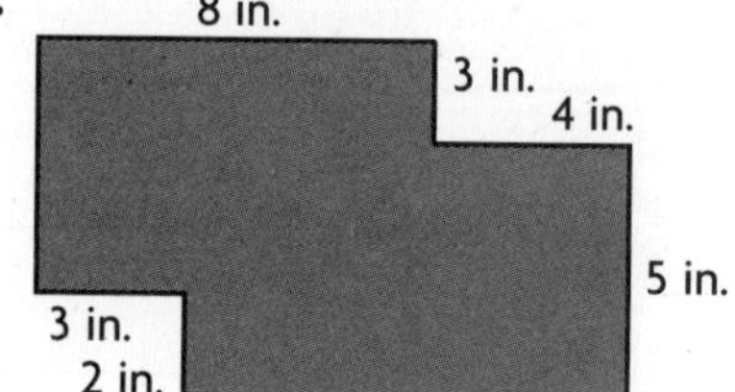

78 in.²

4.

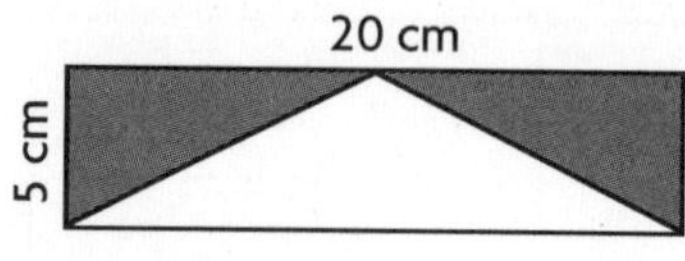

50 cm²

5.

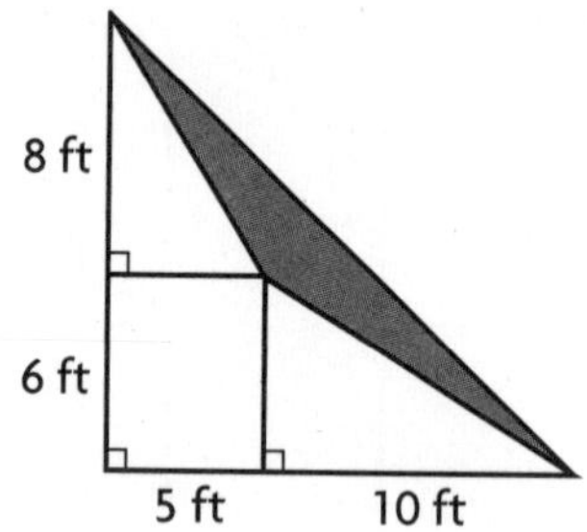

25 ft²

6.

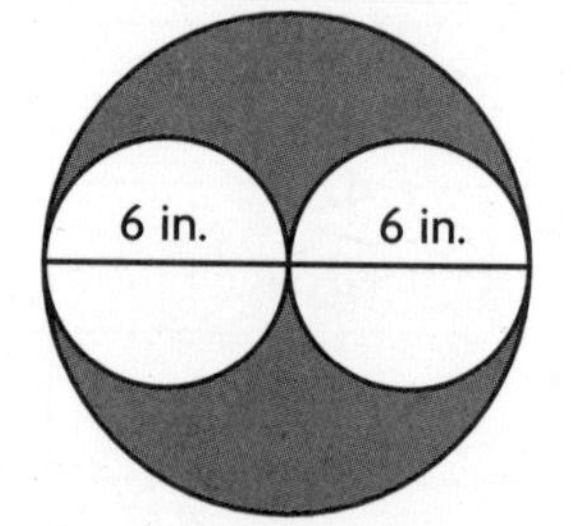

18π in.² ≈ 56.52 in.²

7.

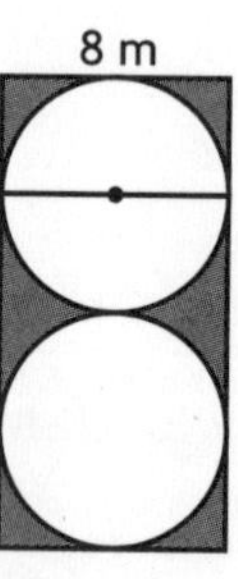
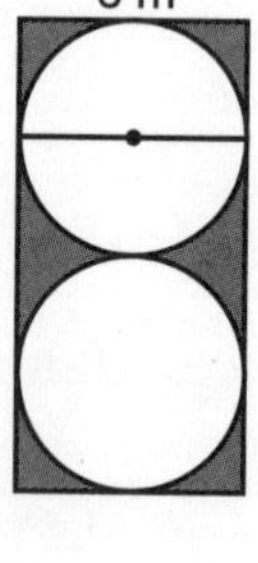

about 27.52 m²

8.

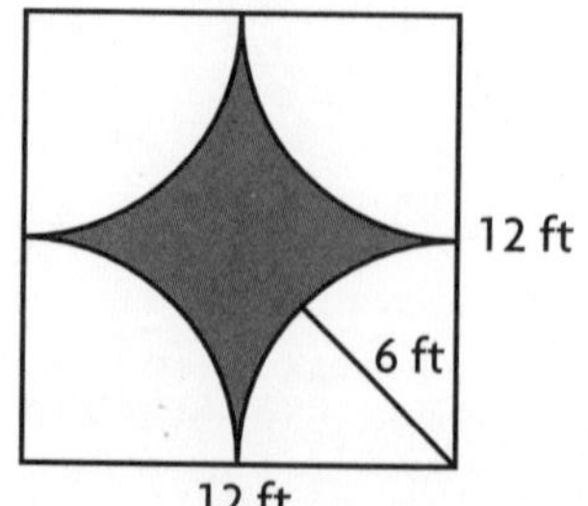

about 30.96 ft²

9.

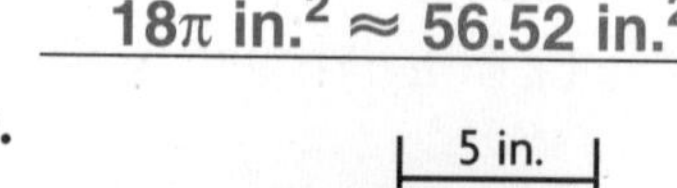

16π in.² ≈ 50.24 in.²

Name ____________________

From Start to Finish

Find your way to the solution. Pass through each square only once as you perform the indicated operation.

1.

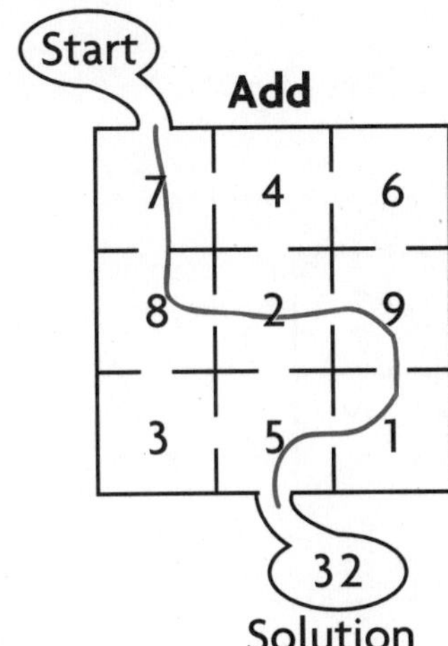

2.

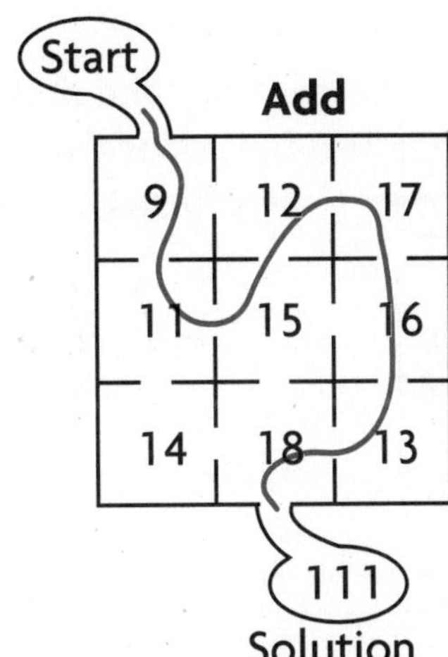

3.

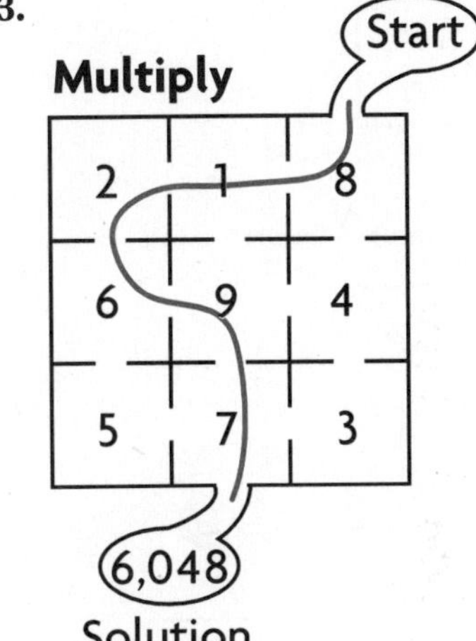

4.

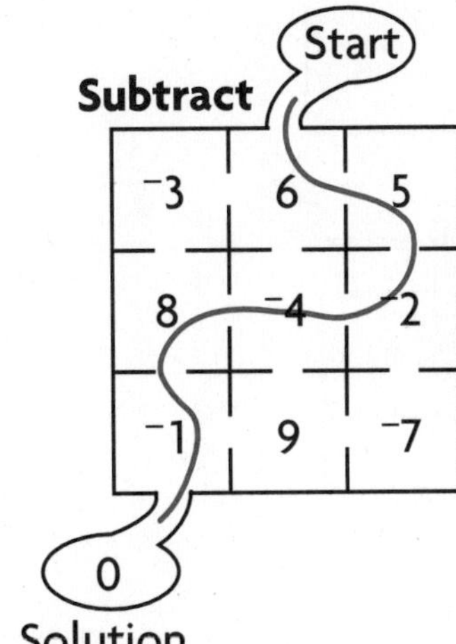

5.

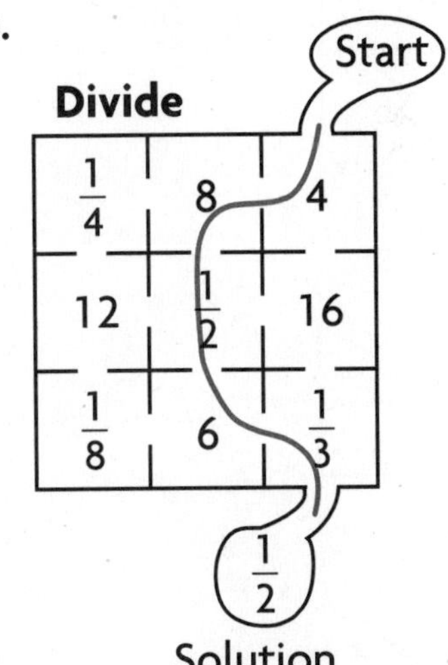

6.

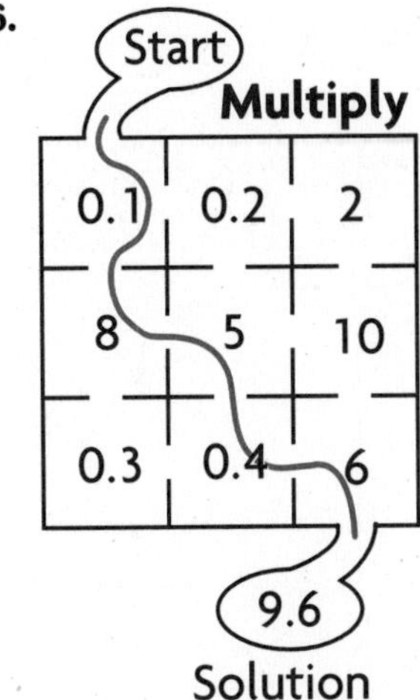

Name ______________________________

LESSON 25.1

Raise the Flag

Find the fraction $\frac{\text{area of color}}{\text{area of flag}}$ for each color. Be careful; sometimes a color is in more than one place on a flag. Combine colors before finding the fraction.

Use your knowledge of symmetry and area to solve. Lines intersecting the edges divide them into halves or thirds. (R = Red, B = Blue, W = White, G = Green, Y = Yellow)

1.

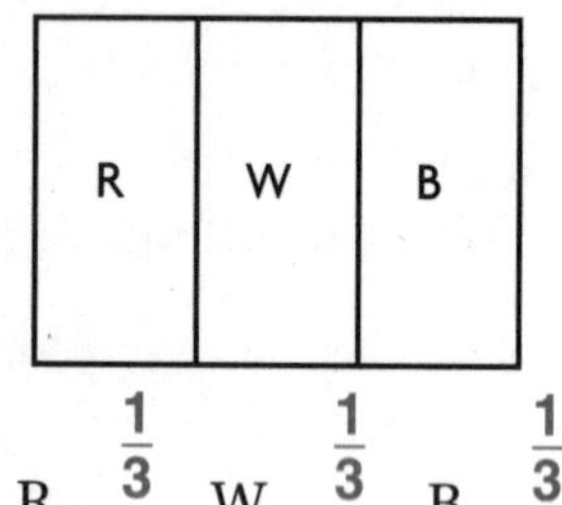

R $\frac{1}{3}$ W $\frac{1}{3}$ B $\frac{1}{3}$

2.

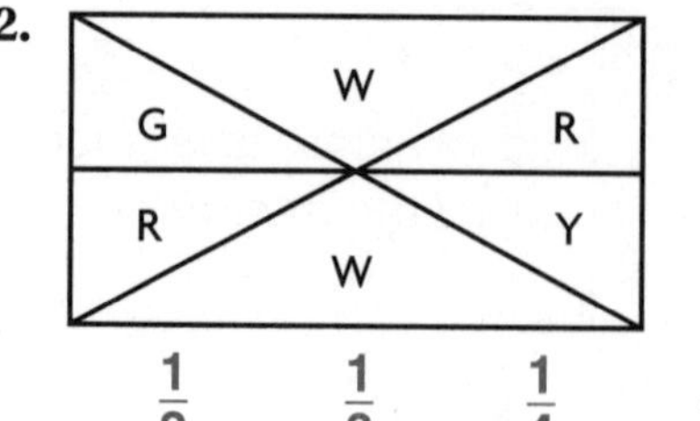

W $\frac{1}{2}$ G $\frac{1}{8}$ R $\frac{1}{4}$ Y $\frac{1}{8}$

3.

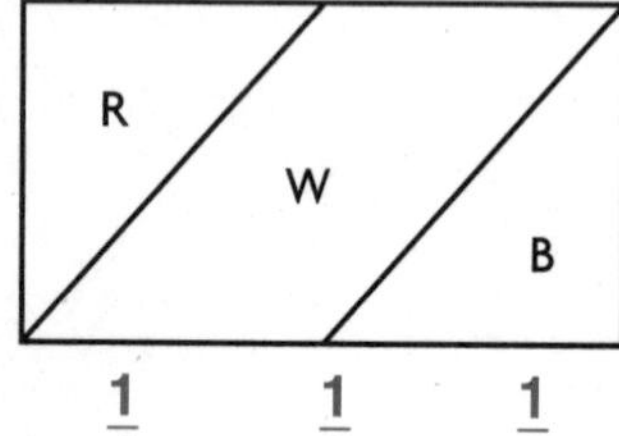

R $\frac{1}{4}$ W $\frac{1}{2}$ B $\frac{1}{4}$

4.

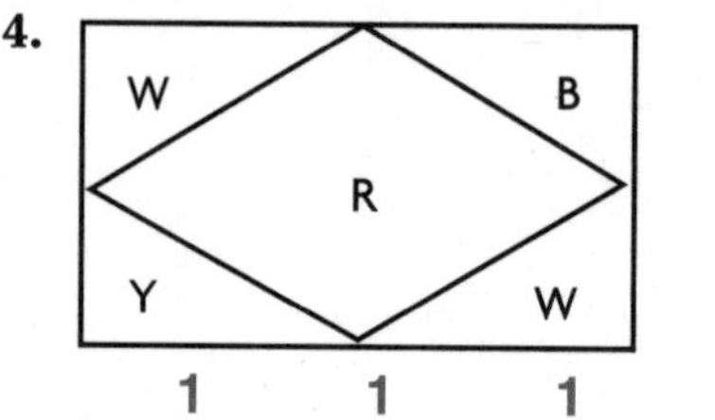

W $\frac{1}{4}$ R $\frac{1}{2}$ B $\frac{1}{8}$ Y $\frac{1}{8}$

5.

R	W	B
W	R	W

R $\frac{1}{3}$ W $\frac{1}{2}$ B $\frac{1}{6}$

6.

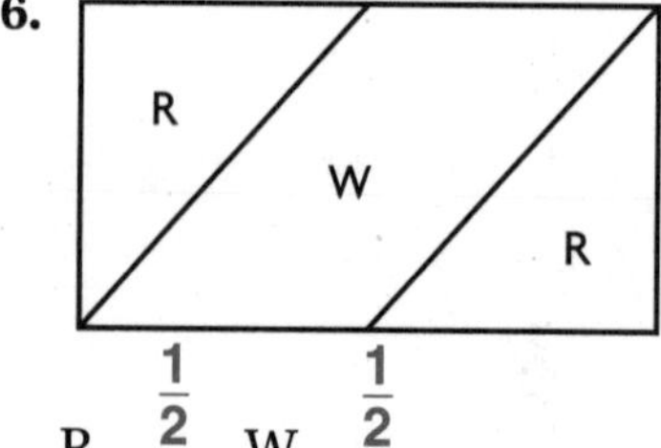

R $\frac{1}{2}$ W $\frac{1}{2}$

7.

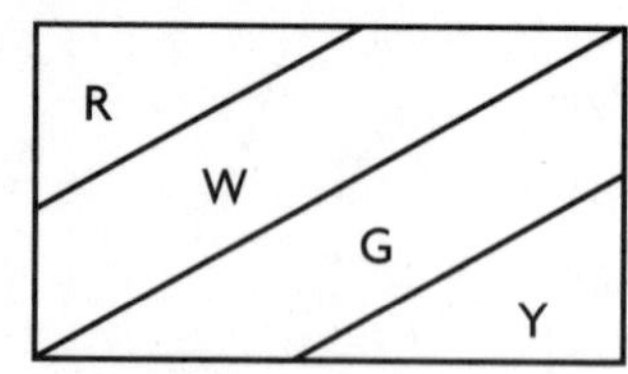

R $\frac{1}{8}$ W $\frac{3}{8}$ G $\frac{3}{8}$ Y $\frac{1}{8}$

8.

R	W
Y	R

R $\frac{1}{2}$ W $\frac{1}{4}$ Y $\frac{1}{4}$

9.

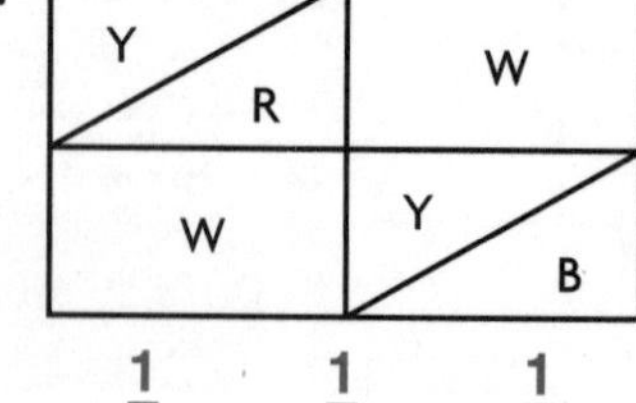

Y $\frac{1}{4}$ R $\frac{1}{8}$ B $\frac{1}{8}$ W $\frac{1}{2}$

10.

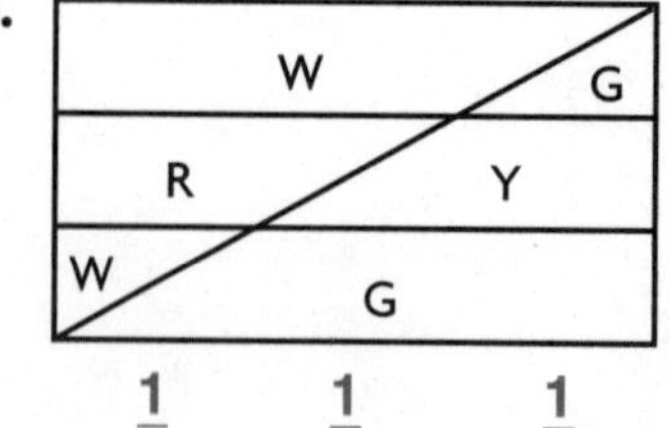

R $\frac{1}{6}$ Y $\frac{1}{6}$ W $\frac{1}{3}$ G $\frac{1}{3}$

Name ____

Play Ball!

Materials needed: metric ruler and compass

A diagram of a baseball field is shown. But it is incomplete. It shows only the foul lines, home plate, and the outfield wall. See if you can complete it by accurately drawing the following:

- first, second, and third bases
- the edge of the outfield grass
- the pitcher's mound
- the warning track

Here is the information you will need.

- The bases are 90 ft apart.
- The edge of the outfield grass is defined by a circle centered on the pitcher's mound with radius of 95 ft.
- The pitcher's mound is centered 60.5 ft from home plate.
- The warning track is 25 ft wide, along the outfield wall.
- The scale is 1 cm: 25 ft, or 1 mm: 2.5 ft.

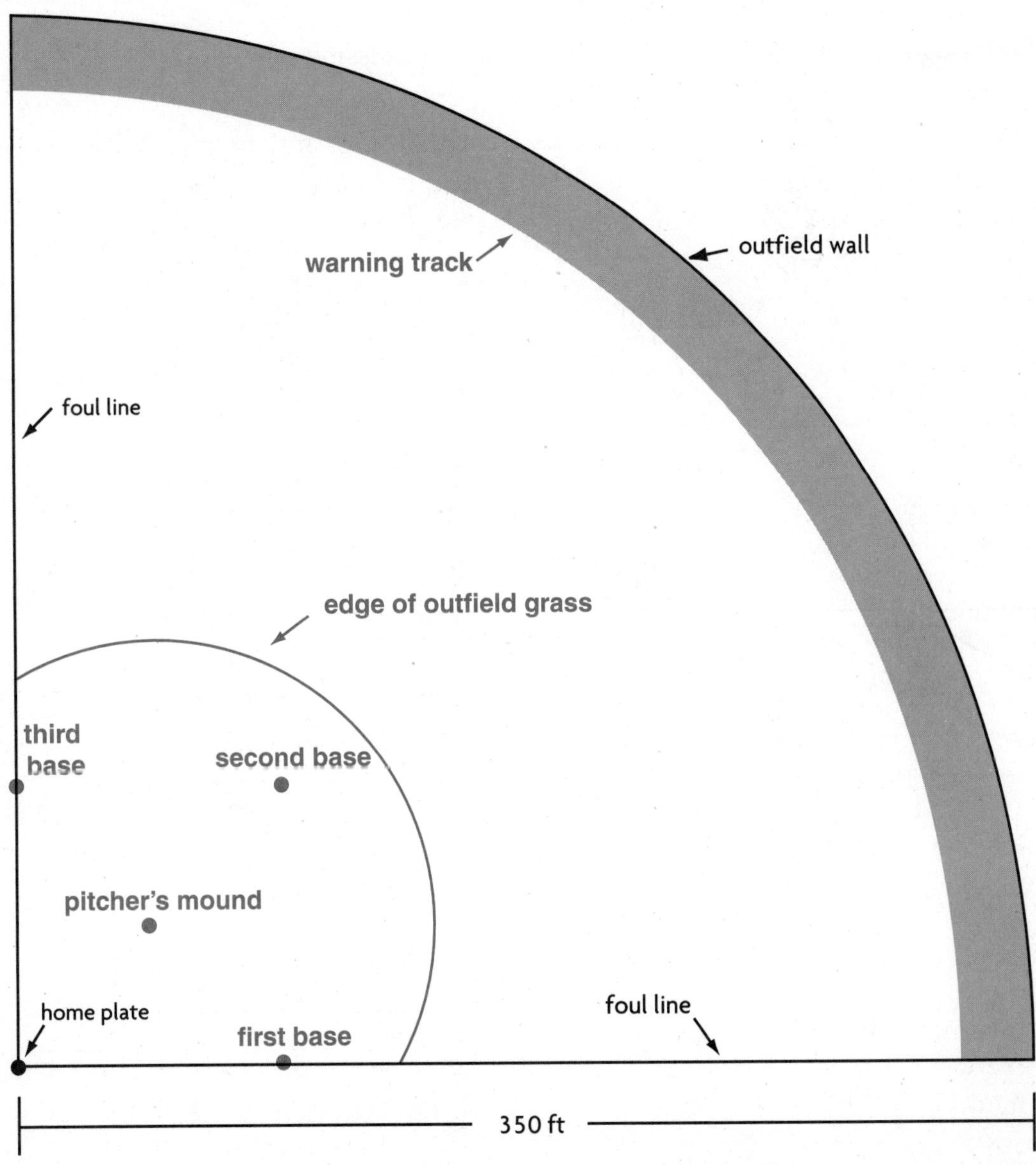

Name ___________________________________

The Part That Isn't There

Sometimes you need to find the volume of a solid figure by first finding the volume of the entire solid and then subtracting a part that is missing.

Use the method of subtracting volumes to find the volume of each figure. Round to the nearest whole number.

1.

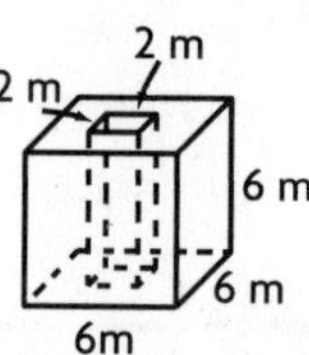

Cube with rectangular prism removed

V of cube: 216 m^3

V of missing part: 24 m^3

V of figure: 192 m^3

2.

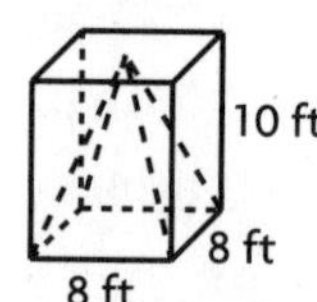

Rectangular prism with pyramid removed

V of prism: 640 ft^3

V of missing part: 213 ft^3

V of figure: 426 ft^3

3.

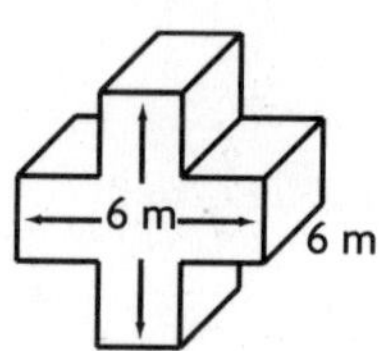

Cube with 2 m × 2 m × 6 m corners removed

V of cube: 216 m^3

V of missing part: 96 m^3

V of figure: 120 m^3

4.

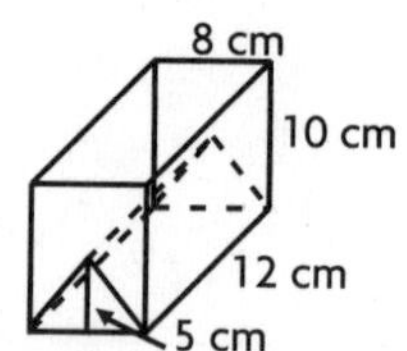

Rectangular prism with triangular prism removed

V of rectangular prism: 960 cm^3

V of missing part: 240 cm^3

V of figure: 720 cm^3

5.

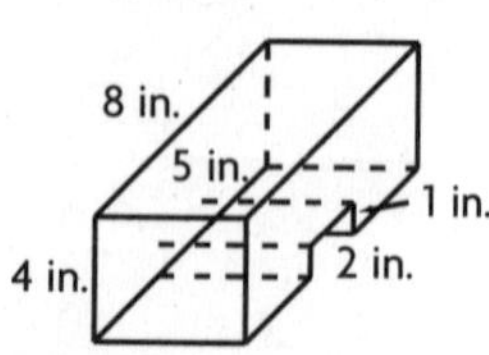

Rectangular prism with rectangular prism removed

V of larger prism: 160 $in.^3$

V of missing part: 10 $in.^3$

V of figure: 150 $in.^3$

6.

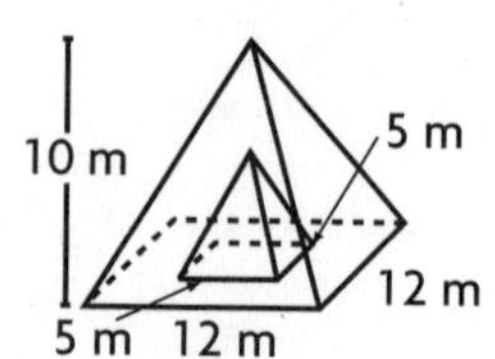

Pyramid (h = 10 m) with pyramid (h = 4 m) removed

V of larger pyramid: 480 m^3

V of missing part: 33 m^3

V of figure: 447 m^3

Name ______________________

The Bigger the Better?

It is important to compare unit prices when you shop. Unit prices are posted for most items so you do not have to calculate them. But this is not always the case.

In a survey of candy stores, students found the jelly bean containers and prices shown below.

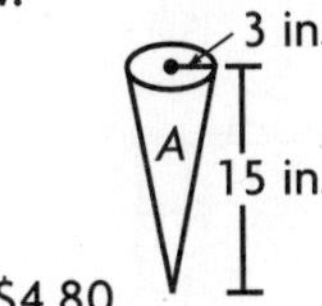

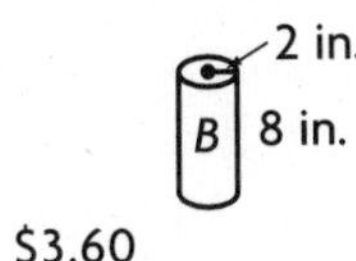

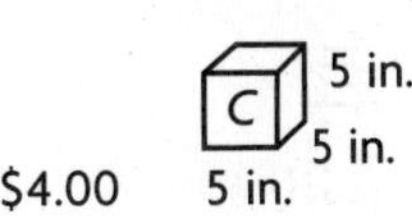

For Exercises 1–7, use $\pi = 3.14$. Round volumes to the nearest cubic inch. Round unit prices to the nearest thousandth.

Complete to find the volume and unit price of each container above.

1. Look at the sizes and prices. Estimate which container has the best unit price, container *A*, *B*, or *C*.

   Answers may vary.

2. Find the volume of each container.

   ***A*: 141 in.^{3}; *B*: 100 in.^{3}; *C*: 125 in.^{3}**

3. Find the unit price of each container by dividing the price by the volume.

   ***A*: $0.034; *B*: $0.036; *C*: $0.032**

4. Which container has the lowest unit price? **the prism**

Compare the cone and the cylinder and their prices.

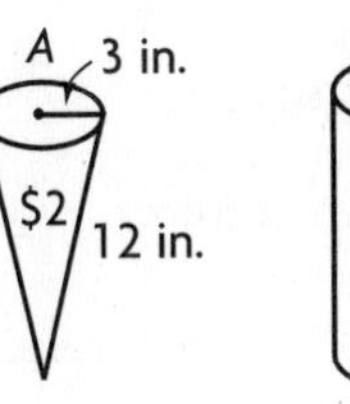

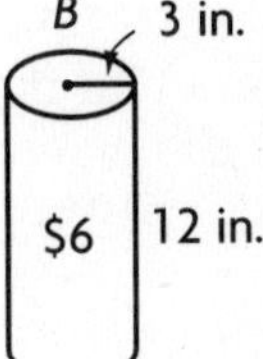

5. Estimate which has the best unit price. Explain your reasoning.

   Answers will vary. Unit price will be the same.

   Volume of cone is $\frac{1}{3}$ volume of cylinder.

6. Calculate the unit price of each container.

   ***A*: $0.018; *B*: $0.018**

7. Draw two containers of different shapes. Give prices for each. Then find the unit price of each. **Check students' work.**

Name ______________________________

LESSON 26.1

Which Shipping Box?

You can change the dimensions of a box without changing the volume.

Molly Manufacturing ships nails to hardware stores. The less cardboard used to make a box, the less the box costs to make.

For each set of boxes, give the missing dimension that will make the volumes of the three boxes equal.

Below each box, write the surface area. Then circle the box in each set that uses the least amount of cardboard.

1.

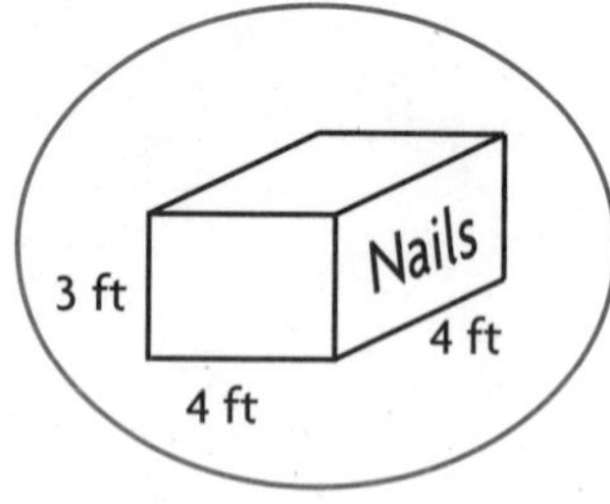

6 ft
Nails
2 ft

width = 4 ft

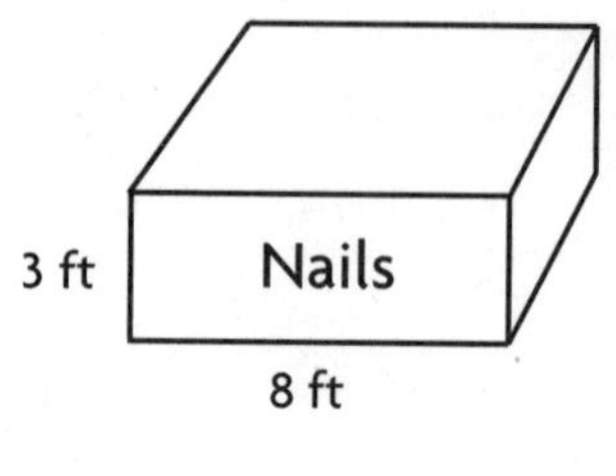

width = 2 ft

surface area = 80 ft²

surface area = 88 ft²

surface area = 92 ft²

2.

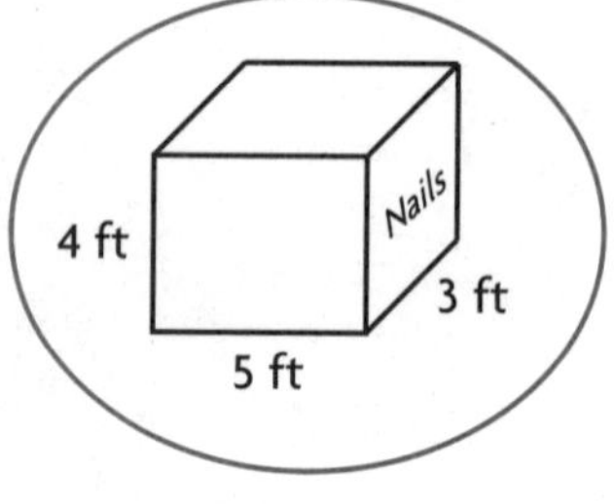

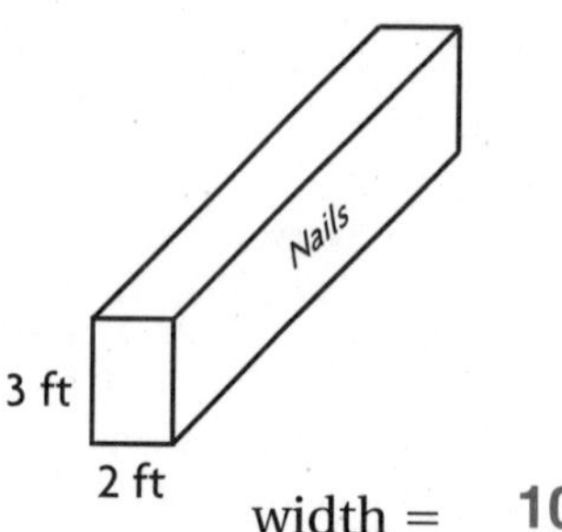

width = 10 ft

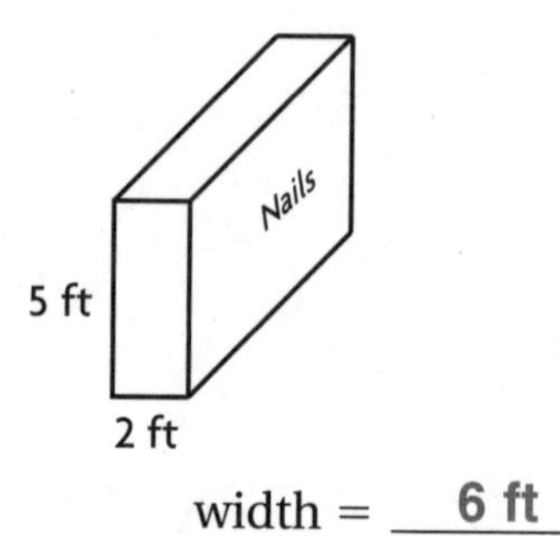

width = 6 ft

surface area = 94 ft²

surface area = 112 ft²

surface area = 104 ft²

3.

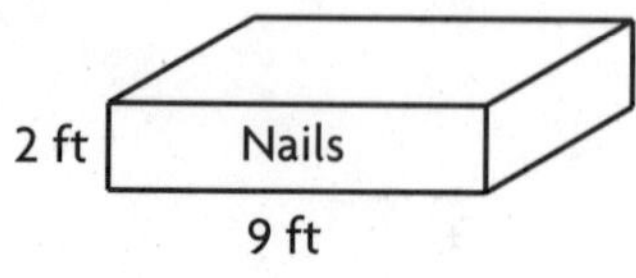

width = 4 ft

surface area = 124 ft²

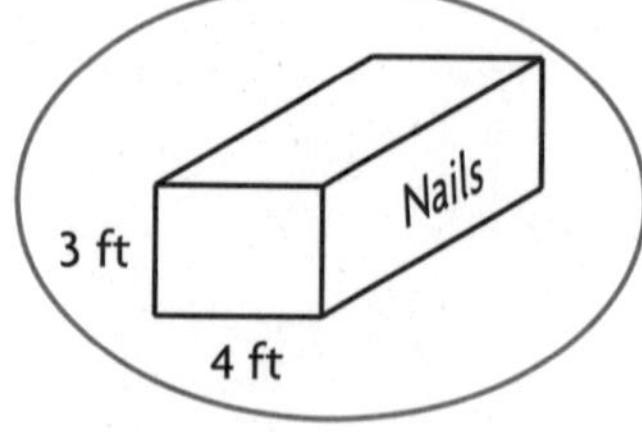

width = 6 ft

surface area = 108 ft²

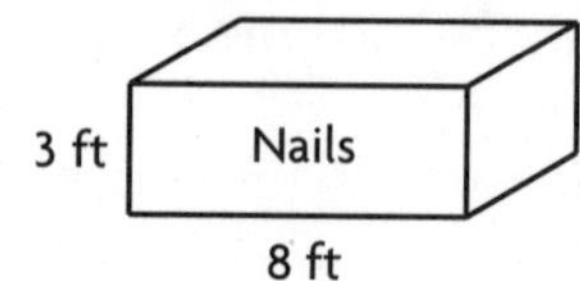

width = 3 ft

surface area = 114 ft²

Name ____

Newspaper Layout

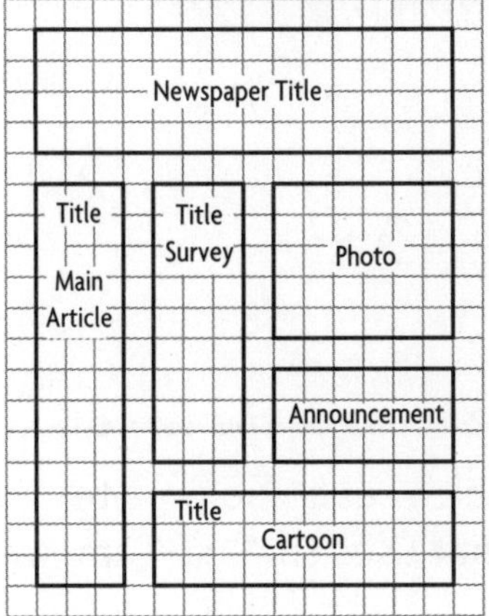

Your job is to lay out the newspaper. The plan at the right shows the space you will use for laying out each part of the front page.

Newspaper Title
Title
Main Article
Title
Survey
Photo
Announcement
Title
Cartoon

Use the scale percentage of 250% for the width and height of each section of the first page to make an enlarged plan.

Draw each section on the graph paper below. Write titles and the announcement, and sketch a photo and cartoon.

Check students' work. Titles and drawings will vary.

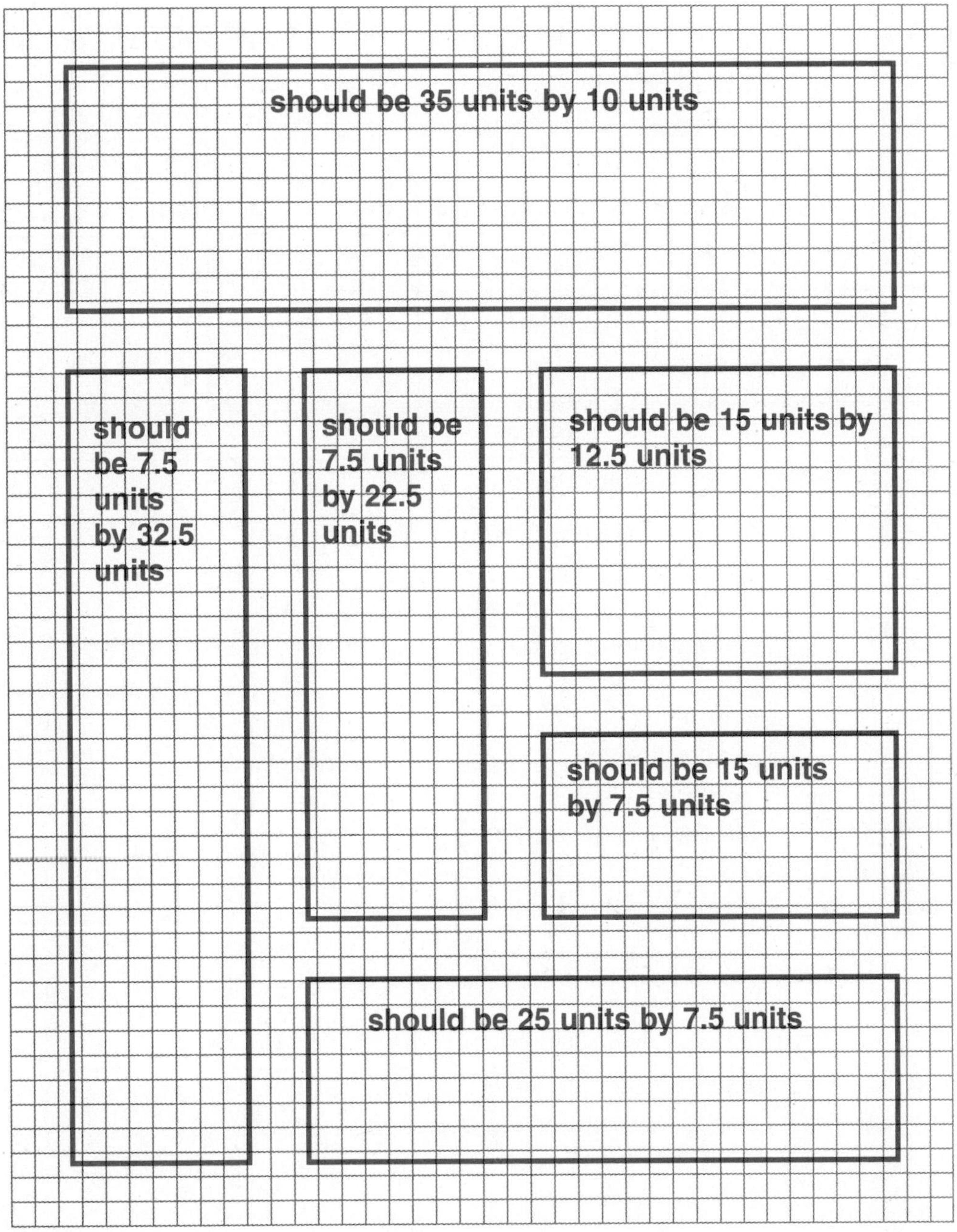

should be 35 units by 10 units
should be 7.5 units by 32.5 units
should be 7.5 units by 22.5 units
should be 15 units by 12.5 units
should be 15 units by 7.5 units
should be 25 units by 7.5 units

Name ______________________________

Nesting Boxes

Russian dolls nest one inside another. You can also make nesting boxes.

1. Complete the table by finding the surface areas and volumes of the patterns for each nesting box series.

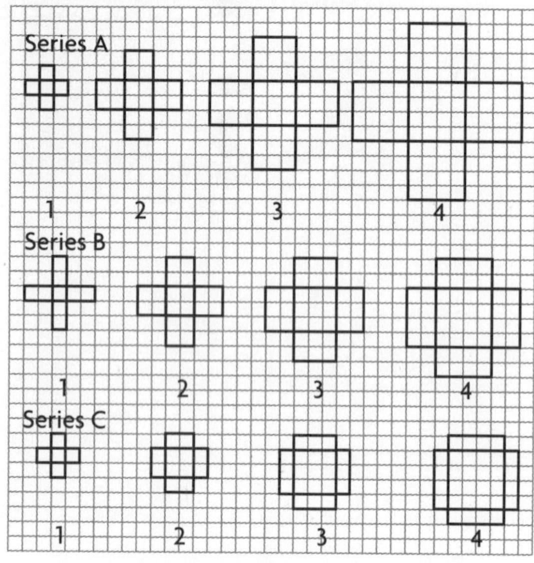

1 unit = 1 foot
1 square unit = 1 square foot

	Box 1	Box 2	Box 3	Box 4
Series A				
Surface Area	5 ft^2	20 ft^2	45 ft^2	80 ft^2
Volume	1 ft^3	8 ft^3	27 ft^3	64 ft^3
Series B				
Surface Area	9 ft^2	20 ft^2	33 ft^2	48 ft^2
Volume	2 ft^3	8 ft^3	18 ft^3	32 ft^3
Series C				
Surface Area	5 ft^2	12 ft^2	21 ft^2	32 ft^2
Volume	1 ft^3	4 ft^3	9 ft^3	16 ft^3

2. What would the surface area and volume of the fifth box in each series be?

Series A

surface area **125 ft^2**

volume **125 ft^3**

Series B

surface area **65 ft^2**

volume **50 ft^3**

Series C

surface area **45 ft^2**

volume **25 ft^3**

3. Make patterns for your own series of five nesting boxes below. Write the surface area and the volume of each box. Which series above are your boxes most similar to? Explain. **Boxes and similarities will vary.**

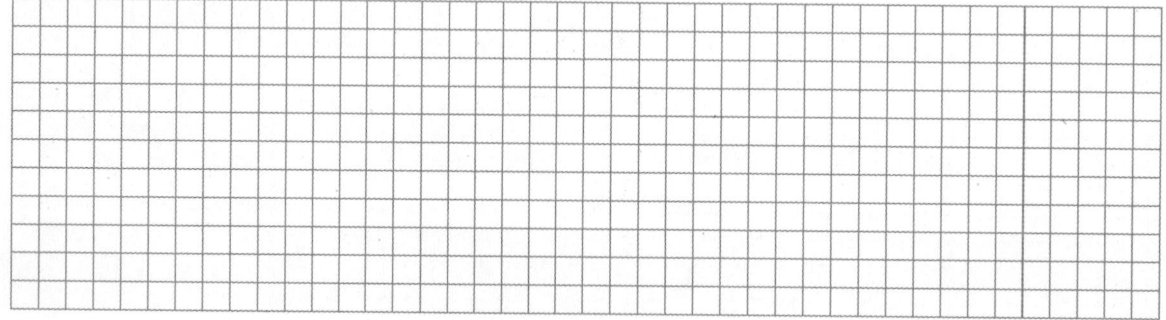

____

Name ______________________________

Packaging Punch

Many cans are not perfect cylinders, but you can still estimate the volume.

For Exercises 1–2, use the can at the right.

1. The punch can is the size of an average 12-oz juice can. What is the approximate volume of the can in cubic inches? Use $\pi = 3.14$, and round to the nearest tenth.

   about 22.1 in.^{3}

2. A 12-oz can holds how many cubic inches if 1 oz $\approx$ 1.8 in.^{3}? Is the can completely filled with punch?

   about 21.6 in.^{3}; no

Find the volume of each can. About how many ounces of punch will each can hold? Round to whole ounces.

3. 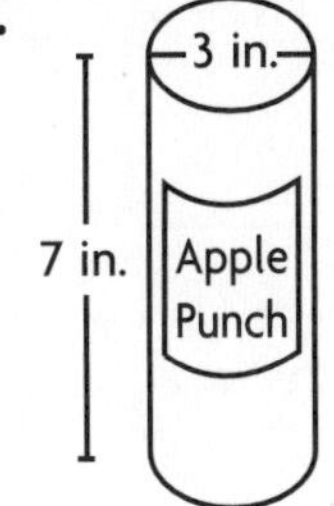

   49.455 in.^{3};

   about 27 oz

4. 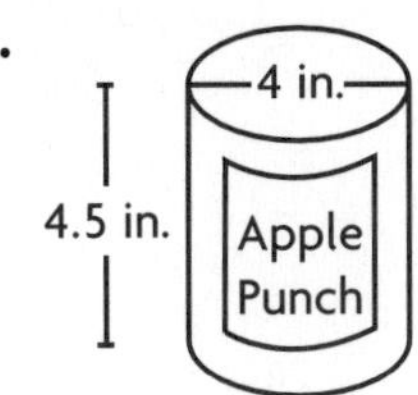

   56.52 in.^{3};

   about 31 oz

5. 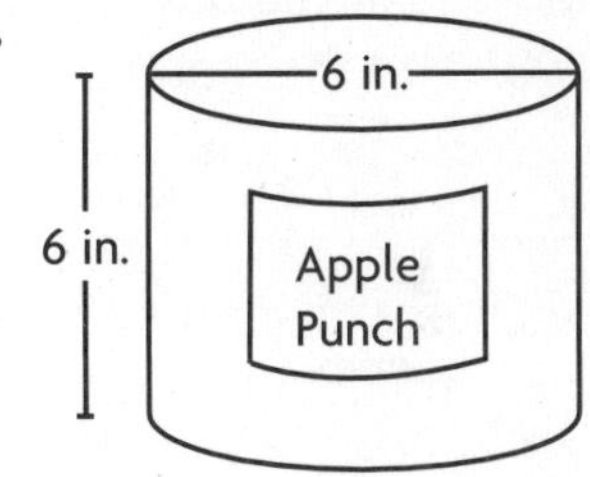

   169.56 in.^{3};

   about 94 oz

6. 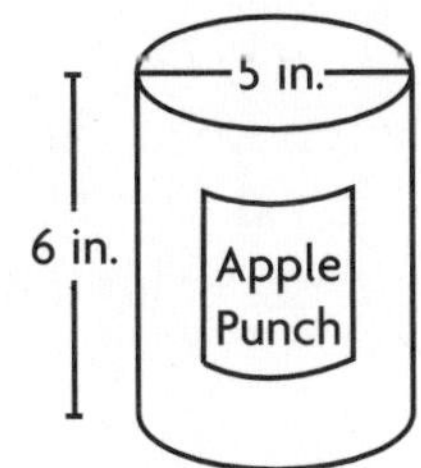

   117.75 in.^{3};

   about 65 oz

7. 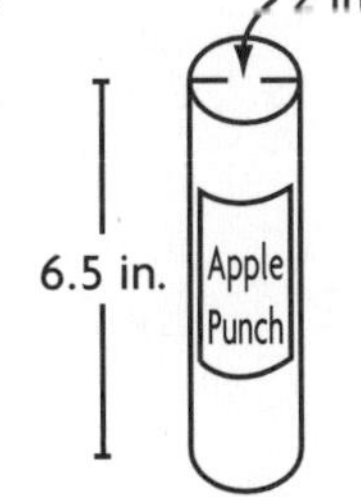

   20.41 in.^{3};

   about 11 oz

8. 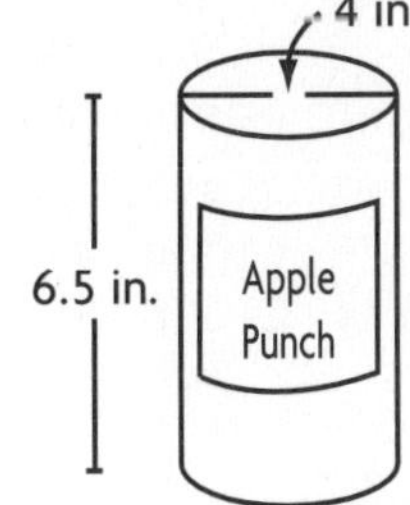

   81.64 in.^{3};

   about 45 oz

Name ____________________

LESSON 27.1

State by State

The table below shows sales tax rates for various states.

Alabama	4%	Florida	6%	Illinois	6.25%	Minnesota	$6\frac{1}{2}$%
California	7.25%	Georgia	4%	Indiana	5%	Mississippi	7%
Colorado	3%	Hawaii	4%	Kentucky	6%	New York	$8\frac{1}{2}$%
Connecticut	6%	Idaho	5%	Louisiana	4%	Oklahoma	4.5%

For Problems 1–14, use the table to solve. Round to the nearest cent. Remember, purchase price + sales tax = total cost.

1. Mrs. Fixx in Louisville, Kentucky buys a hat. The total cost is $21.15. Find the amount of sales tax.

   $1.20

2. John Murphy in Hartford, Connecticut buys a car. The total cost is $13,769.40. Find the purchase price.

   $12,990

3. Mr. Aiello in California buys a TV priced at $425.00. Find the total cost.

   $455.81

4. Lin in Colorado buys a rug for a total cost of $566.50. Find the amount of sales tax.

   $16.50

5. Leilani in Hawaii buys a surfboard priced at $99.00. Find the amount of sales tax.

   $3.96

6. Danny in Oklahoma buys a lamp priced at $45.95. Find the total cost.

   $48.02

7. Julie Estevez in Indiana buys a desk priced at $225.00. Find the total cost.

   $236.25

8. Judy in Mississippi buys a stove for a total cost of $636.65. Find the purchase price.

   $595

9. Ms. Fridie in Birmingham, Alabama buys a copier. The total cost is $349.56. Find the purchase price.

   $336.12

10. Jack in Buffalo, New York buys an answering machine for a total cost of $70.53. Find the purchase price.

    $65

11. Mrs. Klyne in Minnesota buys a set of dishes priced at $59.95 and a frying pan priced at $19.95. Find the total cost.

    $85.09

12. Carlos in Miami, Florida buys two shirts and a hat. The price of each shirt is $9.50, and the price of the hat is $8.90. Find the total cost.

    $29.57

13. Mr. Carver in Idaho buys a truck priced at $19,850.00. Find the amount of sales tax.

    $992.50

14. Lila in Chicago, Illinois buys supplies priced at $4,987.63. Find the total cost.

    $5,299.36

Name ______________________

LESSON 27.2

Pay Early, Pay Less

Companies that sell large amounts of merchandise to stores sometimes offer a discount for payment within a given time. The discount depends on the *terms* which are listed on the *invoice* or bill.

The terms 2/10 offer a 2% discount if the bill is paid within 10 days.
The terms 3/15 offer a 3% discount if the bill is paid within 15 days.

An invoice for $873.20 is dated March 10 and has terms 2/10.

- What is the last day the discount can be taken?

  March 10 plus 10 days is March 20. The discount applies if the invoice is paid on or before March 20. After that, the full amount of $873.20 must be paid.

- What is the discount?

  $873.20 \times 0.02 \approx 17.46$ The discount is $17.46.

- What is the payment?

  $873.20 - 17.46 = 855.74$ The payment is $855.74.

The Casual Clothier receives an invoice for $475.60 dated April 2.
The terms are 3/20.

1. What is the last day the discount can be taken? April 22

2. What is the rate of discount? 3%

3. What is the discount if the invoice is paid within 20 days? $14.27

4. What payment is made on April 15? $461.33

The Pottery Store receives an invoice for $1,245.50 dated November 2.
The terms are 2/15.

5. What is the last day the discount can be taken? November 17

6. What is the rate of discount? 2%

7. What is the discount if the invoice is paid within 15 days? $24.91

8. What payment is made on November 20? $1,245.50

Ace Computer Store receives an invoice for $18,768.20 dated September 20.
The terms are 1/30.

9. What is the last day the discount can be taken? October 20

10. What is the discount if the invoice is paid within 30 days? $187.68

11. What payment is made on October 7? $18,580.52

Name ______________________

Earning a Profit

A store subtracts expenses from sales to find the profit.

During the month of May, the Cozy Corner Book Store had sales of $27,128. Expenses were book purchases, $15,560; rent, $2,200; employee salaries, $5,875.40; utilities and office expenses (electricity, phone, fax, etc.), $1,043.28; and maintenance, $924.70.

Complete to find the amount of profit and the percent of profit. Round to the nearest tenth of a percent.

1.	Sales		$27,128
2.	Expenses: Purchases	$15,560	
3.	Rent	$2,200	
4.	Salaries	$5,875.40	
5.	Utilities and Office	$1,043.28	
6.	Maintenance	$924.70	
7.	Total expenses		$25,603.38
8.	Profit (Sales − Total expenses)		$1,524.62
9.	Percent profit (Profit ÷ Sales)		5.6%

During the month of June, the book store had sales of $24,128. Expenses were book purchases, $13,210; rent, $2,200; employee salaries, $5,675.32; utilities and office expenses, $923.74; and maintenance, $924.70.

Complete to find the amount of profit and the percent of profit. Round to the nearest tenth of a percent.

10.	Sales		$24,128
11.	Expenses: Purchases	$13,210	
12.	Rent	$2,200	
13.	Salaries	$5,675.32	
14.	Utilities and Office	$923.74	
15.	Maintenance	$924.70	
16.	Total expenses		$22,933.76
17.	Profit (Sales − Total expenses)		$1,194.24
18.	Percent profit (Profit ÷ Sales)		4.9%

Name ______________________________

LESSON 27.4

Adding On

Simple interest is the amount of interest earned on the original principal. However, banks let you earn interest on the interest as well as the principal.

Joseph deposits $400 in a bank that pays 5% interest on the principal *and* the interest added to the principal at the end of each year. Find the amount of interest and principal in Joseph's account after 3 years.

Year 1	Year 2	Year 3
$I = prt$	$I = prt$	$I = prt$
$= 400 \times 0.05 \times 1$	$= 420 \times 0.05 \times 1$	$= 441 \times 0.05 \times 1$
$= 20$	$= 21$	$= 22.05$
Interest is $20.	Interest is $21.	Interest is $22.05.

The amount of interest earned after 3 years is $20 + $21 + $22.05 = $63.05

The amount of principal plus interest after 3 years is $400 + $63.05 = $463.05.

There is a faster way to calculate the total of principal and interest if interest is added to the principal at the end of each year.

You can find the total of principal and interest on $400 for 3 years at 5% by multiplying 400 × 1.05 × 1.05 × 1.05 on your calculator. You just found the amount of interest and principal in Joseph's bank account after 3 years, or $463.05.

Find the total amount of interest and principal if interest is added to the principal at the end of the year.

1. $500 for 2 years at 4% **$540.80**

2. $1,200 for 3 years at 4.5% **$1,369.40**

3. $300 for 4 years at 5.5% **$371.66**

4. $750 for 2 years at 5.5% **$834.77**

Use a calculator to find the total of principal and interest if interest is added to principal at the end of the year. Then write the given letter above the answer at the bottom of the page. You will name the type of interest you have been calculating.

5. $400 for 2 years at 5.5% **$445.21**, D

6. $671 for 3 years at 4.25% **$760.24**, U

7. $98 for 3 years at 6.5% **$118.38**, C

8. $1,056 for 4 years at $5\frac{1}{4}$% **$1,295.85**, M

9. $520 for 5 years at $4\frac{3}{4}$% **$655.81**, P

10. $873 for 6 years at 5.2% **$1,183.34**, O

11. $305 for 7 years at 7.3% **$499.46**, N

12. $550 for 6 years at $6\frac{1}{4}$% **$791.30**, O

C	O	M	P	O	U	N	D
$118.38	$1,183.34	$1,295.85	$655.81	$791.30	$760.24	$499.46	$445.21

Name ______________________________

LESSON 27.5

Computer Sense: Buying and Paying

These are some formulas that you can use with a spreadsheet.

= AVERAGE(B2..B9) gives the average of the numbers in cells B2, B3, . . . B9.

= SUM(C2,E2) gives the sum of the numbers in cells C2 and E2.

= SUM(A1..A21) adds the numbers in cells A1 through A21.

= D3–E3 subtracts the number in cell E3 from the number in cell D3.

= D3*1.05 multiplies the number in cell D3 by 1.05.

= ROUND(A3,2) rounds the number in cell A3 to two decimal places.

Use the formulas to complete.

1. What is the difference between ".." and "," in a formula? ".." includes all values between numbers; "," includes only 2 numbers.

2. Write a formula to add the numbers in cells C2 through C6. = SUM(C2..C6)

3. Write a formula to round the number in cell F5 to 1 decimal place.

   = ROUND(F5,1)

The spreadsheet below shows sales, commissions, and other categories for a company during three months.

	A	B	C	D	E	F
1	Month	Sales	Commission	Net Sales	Expenses	Profit
2	January	31,000	1,550	29,450	20,500	8,950
3	February	25,400	1,270	24,130	19,600	4,530
4	March	19,500	975	18,525	17,500	1,025
5	Average	25,300	1,265	24,035	19,200	4,835
6	Total	75,900	3,795	72,105	57,600	14,505

4. What formula is used to find cell C2?

   = B2*0.05

5. What formula is used to find cell B5?

   = AVERAGE(B2..B4)

6. What formula is used to find cell F2?

   = D2–E2

7. What formula is used to find cell E6?

   = SUM(E2..E4)

8. What formula is used to find cell D2?

   = B2–C2

9. What formula is used to find cell F6?

   = SUM(F2..F4)

Name ______________________________

Directly Speaking

Two quantities *vary directly* if they change in the same direction.

- If one quantity increases, then the other increases.
- If one quantity decreases, the other decreases.

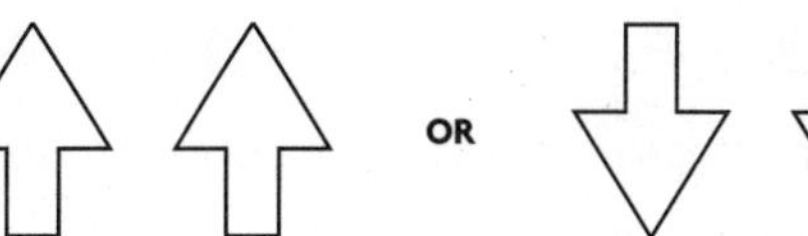

Here are some examples of direct variation:

- amount bought and cost
- number of inches on a map and number of actual miles

If Farmer Jones plants 8 acres that produce 144 bushels of melons, how many acres will produce 1,152 bushels of melons?

- Use the proportion $\frac{\text{acres needed for 144 bushels}}{\text{144 bushels}} = \frac{\text{acres needed for 1,152 bushels}}{\text{1,152 bushels}}$ to solve.

$\frac{8 \text{ acres}}{144 \text{ bushels}} \times \frac{x \text{ acres}}{1{,}152 \text{ bushels}}$ $\quad 144x = 9{,}216 \quad x = 64$

Farmer Jones will plant 64 acres to produce 1,152 bushels of melons.

Complete the proportion to find the answer.

		Both quantities increase or decrease?	Proportion	Answer
1.	If a furnace uses 40 gal of oil in 8 days, how many gallons does it use in 10 days?	both increase	$\frac{40 \text{ gal}}{8 \text{ days}} = \frac{x \text{ gal}}{10 \text{ days}}$	50 gal
2.	If 20 yd of wire weighs 80 lb, what is the weight of 2 yd of the same wire?	both decrease	$\frac{60 \text{ ft}}{80 \text{ lb}} = \frac{6 \text{ ft}}{x \text{ lb}}$	8 lb
3.	A recipe calls for 12 oz of sugar and 18 oz of flour. If only 10 oz of sugar is used, how much flour should be used?	both decrease	$\frac{12 \text{ oz}}{18 \text{ oz}} = \frac{10 \text{ oz}}{x}$	15 oz of flour
4.	The scale on a map is 1 in. = 60 mi. How many inches on the map represent 300 mi?	both increase	$\frac{1 \text{ in.}}{60 \text{ mi}} = \frac{x \text{ in.}}{300 \text{ mi}}$	5 in.
5.	At Mr. Pizza, an 8-in. pizza costs \$6. How much would a 12-in. pizza cost?	both increase	$\frac{8 \text{ in.}}{\$6} = \frac{12 \text{ in.}}{x}$	\$9

Name ____

LESSON 28.2

Inversely Speaking

Two quantities *vary inversely* if they change in opposite directions.

As one increases, the other decreases.

Here are some examples of inverse variation:

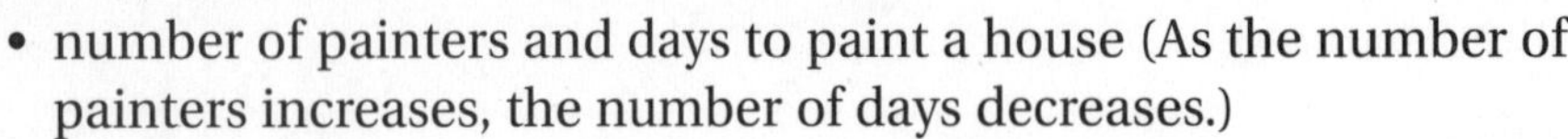

- number of painters and days to paint a house (As the number of painters increases, the number of days decreases.)

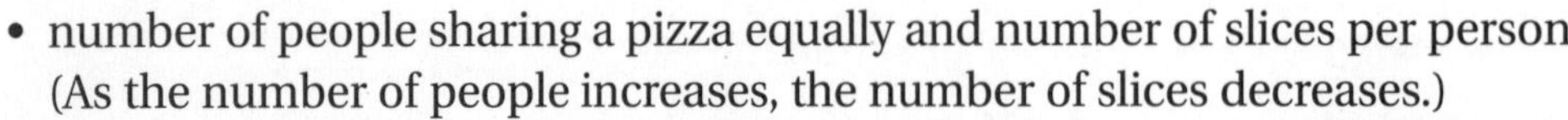

- number of people sharing a pizza equally and number of slices per person (As the number of people increases, the number of slices decreases.)

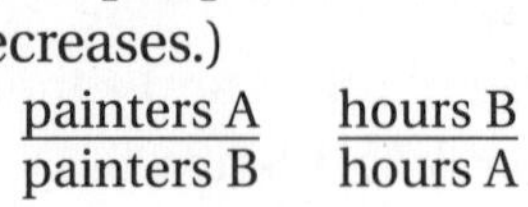

When you write a proportion for an inverse variation, you compare similar items and *invert* the terms of one of the ratios.

$$\frac{\text{painters A}}{\text{painters B}} = \frac{\text{hours B}}{\text{hours A}}$$

- If it takes 4 painters 24 hr to finish a job, how many hours would it take 6 painters to finish the same job?

$\frac{\text{painters A}}{\text{painters B}}$ $\quad \frac{4}{6} = \frac{x}{24} \quad$ $\frac{\text{hours B}}{\text{hours A}}$ $\quad 6x = 96 \quad x = 16$

It would take 16 hr.

Complete the proportion to find the answer.

		Quantities change in opposite directions?	Proportion	Answer
1.	If 125 machines take 10 days to complete a job, how many days would 200 machines take?	yes	$\frac{125 \text{ machines}}{200 \text{ machines}} = \frac{x \text{ days}}{10 \text{ days}}$	$6\frac{1}{4}$ days
2.	Farmer Neale has enough grain to feed 25 cows for 10 days. How many days would the same amount feed 10 cows?	yes	$\frac{25 \text{ cows}}{10 \text{ cows}} = \frac{x \text{ days}}{10 \text{ days}}$	25 days
3.	Nancy weighs 40 lb. She sits 6 ft from the center of a teeter-totter. Sam weighs 45 lb. How far from the center must he sit to balance the teeter-totter?	yes	$\frac{40 \text{ lb}}{45 \text{ lb}} = \frac{x \text{ ft}}{6 \text{ ft}}$	$5\frac{1}{3}$ ft
4.	If Nancy sits 5 ft from the center, how far from the center must Sam sit to balance the teeter-totter?	yes	$\frac{40 \text{ lb}}{45 \text{ lb}} = \frac{x \text{ ft}}{5 \text{ ft}}$	$4\frac{4}{9}$ ft
5.	70 lb — 6 ft — ? ft — 90 lb; balance point	yes	$\frac{70 \text{ lb}}{90 \text{ lb}} = \frac{x \text{ ft}}{6 \text{ ft}}$	$4\frac{2}{3}$ ft

Name ______________________________

Eggs-actly

Materials needed: calculator

The volumes of two similar-shaped figures are proportional to the *cube* of their lengths. But what does this have to do with the price of eggs? Get out your calculator!

Suppose an extra-large egg is 2.5 in. long, compared to a smaller egg 1.25 in. long. What is the ratio of their volumes?

Cube the ratio of their lengths.

$\left(\frac{2.5}{1.25}\right)^3 = \left(\frac{2}{1}\right)^3 = \frac{8}{1}$

The ratio of their volumes is 8:1.

The larger egg has 8 times as much volume, 8 times as much weight, and 8 times as much food.

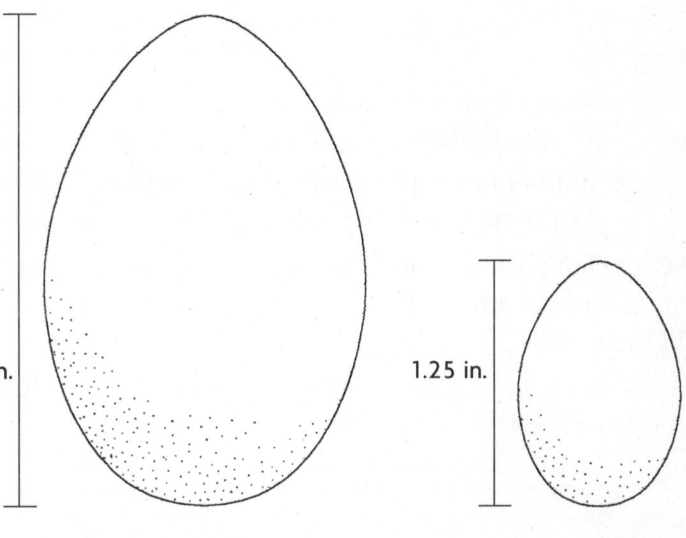

Solve. Show your work.

1. One egg is 2 in. long. Another is 2.75 in. long. How many times greater is the volume of the larger egg?

   $\left(\frac{2.75}{2}\right)^3 \approx \frac{20.8}{8} \approx$ 2.6; about 2.6 times

2. One egg is 2.25 in. long. Another is 1.5 in. long. How many times greater is the weight of the larger egg?

   $\left(\frac{2.25}{1.5}\right)^3 \approx \left(\frac{3}{2}\right)^3 \approx$ 3.4; about 3.4 times

3. The ratio of the lengths of two eggs is 5 to 2. The larger egg contains how many times the food of the smaller egg?

   $\left(\frac{5}{2}\right)^3 = \frac{125}{8} =$ 15.625; about 15.6 times as much

4. Guess and check: An egg is 2 in. long. What is the length of an egg with twice the volume? **about 2.5 in.**

5. Guess and check: An egg is 3 in. long. What is the length of an egg with half the weight? **about 2.4 in.**

6. Guess and check: An egg is 1.75 in. long. What is the length of an egg with twice the food? **about 2.2 in.**

7. Guess and check: An egg is 2 in. long. What is the length of an egg with three times the volume? **about 2.9 in.**

Name ______________________________

LESSON 28.4

A Roller Coaster Ride

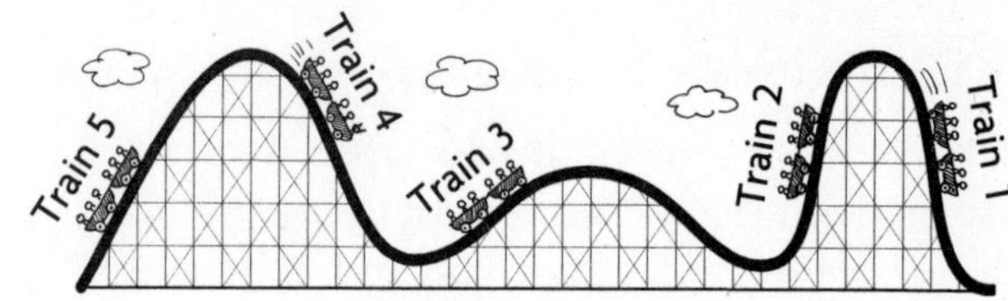

The steepness of a roller-coaster ride depends on the vertical changes and the horizontal changes. This change can be expressed as a ratio, called the *slope.*

$$\text{slope} = \frac{\text{vertical change}}{\text{horizontal change}}$$

- In the picture of the roller coaster, Train 5, Train 3, and Train 2 are climbing, but Train 2 has the steepest climb.
- Train 4 and Train 1 are both going down, but the drop for Train 1 is steeper.

If the cars in each train represent 2 points on a coordinate plane, you can find the slope of the line containing them. This tells you the steepness or slope of the hill.

Find the slope of the line containing point A(4,3) and point B(⁻2,⁻5).

$$\text{slope} = \frac{\text{change in } y\text{-coordinates}}{\text{change in } x\text{-coordinates}}$$

$$= \frac{3 - (^-5)}{4 - (^-2)} = \frac{8}{6}, \text{ or } \frac{4}{3}$$

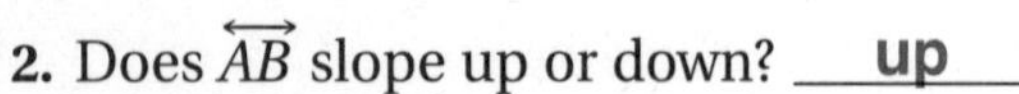

The slope of the line containing points A and B is $\frac{4}{3}$, a *positive* slope.

1. Plot point A and point B on a coordinate plane. Draw $\overleftrightarrow{AB}$.

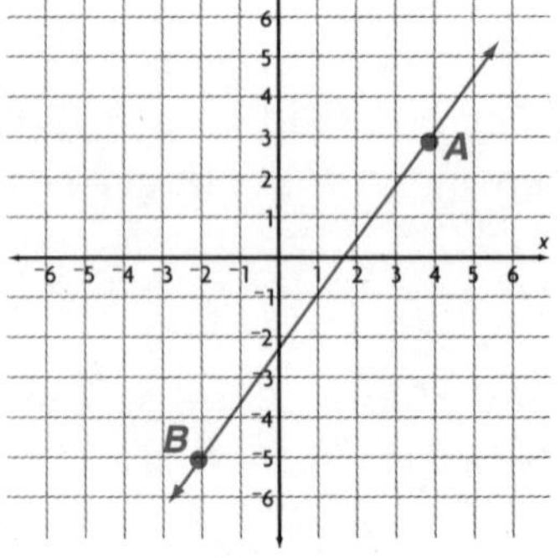

2. Does $\overleftrightarrow{AB}$ slope up or down? **up**
3. Find the slope of the line containing point $C(^-3,2)$ and point $D(1,^-1)$. **$\frac{-3}{4}$**
4. Plot point C and point D on a coordinate plane. Draw $\overleftrightarrow{CD}$.

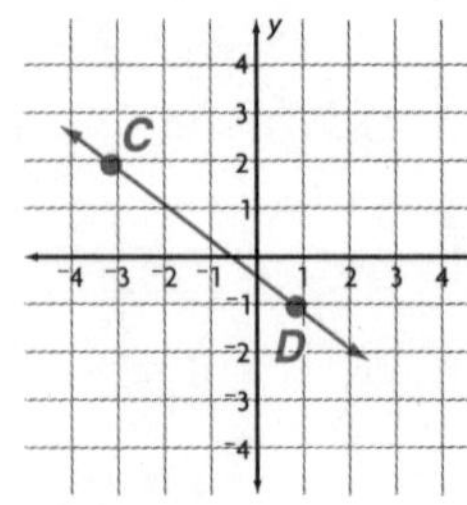

5. Does $\overleftrightarrow{CD}$ slope up or down? **down**

Use the drawing of the roller coaster above.

6. Which trains are on lines that slope up, or have *positive slopes*?

   Trains 2, 3, and 5

7. Which trains are on lines that slope down, or have *negative slopes*?

   Trains 1 and 4